Fun with the Family™ in Oregon

Help Us Keep This Guide Up to Date

Every effort has been made by the author and editors to make this guide as accurate and useful as possible. However, many changes can occur after a guide is published—establishments close, phone numbers change, hiking trails are rerouted, facilities come under new management, and so on.

We would love to hear from you concerning your experiences with this guide and how you feel it could be improved and kept up to date. While we may not be able to respond to all comments and suggestions, we'll take them to heart and make certain to share them with the author. Please send your comments and suggestions to the following address:

The Globe Pequot Press
Reader Response/Editorial Department
P.O. Box 480
Guilford, CT 06437

Or you may e-mail us at: editorial@globe-pequot.com

Thanks for your input, and happy travels!

FUN WITH THE FAMILY™

in OREGON

HUNDREDS OF IDEAS
FOR DAY TRIPS WITH THE KIDS
THIRD EDITION

By CHERYL McLEAN

The Globe Pequot Press

Guilford, Connecticut

Text design by Nancy Freeborn
Maps by M.A. Dubé

ISBN 0-7627-2290-8

Manufactured in the United States of America
Third Edition/First Printing

To our children, and their children, that they will
savor and protect the glorious and diverse beauty that is Oregon's.

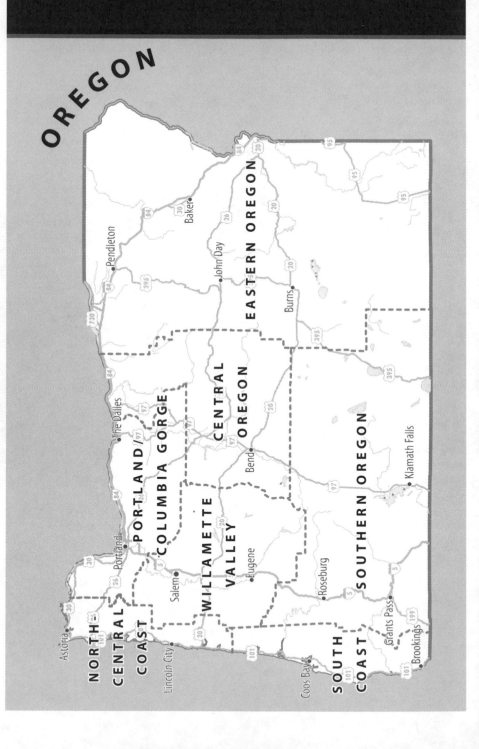

OREGON

Astoria

Pendleton

Baker

The Dalles

Portland

Salem

Lincoln City

John Day

Burns

Bend

Eugene

Roseburg

Grants Pass

Coos Bay

Brookings

Klamath Falls

NORTH & CENTRAL COAST

PORTLAND

COLUMBIA GORGE

WILLAMETTE VALLEY

CENTRAL OREGON

EASTERN OREGON

SOUTHERN OREGON

SOUTH COAST

Contents

Preface to the Third Edition

It's amazing how much can change in just a few years. Since the second edition, several new attractions have sprung up and several old favorites have closed their doors. Opening hours and prices seem to be in constant flux, but I've contacted each listing in the book to make sure everything is as up-to-the-minute as possible.

I've added all the Web sites and E-mail addresses I could find, and in the process discovered how much wonderful information can be found at the click of a mouse. In order to tell you about as many places as possible, I'm not able to tell you as much about each one as I would like. Therefore, the Web can be a tremendous resource for learning more before you go.

Other terrific resources are the local chambers of commerce or visitors bureaus. Each chapter lists the relevant organizations for the areas covered, and most have Web sites that will direct you to area attractions and businesses. You can also call ahead to ask for brochures and maps that will help in planning your trip—and all these services are free.

Sources for Oregon Information

Welcome to Oregon Web site: *www.el.com/to/oregon. This site also has city pages with links to various local attractions.*

State Campground Guide: *(800) 547–7842.*

State Park Campsite Reservations and Information: *(800) 452–5687 for reservations; (800) 551–6949 for general information; www.oregonstateparks.org.*

Bureau of Land Management in Oregon: *www.or.blm.gov/recreation.htm.*

Whale-watching information: *(541) 563–2002; www.whalespoken.org.*

Oregon Department of Fish and Wildlife: *(503) 872–5264 ext. 5528 for information on tidepools.*

Oregon Coast Visitors Association: *(888) 628–2102; (541) 574–2679; www.VisitTheOregonCoast.com.*

Central Oregon Coast Association: *(800) 767–2064; (541) 265–2064; www.orcoast.com/coca.*

As I've worked on revising the book, my delight in my home state has been renewed. There are so many diverse ways to enjoy yourself in Oregon—indoors and out—that it will take a lifetime to explore them all. My family has been enjoying Oregon's bounty all my life, and I know there's more to discover— even after touring the entire state while researching the first edition of this book.

I've also appreciated the warm friendliness and helpfulness of everyone who provided information to be included in the book. Their welcome to you when you visit will be just as warm!

Introduction

I've lived in Oregon most of my life and traveled extensively along its highways and back roads, yet I still have more to discover. I've always marveled at the variety to be found in this state—ocean, mountains, gently rolling pasture-lands, verdant valleys, giant old-growth forests, sagebrush deserts, mesas and canyon lands, and wide stretches of volcanic wasteland. The opportunities for family adventure are just as varied and vast as the landscapes.

Oregon has far more attractions, amusements, and family fun opportunities than can possibly be covered in a book this size, but in the following pages I've included those that have stood the test of time—or the test of Cassidy, my daughter.

In addition to the specific attractions listed in the book, here are some ideas for family fun in just about any town in Oregon:

- Head over to family swim time at the local pool.

- Visit the police department, fire station, and city or county government center or courthouse (call first to see if they'll give you a tour).

- Join family hour at the roller skating rink.

- Grab a lane at the bowling alley (most now have inflatable gutter guards to help little ones play).

- Tour a recycling center, local industry, fast-food franchise restaurant, hospital, post office, television, or radio station (call in advance).

- Visit a U-pick farm and gather berries, beans, or whatever's in season.

- In winter, grab your mittens and scarves, don your warmest coats, and head for the nearest snow hill with sleds, inner tubes, or just a cardboard box.

- In summer, find a swimming hole at the nearest stream, river, or lake (there are plenty in just about every corner of Oregon).

- Find a wide open space (no overhead wires and few trees) where you can fly a kite on a windy day.

We're looking forward to going back to many places and making more discoveries for family adventure in Oregon. I hope you'll contribute your ideas and experiences for future editions. Meanwhile, have fun!

—Cheryl McLean

Rates for Lodging

$	up to $50
$$	$51 to $70
$$$	$71 to $90
$$$$	$91 and up

Rates for Restaurants

$	most selections less than $5
$$	most $6 to $10
$$$	most $11 to $20
$$$$	most more than $20

A note about prices: Although many establishments have pricing for seniors, I chose not to include that in the interest of saving space. Also, all prices and hours of operation are subject to change.

Attractions Key

The following is a key to the icons found throughout the text.

 Swimming

 Plants/Gardens/ Nature Trails

 Boating / Boat Tour

 Animal Viewing

 Historic Site

 Food

 Hiking / Walking

 Lodging

 Fishing

 Camping

 Biking

 Museums

 Amusement Park

 Performing Arts

 Horseback Riding

 Picnicking

 Skiing/Winter Sports

 Playground

 Park

 Shopping

The North and Central Coasts

O regon's Pacific Coast National Scenic Byway follows the entire 400-mile coastal edge. Plan at least two days to explore the many parks, waysides, lighthouses, and public beaches found along the north and central coastline. Within the stretch of broad, sandy beaches and rocky headlands, you and your kids can experience the power of the Pacific Ocean, the lush natural beauty of coastal rainforests, and the fascinating animal and plant life found in tidepool wonderlands. Thanks to the foresight of the state legislature and the leadership of the late Governor Tom McCall, who in 1967 enacted the Beach Bill, all of Oregon's beaches are open to the public. No individual can own any of the beaches in the state, so you're free to roam and explore. Oregon's shoreline is among the least populated in the country, too, so you can frequently find long stretches of beach where you're the only person in sight.

The Oregon coast is a popular vacation spot in the summer for locals and out-of-state travelers. Traffic on the winding scenic highway sometimes seems to crawl in the early afternoon. Try leaving for your destination by 9:00 A.M. to avoid waiting in traffic or in lines at tourist attractions. During the fall and winter the coastal highway is less congested. Lines shrink in restaurants and on beaches, and life gets a little more laid-back. Winter is also the best time to view the gray whale migration and to visit the many historical museums that enrich Oregon's coastal communities. And your kids might end up having the entire beach to themselves.

This region provides the backdrop for all kinds of family fun, but you should carry some essential ingredients with you: Frisbees and other things to toss to one another; simple sand pails with shovels for building sandcastles and digging clams; kites to fly on blustery coastal days; blankets for relaxing on the sand; towels for drying off; snacks to replace the energy kids expend running on the beach; binoculars for spotting whales, birds, and other kinds of wildlife; and, of course, a bag of marshmallows for roasting when the sun goes down.

THE NORTH AND CENTRAL COASTS

Astoria

30

26

Seaside

Cannon Beach

101   53   26

Manzanita

Rockaway

Garibaldi

Tillamook

101

22

Lincoln City   18

Depoe Bay

101

Newport   20

Waldport

34

Yachats

SAFE FUN ON THE BEACH

Keep in mind the following guidelines for beach safety and conservation. "Sneaker" or "rogue" waves are especially dangerous in areas such as jetties or rocky headlands where obstructions cause waves to crash with greater force. Rip tides and undertows can pull adults as well as children underwater and out to sea.

Driftwood also can present dangers. If you see a log drifting in the surf, stay well away, and keep away from piles of logs on shore when waves are nearby. It's legal to build fires on the beach, but remember: Never build a fire in a large pile of driftwood or near grassy slopes that could keep burning after you leave. Before you go, douse the fire with water or wet sand. Don't bury hot coals, because someone walking along shortly after you've gone could be burned.

In several places along the coast, the position of the tide will make a difference in both enjoyment and safety. Pick up a tide table when you get into the area and use it to plan your tide pooling, beachcombing, and hiking to ensure the maximum fun for your family.

PRESERVING THE COAST FOR EVERYONE

The Oregon coast is a popular destination for tourists because of its natural beauty and the many recreational opportunities to enjoy along its shores. Explain to your children the importance of leaving everything as they find it. As the saying goes, take nothing with you but memories; leave nothing but your footprints in the sand.

THE NORTH COAST

Astoria

Astoria was the first settlement west of the Rocky Mountains, and it remains an important shipping port. Huge ships pass daily under the bridge that crosses the 4¹⁄₁₀-mile-wide Columbia River to Washington. On the waterfront you'll find piers to walk on and shops to browse in. At **Smith Point** you can watch the shipping activity from a large viewing deck just west of Pier 1. Kids love watching the enormous cranes at work, lifting whole railroad cars onto ships that make everything else in the vicinity seem minuscule.

Take a Stroll

Take a Stroll The Astoria Walkway at the historic Astoria Waterfront features an ever-changing parade of sea lions, birds, freighters, tug boats, and fishing vessels. It's the perfect place for a pre-dinner walk with your active toddlers and preschoolers.

ASTORIA COLUMN (ages 5 and up)

Reach Coxcomb Hill by driving south on Jerome Avenue and turning east onto Fifteenth Avenue. Continue into the park entrance at Coxcomb; (800) 875–6807 or (503) 325–2963; www.oldoregon.com/Pages/AstoriaColumn.htm. Open daily, 9:00 A.M.–dusk. **Free**.

This 125-foot landmark tower standing on the hill above the town is a favorite with children. The mural painted on the monument's outside walls tells the history of the area as it spirals upward. To get a good view of the other community landmarks, climb the 166 winding steps.

HERITAGE MUSEUM (ages 8 and up)

1618 Exchange Street; (503) 325–2203; www.oldoregon.com/Pages/CC HistoricalSociety.htm. Open daily except Sunday and Monday, May through September, 10:00 A.M.–5:00 P.M.; October through April, 11:00 A.M.–4:00 P.M. $3.00 adults; $2.00 seniors and students; $1.00 ages 6–17; under 6 **Free**.

The Heritage Museum, run by the Clatsop County Historical Society, is housed in the 1904 City Hall. The exhibits encompass all ingredients of the area's history—Native Americans, fur traders, pioneer settlers, geology and natural history, and timber and maritime industries.

FLAVEL HOUSE (ages 8 and up)

441 Eighth Street and Duane Avenue; (503) 325–2203. Open daily, 10:00 A.M.–5:00 P.M. $5.00 adults; $4.00 seniors and students; $2.00 ages 6–17; under 6 **Free**; *family ticket (up to three adults and four children) $15.00.*

The Flavel House was built in 1885-87 by Captain George Flavel, the state's best-known Columbia River bar pilot. You'll start your tour in the rehabilitated Carriage House, which is now an interpretive center.

UPPERTOWN FIRE FIGHTERS MUSEUM (ages 5 and up)

Thirtieth Street and Marine Drive; (503) 325–2203. Hours vary; call first. $2.00 adults; $1.00 ages 6–17; under 6 **Free**.

The Uppertown Fire Fighters Museum has lots of kid appeal with its extensive collection of old firefighting equipment, including a horse-drawn fire wagon in use here in 1877.

ASTORIA AQUATICS CENTER (ages 5 and up)

Twentieth Street and Marine Drive; (503) 325–7027. Open Monday through Friday, 5:30–8:00 P.M.; till 7:00 P.M. Friday; Saturday, noon–7:00 P.M.; Sunday, noon–4:00 P.M. $4.00 adults; $3.00 ages 2–17; $3.50 seniors; under 2 years **Free**.

Opened in 1998, the Aquatic Center has four pools and almost 200,000 gallons of water. Locker rooms are available for men and women and parents with small children will appreciate the family changing rooms. The center also has a weight room and a concession stand.

COLUMBIA RIVER MARITIME MUSEUM (ages 5 and up)

Seventeenth Street and Marine Drive; (503) 325–2323. Open daily, 9:30 A.M.– 5:00 P.M. $5.00 adults; $4.00 senior citizens; $2.00 ages 6–17; under 6 years **Free**.

The museum is undergoing complete renovation, adding interactive exhibits and oral histories that bring maritime history to life. The museum houses many miniature ships and several full-size vessels. Call for information on monthly children's programs.

FORT CLATSOP NATIONAL MEMORIAL (all ages)

92343 Fort Clatsop Road; (503) 861–2471. Open daily, summer hours, 8:00 A.M.–6:00 P.M.; winter hours, 8:00 A.M.–5:00 P.M. Closed December 25. $3.00 for 17 and older or $5.00 per car.

An Adventure to Remember Fort Clatsop National Memorial gives a lively lesson in nineteenth-century history and many rich details about the courageous Lewis and Clark expedition. From mid-June through Labor Day, buckskin clad rangers demonstrated the art of candlemaking and canoe-building and described the trials of the thirty-three-member party who camped here in the winter of 1805–06. A replica of the explorers' 50-foot by 50-foot fort is the centerpiece for this 125-acre park. The rustic fort, a historic canoe landing, and a natural spring are surrounded by lush coastal forests and wetlands that merge with the Columbia River Estuary. There is a visitor center with exhibits and audio visual programs. Walking trails, which connect the visitor center, fort, and canoe landing, are about one mile in length and easy for preschoolers to navigate. Allow one to two hours to visit Fort Clatsop. At $5.00 per family, this is a best buy .

Transport your kids into the early nineteenth century with a visit to Fort Clatsop, which contains an exact replica of the stockade used by explorers Lewis and Clark when they led their Corps of Discovery into this area in 1805.

op Astoria Events

APRIL

Astoria-Warrenton Crab & Seafood Festival. This celebration of the sea's bounty is held at Hammond Mooring Basin.

JUNE

Rose Festival Fleet. The ships stay in port for a couple of days, welcoming visitors aboard. If you plan well in advance, you can board in Astoria and ride with the fleet 100 miles upriver to Portland. (503) 227–2681.

Scandinavian Midsummer Festival. This festival includes dances, food and craft booths, a beer garden, and performances by traditionally garbed singers and dancers.

AUGUST

Clatsop County Fair. The fair is located in the Astoria fairgrounds, and features carnival rides, games, exhibitions, and a tempting array of foods. (503) 325–4600.

Astoria Regatta. The regatta is a week full of activities along the waterfront. Kids enjoy the demolition derby, Coast Guard drills, and boat races.

NOVEMBER

St. Lucia Festival of Lights. This holiday event celebrates the coming of Christmas and pokes fun at the area's rainy winter weather.

For information on Astoria events, call (800) 875–6807 or (503) 325–6311 or visit www.oldoregon.com.

FORT STEVENS STATE PARK AND FORT STEVENS HISTORIC AREA (all ages)

Located 10 miles west of Astoria off U.S. 101; (800) 551–6949 or (503) 861–3170; (800) 452–8657 for reservations; www.oregonstateparks.org. Historic area open daily, summer hours, 10:00 A.M.–6:00 P.M.; rest of year, 10:00 A.M.–4:00 P.M. Park hours vary. $3.00 daily use fee, or $25.00 annual permit for all state park day-use areas.

Fort Stevens State Park and the adjacent Fort Stevens Historic Area, which stretch north to the mouth of the Columbia River at Clatsop Spit, are well worth a visit.

Fort Stevens State Park encompasses sandy beaches, wetlands, forested areas of spruce and pine, and several shallow lakes. The largest of these, Coffenbury Lake, is popular with sailboarders, hikers, and anglers. You can circle the lake on a 2-mile trail. The park's 8-mile system of paved bicycle trails is a real treat for parents with active children.

Fort Stevens Historic Area is the only mainland military installation to receive enemy fire since the War of 1812. An interpretive center displays photographs of the fort's guns in action. Access to the still-visible 1906 shipwreck of the four-masted British ship, the *Peter Iredale*, is through the park campground, at the end of a 1-mile road and a trail that both lead to the beach.

ASTORIA RIVERFRONT TROLLEY (ages 3 and up)

On the Columbia Riverfront between the Port of Astoria and the East End Mooring Basin; (541) 861–1031; www.oldoregon.com/Pages/AstoriaRiverfront Trolley.htm. Hours vary; generally 3:00–9:00 P.M. weekdays and 10:00 A.M.– 9:00 P.M. weekends. $1.00.

Old Number 300, built in 1913 and restored as part of a long-term loan from the San Antonio Museum of Art, now carries passengers along the riverfront. You can ride as long as you want, but you'll pay a dollar each time you get on. A sheltered viewing deck at the end of 6th Street and the dock at 17th Street provide views of the river and two Coast Guard cutters. The 14th Street ferry dock includes interpretive displays.

ECO CRUISES ON THE COLUMBIA RIVER ESTUARY (ages 10 and up)

At the West Mooring Basin; (541) 325–7818; www.oldoregon.com/Pages/Eco Cruises.htm. Call for reservations. Tours range from $15 to $90 for ninety-minute to all-day tours.

Explore the rich diversity of the estuary and get a close-up view of the industrial side of the waterfront. You'll learn about the sturdy tugboats and watch the intrepid river pilots who guide ocean-going vessels over the bar. The islands you'll pass are, in some cases, the result of dredge disposal, but they've become outstanding habitats for birds. Long Island offers a bit of history, with a shipwreck, ghost towns, and old lighthouses.

Seaside

Seaside has been a haven for families since pioneer settlers in the Tillamook Bay area stopped over for a rest on their way home from Portland. In 1920, Seaside built the **Promenade,** now a pedestrian walkway atop a concrete wall, paralleling an 8,000-foot stretch of beach. At the center of the Promenade, or "Prom," the **Turnaround** marks the point where Lewis and Clark ended their westward journey.

From the Turnaround, Broadway is lined with amusements such as bumper cars, shooting galleries, video arcades, and miniature golf. Locals refer to this street as "Million Dollar Walk," no doubt because of the millions of quarters that kids have wheedled out of their parents over the years.

 SEASIDE AQUARIUM (all ages)

200 North Promenade; (503) 738–6211. Open in summer, Sunday through Thursday, 9:00 A.M.–6:00 P.M.; Friday through Saturday, 9:00 A.M.–8:00 P.M.; Wednesday through Sunday, 9:00 A.M.–5:00 P.M., rest of year. $6.00 adults; $3.00 ages 6–13; under 6 **Free** *with paid adult; $19 family (up to six).*

The aquarium is home to a room full of rowdy harbor seals. You can buy a bag of fish to throw to the barking, baying bunch. Touch tanks give kids an opportunity to get close to the tide pool denizens. There's also a rubbing table and a new interpretive center.

 A Seaside Ride Try riding horses along the surf as an alternative to bicycles.

- **North Coast Horse Rentals (ages 7 and up).** *Operates out of Fort Stevens State Park; (508) 791–5617. Call for appointments and prices.*

- **Faraway Farms (ages 10 and under).** *On Hamlet Road off U.S. 101, immediately south of Seaside; (503) 738–6336. Pony rides. Call for appointments and prices.*

 THE SEASIDE HISTORICAL MUSEUM (ages 5 and up)

570 Necanicum Drive at Fifth Street; (503) 738–7065. Open daily, end of March through October, 10:00 A.M.–4:00 P.M.; Sunday noon–3:00 P.M.; November until late March, noon–3:00 P.M. $2.00 adults; $1.00 students 13–20; 12 and under **Free***.*

Lewis and Clark are the focus of many new exhibits, along with Native American displays and depictions of the town's development as the ultimate family beach resort, charm parents and children alike. Kids love the photographs of Seaside's early bathing beauties.

*S*easide Amusements (ages 6 and up) Amusement

rides and arcades are found along Broadway—bumper cars, a carousel, and video arcades. A few miles south of town off Highway 101, you'll find miniature golf and go-carts. In addition, more fun can be found at these locations:

- **Funland Entertainment Center.** 201 Broadway (503) 738-7361. Saltwater aquarium, video games, pinball, shooting gallery, and air hockey; pizza restaurant and big-screen TV.
- **Town Center Mall.** 300 Broadway; (503) 738-6728. Indoor carousel.
- **Cannes Cinema.** 1026 12th Avenue; (503) 738-0671. Local movie house.
- **Evergreen Lanes and Coffee Shop.** 3578 Highway 101 North; (503) 738-5333.
- **Sunset Empire Park & Recreation.** 1140 Broadway; (503) 738-3311. Year-round swimming pool, spa, recreation programs, skate park, and playground equipment.

PROM BIKE SHOP

622 Twelfth; (503) 738–8251. Open 10:00 A.M.–6:00 P.M. Rental prices vary.
Explore Seaside on wheels—bicycles or in-line skates. You'll be amazed at the variety of transportation modes available from this rental shop—bikes, tandems, adult two-seater trikes, strollers, skates, rollerblades, scooters, and surries (four-person pedal carts).

*F*un Fact Lewis and Clark ended their 4,000-mile journey to the Pacific here, a fact that's commemorated with a statue of the explorers.

BROADWAY PARK (all ages)

Located off Broadway at the east end of town along the banks of Neawanna Creek; (800) 444–6740. **Free.**
You'll find covered picnic shelters and plenty of games for your family to play here. In summer, as part of Lewis and Clark historical reenactments, you can participate in the forgotten art of saltmaking on the beach (at the end of Avenue U).

Top Seaside Events

JULY

Miss Oregon Pageant. This annual event charms many families who have never witnessed a beauty pageant live. (800) 394–3003.

Prom Walk & Sand Games. Here's a midsummer event that will appeal to the whole family.

SEPTEMBER

Dahlia Festival Parade. This parade is designed especially for children.

Sandcastle Contest. Beach sculpting for both amateurs and pros.

For more information on these Seaside events, call (800) 444–6740 or (503) 738–6391.

Cannon Beach

Cannon Beach, like Rockaway Beach to the south, developed as a resort community. The town combines quaint old-time charm with a thriving cultural community, good restaurants, and interesting shops—all within view of the most picturesque stretches of beach in the state.

HAYSTACK ROCK (ages 5 and up)

One-half mile south of Cannon Beach off U.S. 101; (503) 436–2623; www.cannonbeach.org (click on "Haystack Rock"). Always open, though cut off from land at high tide. **Free.**

This ocean landmark has graced many a calendar and coffee-table book. A designated marine garden and bird sanctuary, the 235-foot Cannon Beach Haystack is one of the world's

Fun Facts

Just a few miles north of Cannon Beach at the U.S. 101 and State Highway 26 junction is the **world's tallest Sitka spruce.** Located in an old-growth fir and spruce forest in **Klootchy Creek Park,** the 216-feet-high tree has a trunk that is 52 feet in circumference. It's believed to be more than seven centuries old.

largest free-standing monoliths. Enjoy the tide pools around its base that are accessible at low tide.

ECOLA STATE PARK (all ages)

Two miles north of Cannon Beach just off U.S. 101; (800) 551–6949 or www. oregonstateparks.org. Open until dusk. Summer admission fee $3.00 or $25 annual state park pass.

This day-use area provides an incredible view from the picnic tables, where brazen seagulls will beg your kids for handouts. Children love exploring **Indian Beach,** a tiny cove littered with driftwood and rocks.

Top Cannon Beach Events

APRIL

Puffin Kite Festival. This festival includes a workshop for kids on how to make and fly kites. (800) 547–6100.

JUNE

Cannon Beach Sandcastle Contest. Bring your sand-carving tools to this international event that offers cash prizes. (503) 436–2623 or www.cannonbeach.org.

JULY THROUGH LABOR DAY

Sunday Concerts in the Park. Cannon Beach City Park. Bring a picnic, spread out a blanket, and kick back and enjoy the music. (503) 436–2623 or www.cannonbeach.org.

ALL YEAR

Coaster Theatre. This theatre company hosts many productions with kids in mind. (503) 436–1242.

HUG POINT STATE RECREATION SITE (all ages)

Located 5 miles south of Cannon Beach off U.S. 101; (800) 551–6949 or www.oregonstateparks.org. Always open. **Free.**

This park, named for the way pioneers traveling the beach "highway" had to hug the point at low tide in order to pass, has caves and sections of the old road carved out of rock to explore, though these are cut off when the tide comes in.

Other Things to See and Do in Cannon Beach

It's almost impossible to visit Cannon Beach without wandering through its many attractive stores. Kids can buy trinkets and treasures at **Geppetto's Toy Shoppe**, 200 North Hemlock Street (503-436-2467), and collections of stuffed critters at **Animal Crackers of Oregon**, 123 South Hemlock Street (503-436-0536). You might even lure the children through some of the many art galleries in the area with the promise of a stop at **Bruce's Candy Kitchen**, 256 North Hemlock, (503-436-2641) (watching the taffy-pulling machines is mouthwatering); or the **Lazy Susan Grill and Scoop**, 156 South Hemlock (503-436-9551), where kids can enjoy ice cream cones while you get a lift from a shot of espresso.

Manzanita

One of the most delightful beaches on this stretch of the north coast is the lesser-known Manzanita, a small community that sits a few miles off U.S. 101. Walk the beach in relative solitude, or blend the sound of pounding horse hoofs with the pounding surf on a horseback ride along the shore (call **Sundown Beach Rides** at 503-368-7470). The solitude makes this a nice place to stay. Cafes, a few stores, and a small library are all nearby when you want to wander away from the beach.

NEAHKAHNIE MOUNTAIN (ages 8 and up)

The mountain trailhead is one-half mile off U.S. 101, 1.5 miles north of Manzanita to hiker sign; turn east on rocky access road .5 mile to trailhead. Neahkahnie Mountain is in Oswald West State Park, which stretches to the north beyond Cape Falcon and Smuggler's Cove; (800) 551–6949 or www.oregonstateparks. org. **Free.**

To get a bird's-eye view of the beach and bay, walk to the top of Neahkahnie Mountain, which rises 1,631 feet above the surf. The 1½-mile trail takes you through forest and, in spring, beautiful wildflower meadows. Legend tells of buried treasure on the mountain, an enticing tidbit to entertain kids along the way. Allow an hour to get to the rocky summit, where children must use caution.

OSWALD WEST STATE PARK (ages 5 and up)

Located 10 miles south of Cannon Beach off of U.S. 101; (800) 551–6949 or www.oregonstateparks.org. **Free**.

Strewn with red needles, the path through this enchanting rain forest is so peaceful that you can easily forget the ocean waves crashing on the cape just beyond. The trees form such a dense canopy that even if it's raining, you'll hardly notice. From the **Short Sand Beach** parking lot, follow a trail that parallels Short Sand Creek to where it merges with Necarney Creek at the ocean shore. Camping is for tents only because the sites are a quarter mile away from the parking area. Wheelbarrows are provided for transporting your gear along paved pathways.

*F*ishing in Nehalem Bay

Nehalem Bay, according to locals, is one of the richest estuaries for both clamming and crabbing. If you don't have your own equipment, the following outlets can get you set up with buckets, shovels, and such.

Nehalem Bay fisheries (ages 10 and up)
Rent crab rings or clam shovels, as well as boats and motors from either of these fisheries:

- *Brighton Marina, on U.S. 101 3½ miles south of Wheeler; (503) 368–5745. $6.00 for baited crab ring rentals. Boat rentals $45 for three hours and three baited crab rings. Call for hours.*

- *Wheeler Marina, 2 miles south of Nehalem off U.S. 101; (503) 368–5780. Call for hours. Boat rental $35 for three hours; $3 for crab rings; $2 for bait.*

Rockaway Beach and Garibaldi

Rockaway and Garibaldi are small towns whose livelihoods depend on the sea, but in very different ways. Rockaway grew up as a resort community, while Garibaldi, one of the earliest settlements on the coast, is very much a working community.

ROCKAWAY BEACH STATE PARK (ages 5 and up)

Located right in the center of Garibaldi; (800) 551–6949 or www.oregon stateparks.org. Call for hours, fees.

Rockaway Beach State Park is a great family spot for beachcombing, kite flying, and long walks.

 GARIBALDI MARINA LOCATION (ages 8 and up)
302 Mooring Basin Road; (503) 322–3312. Open daily, 5:00 A.M.–5:00 P.M. $3.00 for crab ring rentals; $40 for three-hour boat rentals.
Rent crab rings at the Garibaldi Marina and catch your own appetizers. Boat rentals let you get out on the bay, and charters are available for deep-sea fishing.

 BARVIEW JETTY (ages 8 and up)
Barview Jetty is located just north of Garibaldi off U.S. 101; (503) 322–0301 or garibaldi@oregoncoast.com. Always open. **Free**.
This is a great place for surf fishing, and the beach to the north of the jetty gives the kids a place to roam.

 MEMORIAL LUMBERMAN'S PARK (ages 5 and up)
Third and American Streets; (503) 322–0301. Always open. **Free**.
For a picnic and a bit of local industrial history, stop by this park. Old logging and railroad equipment placed throughout the park invite children to climb.

 op Rockaway Beach Events

MAY

Rockaway Kite Festival. During the day kids get help from the Oregon Kiters Association to make their own kites. A teddy bear drop and hobby horse races add to lots of family-oriented fun. When the weather's right, a lighted kite flight in the evening requires blankets for snuggling together on the beach.

SEPTEMBER

Valley Annual Autumn Festival and Sandcastle Contest. This isn't a pros-only contest—kids are expected to join in (503) 355–8108.

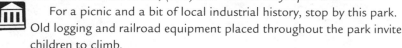 **Tillamook Bay**

Most Oregonians know about Tillamook, if only because of the delicious cheddar cheese to be found in every grocery store cold case. Tillamook is a small community, well inland from the ocean but enjoying the generally mild climate associated with the coast.

 TILLAMOOK CHEESE FACTORY (all ages)
4175 U.S. 101 North; (503) 815–1300; www.tillamookcheese.com. Open daily, summer hours, 8:00 A.M.–8:00 P.M.; rest of the year, 8:00 A.M.–6:00 P.M. **Free**.
The Tillamook Cheese Factory is a favorite for all ages, with its **Free** offerings of cheese samples. Be sure to take a quick tour to learn about the cheesemaking process. Then stop by the deli to purchase a variety of packaged cheeses for vacation snacks or to send home or an ice cream cone from up to forty flavors of Tillamook ice cream.

 BLUE HERON FRENCH CHEESE COMPANY (all ages)
Located one mile north of Tillamook off U.S. 101; (800) 275–0639. Summer hours, 8:00 A.M.–8:00 P.M.; winter hours, 9:00 A.M.–6:00 P.M. **Free**.
The Blue Heron is a less well-known (and less crowded) cheese company in the area that offers equally delicious samples of creamy Bries as well as home-smoked sausages. Blue Heron sells its products at an on-site deli-restaurant. Have a snack, then head for the on-site petting farm, filled with goats, llamas, ducks, rabbits, cows, and sheep.

 TILLAMOOK COUNTY PIONEER MUSEUM (ages 5 and up)
2106 Second Street; (503) 842–4553 or www.oregoncoast.com/Pionrmus. htm. Open Monday through Saturday, 8:00 A.M.–5:00 P.M.; Sunday, 11:00 A.M.–5:00 P.M. $2.00 adults; $1.50 seniors; 50 cents ages 12–17; under 12 **Free**.
This large museum contains more than 35,000 artifacts of area pioneers and Native Americans who lived in this area and features natural history dioramas of animals, birds, insects, and shells.

Money-saving Travel Tips

- Be sure to ask if a complimentary breakfast is included in the hotel rate. Enjoying a simple continental breakfast with the children in the room is often more relaxing the first thing in the morning.

- A room with a small refrigerator saves money when you load it up with fruit, juice, and yogurt for the kids to snack on.

TILLAMOOK NAVAL AIR STATION MUSEUM (ages 5 and up)

6030 Hangar Road, 2 miles south of Tillamook off U.S. 101; (503) 842–1130; www.tillamookair.com. Open daily, year-round, 10:00 A.M.–5:00 P.M. Call for admission rates. Group rates available.

This museum is enclosed inside a World War II blimp hangar, with fighter planes and blimps that are fascinating for kids. The largest clear-span wood building in the world, the hangar is as wide as a football field is long and stretches 1,072 feet from end to end. The ceiling is fifteen stories high—195 feet—making everything inside seem tiny by comparison. The hangar housed blimps that patrolled the ocean for enemy submarines during the war.

CAPE LOOKOUT STATE PARK

Located twelve miles southwest of Tillamook on Whiskey Creek Road; (800) 551–6949; (800) 452–5687 for camping reservations; www.oregonstateparks.org. Open year-round; $3.00 day-use fee.

This is part of the **Three Capes Loop drive,** which takes you off U.S. 101 for about 35 miles between Tillamook and Neskowin to view three outstanding natural areas. The park extends north along the Netarts Spit, which forms the boundary of Netarts Bay. Many campsites have ocean views or direct beach access. Yurts—canvas-walled circular buildings—and teepees are also available to campers who aren't traveling with their own tents.

CAPE MEARES STATE SCENIC VIEWPOINT (ages 5 and up)

Located 9 miles northwest of Tillamook using Whiskey Creek Road; (800) 551–6949; www.oregonstateparks.org. Open daily, May through September, dawn to dusk; lighthouse open 11:00 A.M.–4:00 P.M. April through October, weather permitting. **Free**.

The 1890 **Cape Meares Lighthouse** and the nearby giant spruce **Octopus Tree** are perennial favorites of kids. Oregon's largest seabird colonies thrive at **Three Arch Rocks National Wildlife Refuge**, offshore where species include common murres, tufted puffins, storm petrels, and pigeon guillemots.

CAPE KIWANDA STATE NATURAL AREA (ages 5 and up)

Located south of Cape Lookout, 15 miles southwest of Tillamook on Whiskey Creek Road; (800) 551–6949 for information; www.oregonstateparks.org. Day use only. **Free**.

You can watch Pacific City dories launch if you're here early in the morning, but it's even more fun to be standing on the beach just south of the park when they're heading for shore. They head straight for the sand, riding to ground on a high wave.

 MUNSON CREEK FALLS (ages 5 and up)
Located about 6½ miles south of Tillamook on U.S. 101; (503) 842–7525. Always open. **Free.**
Here you'll find a trailhead that takes you through old-growth forest to the highest waterfall in the Oregon Coast Range. The 1.5-mile road into the small parking area is a bit rough, but the quarter-mile walk to the falls is worth the ride.

THE CENTRAL COAST

Lincoln City

The largest of the coastal resort towns, Lincoln City has almost 8 miles of wide open sands where families can walk, fly kites, jump over waves, and soak up the sun or—since this is, after all, the Oregon coast— the rain. With fifteen beach access spots in town, you'll have no problem finding your way onto the sand.

Devils Lake has an interesting history, according to Indian folklore. Once known as Indian Bay, the lake was supposedly inhabited by an evil spirit. Sometimes Siletz warriors mysteriously disappeared in the lake. The legend remains

 **un Facts**

- Lincoln City is the **"Kite Capital of the World,"** because kites are frequent sky decorations, especially along the beach around the D River. (**Catch the Wind Kite Shop**, 266 Southeast Highway 101, south of the D River wayside, sells kites of all shapes and sizes for parents and kids who want to try their own hand at kite flying.)

- The **D River** is the world's shortest river, flowing from Devils Lake a brief 120 feet to the ocean.

that if a boat crosses the moon's reflection in the center of the lake, the passengers will feel a chill of fear rise up from the lake.

NORTH LINCOLN COUNTY HISTORICAL MUSEUM
(ages 5 and up)

4907 Southwest Highway 101; (541) 996–6614. Call first for exact hours; usually open Tuesday through Saturday, noon–4:00 P.M. Free *but donations accepted.*

Several rooms are set up as they would have looked in the early days of the pioneers. Displays include a variety of Native American baskets and beadwork as well as a hands-on table with some pioneer and Native American artifacts they can handle, plus puppets and coloring activities.

OCEAN TRAILS RIDING STABLES (ages 10 and up)

Located in Neskowin, 6 miles north of Lincoln City; call for appointment; (541) 994–4849. Beach rides $35 per hour; pony walks $5 for fifteen minutes or $20 per hour.

Call a few days ahead of time for reservations.

Devil's Lake Parks (all ages) Today, five parks offer

recreation on Devil's Lake, from fishing and boating (in daylight, of course) to camping and picnicking. Call for hours, fees: (800) 551–6949, (541) 994-8378, (541) 994-2131.

- **Blue Heron Landing**, 4006 West Devil's Lake Road (541–994–4708), has plenty of choices for water play. Canoes, paddleboats, bumper boats, and motorboats are available for rent by the day, or by the hour.

- **Regatta Grounds Park** is located on Devil's Lake, ¾ miles east off U.S. 101. You can take advantage of a half-mile exercise and jogging path while your kids try out the playground equipment, then head to the swimming area.

- **Sand Point Park**, located off East Devil's Lake Road on a point of land jutting into the lake, has a swimming beach and picnic tables.

- **Devil's Lake State Park**, 1452 Northeast Sixth Drive, has camping facilities straddled between the lake and the ocean. It's open year-round, and you can make reservations in advance by calling (800) 452-8657.

- **Holmes Road Park**, on Holmes Road 8 blocks off U.S. 101. A small dock allows acccess to the lake, and the picnic tables in this little park have a great view.

Top Lincoln City Events

MAY

Spring Kite Festival. Another kite extravaganza that offers prizes for the best children's kites, among other categories.

LATE SUMMER

Sandcastle Competition. Fun in the sand for the whole family. If you aren't up to sculpting your own, you can watch the pros at work.

OCTOBER

International Kite Festival. *D River Wayside.* The biggest and most spectacular of Lincoln City's annual events. Kids are thrilled by skydivers gliding on gigantic kite-like, colorful parachutes; kite battle and team choreography; and nighttime lighted kite flying.

Glass Float Search. From October through Memorial Day, handblown glass floats by local artisans are hidden above the high-tide level. If you find one, take it to the Visitor Center (801 SW Hwy 101) for a certificate and description of the artist.

For information about Lincoln City events, call (800) 452–2151 or (541) 994–8378; www.oregoncoast.org.

 ### CASCADE HEAD (ages 5 and up)

Located 4 miles north of Lincoln City at the west end of Three Rocks Road; (503) 392–3161 or (541) 994–5564. Open dawn to dusk. **Free**.

An area of outstanding scenic beauty just 4 miles north of Lincoln City, Cascade Head offers hiking trails to suit all ages. Within the **Cascade Head Scenic Research Area,** two trails maintained by the Nature Conservancy and two U.S. Forest Service trails take you through a variety of ecosystems, and on one, a self-guiding brochure lets your child be the guide, pointing out old-growth Sitka spruce, or the scars left by forest fires.

 ### TAFT WATERFRONT PARK (all ages)

Located at the mouth of the Siletz River, off Fifty-first Street on the south side of town.

Sea lions often congregate here on the northern edge of the Salishan Spit, which forms the south edge of the Siletz River mouth. A small parking area has restrooms, and **Mo's Restaurant** (541-996-2535), famous for its clam chowder, lies just up the street. Crabbing is good October through February, off the public crabbing dock adjacent to the restaurant. Rent crab rings from Eleanor's Undertow (541-996-3800), a restaurant and take-out at 869 SW Fifty-first Street, for $10 for twenty-four hours.

*S*uper Shopping Factory Outlet Stores. *U.S. 101 at East Devil's Lake Road; (541) 996-5000. Open Monday–Saturday 10:00 A.M.–8:00 P.M., Sunday 10:00 A.M.–6:00 P.M.* No discussion of activities in Lincoln City can ignore the presence of this mammoth shopping center. The collection of big-name factory stores include at least a few to keep the kids happy: **Toy Liquidators, OshKosh B'Gosh, Carter's Childrenswear,** and the **Book Warehouse.** There's also an ice cream shop tucked in the mall, offering rewards for patience and good behavior!

Gleneden Beach

Here you'll find a small marketplace ideal for browsing or picking up picnic supplies, a golf course, and a resort that makes any trip to the coast very special. **Westin Salishan Lodge** (888-725-4742 or 503-764-3600; www.salishan.com), a well-known five-star resort, has something for the whole family: tennis courts, swimming pool, exercise room, large whirlpool spa, sauna, nature walks, jogging path, playground, and video arcade.

*S*uper Shopping Siletz Tribal Smokehouse. *272 U.S. 101 South in Depoe Bay; (541) 765-2286; www.oregonsmokedfoods.com.* You can purchase mouthwatering smoked Chinook or Coho salmon and other products here.

Depoe Bay

A small fishing village that claims the world's smallest harbor, Depoe Bay sits midway between the larger towns of Lincoln City and Newport. Your kids will be more fascinated by the spouting horns, a pair of ocean-driven geysers that spout plumes of water with the crashing of the waves, especially at high tide or after a storm. Watch out, though; if the waves are strong, you're in for a dousing! From the bridge it's fun to watch the boats navigate the narrow, rocky channel that leads into the tiny harbor.

TRADEWINDS CHARTERS (all ages)

Located at north end of the bridge in Depoe Bay; (541) 765–2345 or www. tradewindscharters.com. Call for hours. Whale-watching tour: $13.00 adults; $11.00 seniors and teens; $7.00 ages 5–12; under 5 **Free***.*

To experience the passage from the deck of a boat, try a whale-watching or fishing charter trip.

FOGARTY CREEK STATE PARK (all ages)

Two miles north of Depoe Bay on U.S. 101; (800) 551–6949; www.oregonstate parks.com. Day use only; $3.00 fee or $25 annual state park pass.

This is a beautiful spot to spend the day. You can walk on the path alongside the creek as it lazily winds through the park, crossing picturesque arched footbridges at several points. Spread out a picnic feast at the charming cove where Fogarty Creek meets the sea, and explore the tidepools at low tide.

ROCKY CREEK STATE PARK (ages 5 and up)

Two miles south of Depoe Bay; (800) 551–6949. Call for hours, fees.

Rocky Creek offers an excellent viewpoint for whalewatching. Sitting on a bluff over the ocean, the day-use park has picnic facilities as well as broad areas of grass where the kids can run and play.

Top Depoe Bay Event

SEPTEMBER

Depoe Bay Indian Salmon Bake. Sample delicious salmon prepared on alder stakes over open fire pits. The Siletz Dancers often perform traditional tribal dances for this event. (503) 765–2889.

Newport

This central Oregon coast community has developed a successful tourist industry that works hard to give people experiences worth coming back for. Fishing, centered at the **Newport Bayfront,** is still one of the town's economic mainstays. **Nye Beach,** which became a beloved vacation spot at the turn of the twentieth century, still has the lingering feel of an old-fashioned neighborhood and boasts several small cafes and shops to explore.

OREGON COAST AQUARIUM (ages 6 and up)

2820 Southeast Ferry Slip Road; (541) 867–3474; www.aquarium.org. Open daily, summer hours, 9:00 A.M.–6:00 P.M.; winter hours, 10:00 A.M.–5:00 P.M. $10.25 ages 14 and older; $9.25 senior citizens. $6.25 ages 4 to 13, under 4 **Free**.

The twenty-nine-acre state-of-the-art aquarium is an impressive complex nestled on the south shore of Yaquina Bay. Everything is geared to give your children an educational experience they'll only remember as fun. A favorite with kids of all ages is the rocky shores exhibit, where they can "drive" a television camera through a deep pool for close-up views as if they were underwater divers. On busy summer weekends you can purchase your tickets in advance at the Lincoln City Visitors Center (801 U.S. 101S).

MARK O. HATFIELD MARINE SCIENCE CENTER (ages 5 and up)

Marine Science Drive, south side of Yaquina Bay and east of U.S. 101; (541) 867–0271; www.hmsc.orst.edu/visitor. Open daily, summer hours, 10:00 A.M.–5:00 P.M.; rest of the year, 10:00 A.M.–4:00 P.M. **Free** *but donations appreciated.*

This is a terrific, long-beloved option for coastal education. Your children will love the touching pool, where they can have close encounters with starfish, sea urchins, anemones, sculpin, and the deliciously yucky sea cucumber. The resident octopus is another favorite.

Kids' Books on Oregon

A Historical Album of Oregon. Charles A. Wells. Ages 9–12. A history of Oregon from its early exploration and settlement to the present day.

The Oregon Trail. Leonard Everett Fisher. Ages 9–12. This tale charts the journey of those who followed the Oregon Trail in the first half of the nineteenth century.

RIPLEY'S BELIEVE IT OR NOT (ages 10 and up)
WAX WORKS (ages 10 and up)
UNDERSEA GARDENS (ages 8 and up)

All open daily, 9:00 A.M.–6:00 P.M. Admission to each center: $6.95 adults, $3.95 ages 5–12, under 4 **Free**. *Combo rates for all three: $13.80 adults, $7.80 children. (541) 265–2206.*

These kid-centered buildings all are located at **Mariner Square,** 250 Southwest Bay Boulevard.

 YAQUINA HEAD OUTSTANDING NATURAL AREA
 (ages 5 and up)

2 miles north of Newport off U.S. 101; (541) 574–3100. Open dawn to dusk daily. $5.00 per car (covers entire natural area).

Visitors are in for a real treat here. During whale migrations, there's often a park ranger on hand with strong binoculars or a spotting scope to help you see the whales. During summer, some resident gray whales have taken to feeding offshore here. You can also get a look at a wandering sea lion or, on the rocks below, some of the offshore bird species, such as the elusive tufted puffin or the endangered guillemots. Wheelchair-accessible tidepools and an interpretive center make this a place for everyone to enjoy.

 YAQUINA HEAD LIGHTHOUSE (ages 8 and up)

Located off U.S. 101, 3 miles north of Newport; (541) 574–3100. Lighthouse and Interpretive Center open noon–4:00 P.M. daily. $5.00 per person.

A 93-foot-high tower that stands 162 feet above sea level makes this Oregon's tallest lighthouse. You can tour the authentically refurbished 1873 lighthouse year-round, weather permitting.

 MARINE DISCOVERY TOURS

345 Southwest Bay Boulevard; (541) 265–6200 or (800) 903–2628. Call for hours. (The Chamber of Commerce can provide a list of other charter services; call 800–262–7844.) Two-hour Discover tour Sealite cruise $22 adults; $18 ages 13–16; $12 ages 4–12; under 4 **Free**. *More adventuresome Oregon Rocket one-hour wave-jumping tour $28 adults; $18 ages 8–16.*

To see the whales up close, a number of tour operators take charter trips into the ocean for whalewatching and offer both a one-hour bay tour and a two-hour whale-watching cruise. Marine Discovery Tours has a naturalist on board who leads the kids in fun learning activities during the two-hour ride.

BAYFRONT CHARTERS (ages 8 and up)

890 South East Bay Boulevard; (541) 265–7558 or (800) 828–8777. Open daily, 6:00 A.M.–8:00 P.M. $15.00 per hour boat rental; $8.00 crab ring and bait.

Located at the Embarcadero Marina, Bayfront Charters rents 14-foot motor boats for crabbing in the bay. Charter fishing trips are also available.

NEWPORT MARINA AT SOUTH BEACH (ages 8 and up)

2122 Southeast Marine Science Drive; (541) 867–4470. Open daily 5:30 A.M.– 9:00 P.M. $5.50 per day for crab rings; $55.00 for four-hour boat ride with crab gear.

This South Beach marina rents crab rings at its marina store and at the fuel dock. The long public pier adjacent to the marina is a perfect place to toss your crab rings into the water and wait for those delicious Dungeness to take the bait.

*S*uper Shopping On Saturdays, May through October, you can pick up fresh organic produce, cut flowers, catch-of-the-day seafood, and local arts and crafts at the **Newport Saturday Market.** Open 9:00 A.M.– 1:00 P.M., ¼ mile north of the Yaquina Bay Bridge in the lot between Alder and Fall Streets. (541) 574–4040.

NEWPORT VISUAL ARTS CENTER (ages 8 and up)

777 Nye Beach Turnaround; (541) 265–6540. Open Tuesday through Sunday, 11:00 A.M.–6:00 P.M. April through October; 11:00 A.M.–5:00 P.M. rest of the year. **Free***, donations welcome.*

The center looks out over a renovated beach access area, with benches and an attractive walkway to Nye Beach. The Center offers exhibits of local artists, touring exhibits, and frequent workshops.

NEWPORT PERFORMING ARTS CENTER (ages 8 and up)

777 West Olive; (541) 265–2787 or (541) 265–9231. Call for hours, prices, and schedule of events.

Newport's Performing Arts Center brings touring companies into the community but also presents local productions, with several directed at family audiences.

LINCOLN COUNTY HISTORICAL SOCIETY MUSEUMS (ages 5 and up)

545 Southwest Ninth Street; (541) 265–7509. Open Tuesday through Sunday, 10:00 A.M.–5:00 P.M. in summer; 11:00 A.M.–4:00 P.M. in winter. **Free** *but donations appreciated.*

The Lincoln County Historical Society operates both the **Log Cabin Museum** and the **Burrows House.** The 1895 Victorian Burrows House includes Native American, maritime, and coastal settlement exhibits.

U.S. COAST GUARD STATION (ages 8 and up)

Located on the east end of Bay Boulevard on the Newport waterfront; (541) 265–5381. Open daily, 1:00–4:00 P.M. **Free.**

You will get a strong sense of the Coast Guard's role on the Oregon Coast here, both past and present. It's also a great chance for your kids to learn about ocean safety as well as the Coast Guard's dramatic rescue capabilities.

YAQUINA BAY LIGHTHOUSE/STATE PARK (all ages)

8465 Southwest Government Street at the north end of the bay bridge; (541) 867–7451. Lighthouse open 10:00 A.M.–5:00 P.M. daily in summer and on weekends noon–4:00 P.M. the rest of the year. Park is day use only. **Free.**

Built in 1871, the lighthouse is Newport's oldest building. It operated for only three years before giving way to the more powerful lighthouse at Yaquina Head. Your kids will appreciate the tale of the lighthouse "ghost"; look for a pamphlet at the museum that tells the story.

Fun Facts At Yaquina Head, you'll see the world's first barrier-free tidal zone. It was constructed in an old quarry site, with gently sloping paths winding around the tide pools, the perfect alternative for parents with strollers as well as for people who are physically challenged.

F ree Things to Do in Newport

WHALEWATCHING (ages 8 and up)

■ **Cape Foulweather.** *To reach Cape Foulweather, take U.S. 101 north to the Otter Crest Loop Drive, which winds to a viewpoint overlooking the Pacific.*

■ **Yaquina Head.** *Located 2 miles north of town off U.S. 101.*

Volunteers are often stationed at these sites (and others along the coast) on peak whale-watching weekends in spring (last two weeks in March) and winter (late December and early January). For information on migrating whales, visit www.whalespoken.org.

CLAMMING (ages 8 and up)

■ **South Beach Marina.** *Out under the bridge adjacent to the marina.*

Clamming is popular in the bay's tide flats during spring or summer minus tides (check the tide tables). This spot gives the best access to gaper clams. Grab a shovel and bucket, roll up your jeans, and get ready to have a ball and make a mess. Be sure to check that there isn't a red tide, a rare occurrence in Oregon but potentially fatal.

BEACHCOMBING (ages 5 and up)

■ **Agate Beach.** *Located on the north edge of town off Ocean View Road.* Agates are commonly found among the loose gravel on top of the sand, especially in off-season months, from October to April. From Agate Beach you've got a clear stretch of beach leading north to **Yaquina Head** or south to **Yaquina Bay.**

■ **Beverly Beach.** *Located 7 miles north of Newport; park on the east side of U.S. 101 and walk under the bridge to the beach. Day-use fee $3.00.* This wonderful park boasts a playground and a lovely stream that flows into the ocean.

 DEVIL'S PUNCHBOWL STATE PARK (ages 8 and up)
Located 8 miles north of Newport off U.S. 101; (800) 551–6949; www.oregon stateparks.org. Day use only. **Free**.
This park is also on Crest Loop Drive with picnic facilities and a walking trail to a view of the punchbowl, a wave-carved rock bowl that fills from a cavern below as the tide thunders in. Another trail leads to the marine gardens, an area of tidepools that is perfect for exploring

during low or minus tides (indicated with a minus sign on the tide table). It can be hazardous during high tides, however, so keep an eye on the water level.

 ### SEAL ROCK STATE PARK (ages 8 and up)
Located 10 miles south of Newport on U.S. 101; (800) 551–6949 or (888) 628–2101. Call for hours, fees.

This lovely park sits atop a bluff next to Seal Rock, a large basalt sea stack just offshore. Picnic tables are nestled along narrow forest paths that lead to the beach below.

Top Newport Events

MAY

Loyalty Days and Sea Fare. This gala four-day event celebrates patriotism with a carnival, a parade, military ship tours, and lots of food and fun.

JULY

Rope in some good-old family fun at the annual **Lincoln County Fair and Rodeo.**

For information on these and other Newport events, call (888) 628–2101 or (541) 574–2679.

Waldport

Waldport means "port of the woods" in German. The early settlers in this Alsea River basin were Germans who came for the brief gold rush and then stayed to develop the timber industry.

 ### ALSEA BAY BRIDGE INTERPRETIVE CENTER (ages 8 and up)
620 Northwest Spring Street, on U.S. 101 just south of the Alsea Bay Bridge; (541) 563–2002 or (800) 551–6949. Open daily in summer; Wednesday through Sunday during rest of the year, 9:00 A.M.–5:00 P.M. Daily bridge tours at 2:00 P.M. **Free.**

In the center, you'll learn the old bridge's story with photographs and a short video. Once the longest cement-poured bridge in the world, it was torn down in 1992 and rebuilt to be more structurally sound.

Attractions kids will appreciate include model replica of the old bridge, displays on the history of transportation, a powerful viewing scope trained on the new bridge, and exhibits about the Alsi Indians who once lived in this area. You can also participate in clamming and crabbing demonstrations; times and locations vary with the tides.

Top Waldport Events

JUNE

Beachcomber Days. These fun-filled days include a sandcastle contest, a treasure hunt, slug races, and a parade.

SEPTEMBER

Valley Alsea Bay Crab Festival. This event features a crab-ring toss, crab-catching contest, crab races, and, of course, a crab feed.

For information call (541) 563–2133 or visit www.waldport.org.

Yachats

Practice pronouncing the name of this tiny coastal town before you venture any questions to the locals. It's "YAH-hots," and comes from the local tribe of Native Americans of that name, which is said to mean "dark waters at the foot of the mountain."

 LITTLE LOG CHURCH MUSEUM (ages 5 and up)
Corner of Third and Pontiac Streets; (541) 547–3976. Open daily except Thursday; 10:00 A.M.–4:00 P.M. Saturday and Sunday, noon–3:00 P.M. weekdays. **Free** *although donations are welcome.*

This tiny museum houses an interesting collection of Native American artifacts as well as pioneer tools and household items, such as a one hundred-year-old crazy quilt, teddy bears, fossils, and a molar from a wooly mammoth.

 YACHATS OCEAN ROAD WAYSIDE (ages 5 and up)
Located immediately south of Yachats, 500 feet off U.S. 101. Day-use area. **Free.**

Access to a wide sandy beach begins here. Tidepooling is great on the rocks that edge the ocean shore. But be very careful, and go out on these rocks only when the tide is well out. Sneaker waves—especially during winter months—can be deadly, and the rocks can be slippery.

SMELT SANDS WAYSIDE (ages 5 and up)

Located at the north end of Yachats; (800) 551–6949. Day-use area. Free.

Both a whale-watching viewpoint and a great kids-oriented hiking trail, this area is located about a half-mile north of town along the oceanfront. From the parking area you can take the Yachats 804 Trail. The trail is wheelchair accessible, so even your youngest will manage the easy, level terrain. It leads along a cliff top above odd-shaped rocks that eroded from the twenty-five-million-year-old Yaquina Formation. The beach is not quite a mile from the trailhead.

CAPE PERPETUA SCENIC AREA (ages 5 and up)

3 miles south of Yachats; (541) 547–3289. Visitor Center open daily, 10:00 A.M.–5:00 P.M. in summer. Call for winter whale-watching information. Day-use fee is $5.00 per vehicle; covers Oregon Dunes National Recreation Area and all of Cape Perpetua.

One of the most beautiful areas on the coast, Cape Perpetua winds along coastal cliffs that jut straight up from the ocean. Stop by the **Visitors Center,** which contains exhibits that explain local geological features, give whale-watching tips, present local history, and describe Native American culture. Maps are available for the area's 23 miles of hiking trails. The Giant Spruce Trail leads for 1 mile to a massive 500-year-old Sitka spruce.

Fantastic Facts About Oregon

- Nearly half of Oregon's 97,073 square miles is forested.

- Oregon has more than 5,800 registered campsites. (Call 800–551–6949 for a copy of the State Campground Guide.)

- Oregon is one of the very few states that still has no sales tax—it's a shopper's paradise for visitors.

DEVIL'S CHURN VIEWPOINT (ages 5 and up)

Located just north of junction at Cape Perpetua Road and U.S. 101; (541) 547–3289. Day-use area. Cape Perpetua Scenic Area fee applies (see above).

Trails near the viewpoint will take you down to the rocks below, where the surf at high tide churns in the deep chasm and crashes onto the rock, throwing sea spray onto everything around—including tourists who get too close! Enjoy the view at high tide from above, which is now a wheelchair-accessible viewpoint. Several other scenic overlooks and turnoffs in this area give you access to sandy beaches, picnic spots, tide pools, and hiking trails.

Family Favorites on the North and Central Coasts

1. Astoria Aquatics Center
2. Fort Clatsop National Memorial, Astoria
3. Haystack Rock Marine Garden, Cannon Beach
4. Tillamook Cheese Factory
5. Tillamook County Pioneer Museum
6. Cascade Head, near Lincoln City
7. Oregon Coast Aquarium, Newport
8. Yaquina Bay Lighthouse, near Newport
9. Cape Perpetua Scenic Area, near Yachats
10. Devil's Churn Viewpoint, near Yachats

Where to Eat

IN ASTORIA

Mr. Fultano's Pizza. *620 Olney; (503) 325–2855.* Fultano's has old-fashioned pizzas, Italian and Mexican dishes, hamburgers, and a salad bar. They'll even deliver to your hotel room. $$

Pier 11 Restaurant & Lounge. *77 Eleventh Street; (503) 325–0279.* Almost all tables here offer a view of the river and frolicking sea lions and seals. Seafood specialties. Breakfast, lunch, dinner. Children's menu. $–$$$

IN CANNON BEACH

Cannon Beach Cookie Company. *239 North Hemlock Street, #1; (503) 436–2832.* Adults can savor an afternoon cup of coffee while the kids work their way through oversized cookies. Sandwiches and pizza also available. $

Lazy Susan Cafe. *126 North Hemlock Street; (503) 436–2816.* A cheerful cafe in a brick courtyard off the main street in downtown Cannon Beach. Highly recommended for breakfast waffles and omelets. $–$$

Mo's Restaurant. *3400 South Hemlock Street; (503) 436–1111.* Casual dining well-suited for families with young children. Fish and chips, and creamy clam chowder are popular mainstays. $–$$

IN MANZANITA

Blue Sky Cafe. *154 Laneda; (503) 368–5712.* Excellent fresh seafood, pasta, beef, and chicken entrees. Special children's entrees served. Cash only. $$–$$$

Manzanita Beach Fireside Inn and Café. *114 Laneda; (503) 368–1001 or (800) 368–1001.* This charming inn offers both rooms and meals, and families and pets are welcome. The menu is varied enough to have something for everyone—fresh seafood, pasta, burgers, vegetarian meals, and chowder. $$–$$$

IN SEASIDE

Dooger's Seafood and Grill. *505 Broadway; (503) 738–3773.* Famous for its rich clam chowder. Wonderful desserts might extend the dinner hour for your family. Breakfast, lunch, dinner. Children's menu available. $$–$$$

Vista Spring Cafe. *150 Broadway; (503) 738–8108.* Casual lunch and dinner fare for the whole family. Pizza, soup, and sandwiches are the specialties here. Clam chowder is a local favorite, but beware—they run out early. $–$$

IN AND AROUND LINCOLN CITY

Lighthouse Brewery Pub and Restaurant. *Located in the Roads End shopping center, 5157 North Highway 101; (541) 994–7238.* The Lighthouse Brewery has burgers, fish and chips, and other kid-oriented fare on the children's menu as well as local ales for mom and dad to try. $–$$$

Mo's. *860 Southwest Fifty-first Street; (541) 996–2535.* This popular seafood coastal chain is a can't miss with little ones. $–$$

60s Cafe. *4157 NW Highway 101, #139; (541) 996–6898.* Nostalgic diner with good burgers. $

IN NEWPORT

Apple Peddler Restaurant. *705 Southwest Coast Highway; (541) 265–5165.* Simple, family-oriented restaurant serving breakfast, lunch, and dinner. $

Kam Meng's Chinese. *837 SW Bay Boulevard; (541) 574–9450.* On the bay with indoor and outdoor seating, this little restaurant serves homestyle Chinese food, fresh crab, and orders to go. $–$$

Cosmos Cafe & Gallery. *740 West Olive Street; (541) 265–7511.* Informal atmosphere featuring celestial decor. Wholesome meals to please the whole family. Breakfast, lunch, dinner. Pick up shortbread cookies before heading over to the beach, which is just a half block away. $–$$

Newport Chowder Bowl. *728 Northwest Beach Drive; (541) 265–7477.* Heaping bowls of chowder make this the perfect stop for lunch. $–$$

IN YACHATS

La Serre. *Second Avenue and Beach Street; (541) 547–3420.* Steaks and seafood prepared in innovative ways. Enticing array of desserts. $$$

The Joe's Town Center Cafe. *251 N. Coast Highway 101; (541) 547–4244 or (877) 233–2850.* You'll find fresh- baked muffins and scones and home-made soups at this breakfast and lunch spot. $-$$

Where to Stay

IN AND AROUND ASTORIA

Crest Motel. *5366 Leif Erickson Drive; (503) 325–3141 or (800) 421–3141 (for reservations only); www.crest-motel.com.* Forty rooms on a picturesque hilltop overlooking the Columbia River. Continental breakfast, spa. Coin laundry. $$-$$$

Rosebriar Hotel. *636 Fourteenth Street; (800) 487–0224 or (503) 325–7427; www.oregoncoastlodgings.com/rosebriar.* Eleven units in a small, classic hotel overlooking the Columbia River. Some kitchenettes. Complimentary breakfast. $$-$$$

Shilo Inn. *1609 East Harbor Drive, Warrenton; (800) 222–2244 or (503) 861–2181.* Sixty-three units. Restaurant. Some kitchenettes. Outdoor swimming pool, hot tub. $$-$$$$

Fort Stevens Campground. *Ten miles west of Astoria off U.S. 101; (800) 452–5687; www.oregonstateparks.org.* Oregon's third largest campground. $-$$

IN CANNON BEACH

Blue Gull Inn Motel. *632 South Hemlock Street; (800) 507–2714 or (503) 436–2714; www.bluegullinn.com.* Just a few steps away from the beach. Twenty-one units. Two-bedroom suites and cottages are ideal for families. $$-$$$$

McBee Motel Cottages. *Check in at the Sandtrap Inn at 539 South Hemlock Street;* *(503) 436–2569; www.mcbeecottages.com.* Twelve units. Cottages a block from the beach and a short walk to downtown. Some kitchens and fireplaces. Well-mannered pets are welcome. $-$$$$

Schooner's Cove Inn. *180 North Larch Street; (800) 843–0128 or (503) 436–2300; www.schoonerscove.com.* Thirty units. Beach access and ocean views from private decks. Kitchens. VCRs. A variety of rooms and suites with fireplaces and fully-equipped kitchens. Oceanfront lawn features gas barbecues, picnic tables, and chaise lounges. $$$$

The Waves Ocean Front Motel. *188 West Second Street; (800) 822–2468 or (503) 436–2205; www.thewavesmotel.com.* Thirty-five units. Above the beach in the heart of town. Kitchens, fireplaces, and views. $$-$$$$

Sea Ranch RV Park. *415 North Highway 101; (503) 436–2815; E-mail: searanch@seasurf.net.* Horseback riding is available in the summer at Sea Ranch. $-$$

RV Resort at Cannon Beach. *345 Elk Creek Road; (800) 847–2231 or (503) 436–2231; www.cbrvresort.com; E-mail: info@cbrvresort.com.* This facility, which offers the closest camping in the Cannon Beach area, has a kids' playground, an indoor pool and spa, and bicycle rentals. $

IN MANZANITA

Sunset Surf Ocean Front Resort. *248 Ocean Road; (800) 243–8035 or (503) 368–5224.* Forty-one units. Oceanfront pool, fireplaces. $$–$$$

Nehalem Bay State Park. *Nehalem Bay; (800) 452–5687; www.oregonstate parks.org.* A children's playground, showers, and a boat ramp into the bay are among Nehalem Bay State Park's amenities. On the beach you can walk 6 miles to the end of the spit at the mouth of the river, where you might see Roosevelt elk, migrating whistler swans, or harbor seals. $

IN ROCKAWAY BEACH

Tradewinds Motel. *523 North Pacific Street; (503) 355–2112 or (800) 824–0938; www.tradewinds-motel.com.* Nineteen units. Fifty feet from edge of beach. Children's playground on beach side of motel. Oceanfront rooms have fireplaces, refrigerators, and coffeemakers. Pets allowed. $$–$$$

Jetty Fishery RV Park & Marina. *27550 Highway 101 North; (800) 821–7697 or (503) 368–5746; E-mail: jetty fishery@nehalemtel.net.* Fourteen spaces. $

IN GARIBALDI

Bayshore Inn. *227 Garibaldi Avenue; (503) 322–2552 or (877) 537–2121; www.bayshoreinn.org; E-mail: information@ bayshoreinn.org.* Twenty-one units with refrigerators, microwaves, and free movies. Pets welcome. $$

IN NEWPORT

Little Creek Cove. *3641 Northwest Oceanview Drive; (800) 294–8025 or (541) 265–8587; www.littlecreekcove.com.* Thirty-one units. Oceanfront accommodations. Studios, one and two bedroom units with fully equipped kitchens and gas fireplaces. $$$$

Shilo Oceanfront Resort. *536 Elizabeth Street; (800) 222–2244 or (541) 265–7701.* One hundred seventy-nine units. Offers a wide variety of rooms and sizes, all with ocean views. Pets welcome. In-room refrigerator, microwave, coffeemaker. $$–$$$$

Vikings Condominiums and Cottages. *729 Northwest Coast Street; (800) 480–2477 or (541) 265–2477.* Twenty-four condominiums and fourteen cottages. Kitchenettes. Oceanfront rooms, family units. Stairs to beach. Pool and spa. $$$–$$$$

Camping

Beverly Beach State Park. *Located 7 miles north of Newport on the landward side of U.S. 101; (800) 452–5687 (for reservations); (541) 265–9278 or (800) 551–6949 for information. www.oregonstate parks.org.* Has 150 campsites and facilities for electrical or full hookup. Yurt camping available. Open year-round. $

South Beach State Park. *About 2 miles south of Newport; (800) 452–5687; www.oregonstateparks.org (for reservations); (541) 867–4715 (for information).* Yurt camping also available. $

IN LINCOLN CITY

Beachwood Oceanfront Motel. *2855 Northwest Inlet; (541) 994–8901 or (800) 889–7037.* Twenty-eight units. Oceanfront lodging on miles of walking beach. Budget-priced rooms and apartments. Balconies, fireplaces, kitchenettes. Walking distance to restaurants, casinos, shops. $$–$$$$

Nordic Oceanfront Lodging. *2133 Northwest Inlet; (800) 452–3558 or (541) 994–8145.* Fifty-two units. Oceanfront units with panoramic views. VCRs, complimentary movies. Kitchens/kitchenettes. Continental breakfast. $$–$$$

Seagull Motel. *1511 Northwest Harbor; (541) 994–2948 or (800) 422–0219.* Twenty-five units. Oceanfront motel with low beach access. Large variety of rooms with kitchens and private spas. Small pets welcome. $$–$$$$

IN GLENENDEN BEACH

The Westin Salishan. *7760 Highway 101 North; (888) SALISHAN or (541) 764–2371; www.salishan.com.* Two hundred five units. Ocean beaches about a half-mile away. Pets allowed. Five-star golf resort on 750 acres with tennis courts, swimming pool, exercise room, large whirlpool spa, sauna, nature walks, jogging path, playground, and video arcade. Three restaurants that offer the best in Oregon coast cuisine. $$$$

IN WALDPORT

Cliff House Bed and Breakfast. *1450 Adahi Street; (541) 563–2506.* Four units. Located south of Waldport just off U.S. 101, this beautiful little house sits atop the cliff, with decks and a sunroom and even an all-glass gazebo, where you can enjoy your morning coffee with an incredible view, but without being buffeted by the coastal winds. $$–$$$

Camping

Beachside State Park. *Located about 3 miles south of Waldport off U.S. Highway 101; (800) 452–5687 (for reservations); (800) 551–6949 (for information); www.oregonstateparks.org.* Open year-round, this park provides sheltered campsites with a measure of privacy not always found in coastal campgrounds. A separate day-use picnic area lies across a small stream. A section of the Oregon Coast Trail, connecting Yachats and Waldport, passes through the campground. Yurts also available. $

IN YACHATS

Fireside Resort Motel. *P.O. Box 313, 1881 Highway 101 North; (800) 336–3573 or (541) 547–3636.* Kitchenettes; coffeemaker and fridge in all rooms. Oceanfront rooms. Pets allowed. $$–$$$

Shamrock Lodgettes Resort and Spa. *105 U.S. 101 South; next to the Yachats Ocean Road Wayside; (800) 845–5028 or (541) 547–3312; www.shamrocklodgettes.com.* Nineteen units. Offers family-size cabins nestled on park-like grounds near the ocean. Each cabin has a fireplace, and some are equipped with kitchens. Spa, sauna, and exercise room. $$$–$$$$

Wayside Lodge. *5773 Highway 101 North; (541) 547–3450; www.pioneer. net/~wayside.* Seven units. All units just a stone's throw from the beach. Kitchenettes. Swings and large lawn area make this inexpensive spot ideal for families with young kids. $$–$$$

For More Information

Astoria-Warrenton Area Chamber of Commerce. *111 West Marine Drive, P.O. Box 176, Astoria, OR 97103; (800) 875–6807 or (503) 325–6311; www. oldoregon.com; E-mail: awacc@seasurf.com.*

Astoria-Warrenton Highway 101 Visitor Center. *143 South Highway 101, Warrenton, OR 97146; (503) 861–1031; www.oldoregon.com; E-mail address: awacc@ seasurf.com.*

Cannon Beach Chamber of Commerce. *Second and Spruce Streets, P.O. Box 64, Cannon Beach, OR 97110; (503) 436–2623; www.cannonbeach.org; E-mail: chamber@cannonbeach.org; .*

Central Oregon Coast Association. *P.O. Box 2094, Newport, OR 97365; (800) 767–2064; (541) 265–2064; www.newportnet.com; E-mail: coca@ newportnet.com.*

Depoe Bay Chamber of Commerce. *P.O. Box 21, 630 Southeast Highway 101, Depoe Bay, OR 97341; (541) 765–2889; www.newportnet.com.*

Greater Newport Chamber of Commerce. *555 Southwest Coast Highway, Newport, OR 97365; (800) 262–7844; (541) 265–8801; www. newportchamber.org; E-mail: chamber@ newportnet.com.*

Lincoln City Visitors & Convention Bureau. *801 Southwest Highway 101, #1, Lincoln City, OR 97367; (800) 452–2151 or (541) 994–8378; www.lcchamber.com.*

Oregon Coast Visitors Association. *P.O. Box 74, 313 SW Second Street, Suite*

D, Newport, OR 97365; (888) 628–2101 or (541) 574–2679; www.VisitTheOregon Coast.com or www.oregon-coast.org; E-mail: ocva@netbridge.net.

Garibaldi Chamber of Commerce. *P.O. Box 915, 235 Garibaldi Avenue, Garibaldi, OR 97118; (503) 322–0301; www.garibaldioregon.com; E-mail: dream@oregoncoast.com.*

Rockaway Beach Chamber of Commerce. *P.O. Box 198; 103 South First Street, Rockaway Beach, OR 97136; (503) 355–8108; www.rockawaybeach.net; E-mail: rbcc@pacifier.com.*

Seaside Visitors Bureau. *Mail to: 989 Broadway; Street Address: 7 North Roosevelt, Seaside, OR 97138-6825; (888) 306–2326 or (503) 738–3097; www.clatsop.com/seaside; E-mail: visit@ seaside-oregon.com.*

Tillamook Chamber of Commerce. *3705 Highway 101 North, Tillamook, OR 97141; (503) 842–7525; www.tillamook chamber.org; E-mail: tillchamber@wcn.net.*

Waldport Chamber of Commerce and Visitors Center. *P.O. Box 669; 620 Northwest Spring Street, Waldport, OR 97394; (541) 563–2133; E-mail: waldport @pioneer.net/~waldport.*

Yachats Area Chamber of Commerce and Visitors Center. *P.O. Box 728, 241 Highway 101, Yachats, OR 97498; (800) 929–0477; (541) 547– 3530; www.yachats.org; E-mail: yachats chamber@pioneer.net.*

The South Coast

The dramatic scenery of Oregon's south coast varies from the vast dunes around Florence to the sandstone cliffs south of Coos Bay and the myriad sea stacks dotting the shore near Brookings, the state's "Banana Belt." Less populated than the north or central parts of the coast, this area is ideal for family getaways. Your adventures can take you on dune buggy rides, hikes through redwood and old-growth myrtlewood forests, and visits to a wildlife petting park, a dinosaur-infested rainforest, and a garden where the plants themselves are carnivores.

Originally populated by adventurers seeking gold dust that washed ashore or was swept down mountain streams, the towns on the south coast quickly turned to the ocean and the forests for economic viability. Tourism now joins these primary industries as communities develop the resources that attract visitors from around the country. Even the weather has become a drawing card: Brookings, just six miles from the California border, claims the mildest, sunniest weather on the Oregon Coast, while Bandon touts itself as the "Storm Watching Capital" to encourage wintertime visits.

Florence

In the last several years, Florence's Old Town has been revitalized with an influx of boutiques, cafes, restaurants, and other attractions. Around Florence you can enjoy all kinds of recreation on more than a dozen lakes covering some 10,000 acres and on dozens of hiking trails.

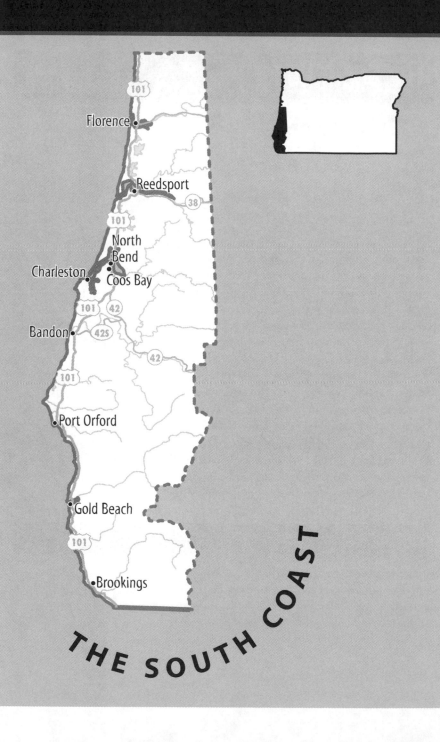

THE SOUTH COAST

WESTWARD HO! STERNWHEELER (ages 5 and up)

Located on Bay Street, next to Mo's Restaurant; (541) 997–9691. Departs 11:00 A.M., 1:00 P.M., 2:00 P.M., and 3:00 P.M. $12. One-hour trips: $14 adults; $10 ages 12 and under. Half-hour trips: $8.50 adults; $7.50 ages 12 and under.

Take the 65-foot *Westward Ho!* sternwheeler for a one-hour or half-hour trip up the Siuslaw River. In the summer, kids enjoy sitting on the boat's top level as the frontier sternwheeler chugs upriver. Lunch and dinner cruises are also available by reservation only.

 OLD TOWN PARK (all ages)

Located on Bay Street at the end of Laurel Street; (541) 997–3128. Always open. **Free.**

This small public park has a boat dock that's fenced to keep kids from falling into the Siuslaw River. Take the opportunity to throw a fishing line or a crab ring in here.

 SIUSLAW PIONEER MUSEUM (ages 5 and up)

85294 U.S. 101 South, just south of the Florence bridge in an old barn-shaped church; (541) 997–7884. Open Tuesday through Sunday, 10:00 A.M.–4:00 P.M. in summer; October–February, 10:00 A.M.–2:00 P.M. $2.00 adults; children under 12 **Free.**

The museum displays here trace the area's past, including exhibits on home life, a general store, and fishing, farming, logging, and shipbuilding industries. A large dugout canoe found at the mouth of the river is a central feature in the museum's collection. The Siuslaw and Siletz trading baskets are beautiful in their simplicity and utility.

Family Favorites on the South Coast

1. Oregon Dunes National Recreation Area
2. Jessie L. Honeyman State Park, near Florence
3. Dean Creek Elk Viewing Area, Reedsport
4. South Slough National Estuarine Research Reserve, Charleston
5. Shores Acres State Park, near Charleston
6. Coquille River Museum, Bandon
7. Bandon Cheese Factory
8. Bandon State Park-Face Rock Wayside
9. Cape Blanco State Park, near Port Orford
10. Samuel H. Boardman State Park

DOLLY WARES DOLL MUSEUM (ages 5 and up)

*3620 U.S. 101; (541) 997–3391. Usually open Tuesday through Sunday, 10:00 A.M.–5:00 P.M. $5.00 adults; $3.00 children 5–12; under 5 **Free**.*
You'll be amazed at the variety within the collection. From a pre-Columbian clay figure to high-fired porcelain from China, the dolls attest to a common human need to play at parenting.

 SILTCOOS LAKE (all ages)

*Located 6 miles south of Florence on the east side of U.S. 101; (541) 997–3128. Always open. **Free**.*
The largest lake in Florence, it covers more than 3,000 acres. You can rent watercraft from pedal boats to motorboats, canoes to jet skis.

 WOAHINK LAKE (all ages)

*Located just north of Siltcoos Lake; (541) 997–3128. Always open. **Free**.*
Woahink offers swimming, water skiing, and fishing.

 JESSIE L. HONEYMAN STATE PARK (all ages)

Located 3 miles south of Florence; (800) 551–6949 (for information); (800) 452–5687 (for reservations); www.oregonstateparks.org. Call for hours, fees.
This park spans a diverse natural landscape, from ocean and sand dunes to lake and forest. On the east side it's bordered by 350-acre Woahink Lake. Cleawox Lake, which covers a mere eighty-seven acres, is the perfect size for paddling around in; you can rent boats at the lodge. The west side of the lake is a big sand dune that's ideal for kids to run down and into the water. Six miles of hiking trails wind through the 522-acre park.

 HONEYMAN PARK LODGE

(541) 997–2718. Call for prices, hours.
Rent canoes, rowboats, kayaks, or pedal-powered boats for Cleawox Lake and purchase snacks here.

 SEA LION CAVES (ages 5 and up)

*Located 11 miles north of Florence; (541) 547–3111; www.sealioncaves.com. Open daily, 9:00 A.M.; closing hours vary; opens at 8:00 A.M. July and August. $7.00 age 16 and older; $4.50 ages 6–15; under 5 **Free**.*

After walking down stairs and a ramp to the elevator, you'll descend nearly 200 feet to the largest sea cave in North America, with a two-acre base and a 125-foot vaulted ceiling. Depending on the time of year, you might see a hundred or more Steller (northern) sea lions in the cave—or just a few. Find out what to expect at the gift shop.

 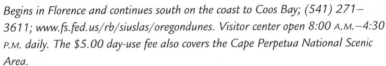

OREGON DUNES NATIONAL RECREATION AREA (ages 5 and up)

Begins in Florence and continues south on the coast to Coos Bay; (541) 271–3611; www.fs.fed.us/rb/siuslas/oregondunes. Visitor center open 8:00 A.M.–4:30 P.M. daily. The $5.00 day-use fee also covers the Cape Perpetua National Scenic Area.

Oregon Dunes National Recreation Area (ODNRA) will make your kids gape with wonder at this seemingly endless sandbox. The ODNRA stretches from Florence to Coos Bay, with a number of dune access roads, campgrounds, and day-use picnic areas along the way. Ten miles south of Florence is the Oregon Dunes Overlook, a nicely constructed series of viewpoints overlooking the dunes. In summer guided tours are offered.

C & M STABLES (ages 8 and up)

Located 8 miles north of Florence at 90241 U.S. 101 North; (541) 997–7540. (Call ahead for reservations). Open daily, year-round, 10:00 A.M.–dusk in summer; 10:00 A.M.–4:00 P.M. in winter. $25 per person for a one-hour dune ride, up to $120 for an all-day boat ride; $8.00 for a 10-minute corral ride for children 5 and under.

Rent a horse for every skill level and ride on the beach or dune trails. You can keep the horses out until dusk, which allows time for enjoying the ocean sunset on horseback.

DARLINGTONIA BOTANICAL GARDENS (ages 5 and up)

Located 5 miles north of Florence, ¼ mile off U.S. 101 on Mercer Lake Road; (541) 997–3128. Call for hours. **Free**.

Here's something to delight the gore-loving imagination of many a youth. A loop trail overlooks thousands of carnivorous plants that flourish in the marshy area of this eighteen-acre park. The *Darlingtonia californica*, better known as the cobra lily or pitcher plant, lures insects with a sticky, sweet-smelling nectar, then traps and eats them.

CROSSWIND AIR TOURS (ages 8 and up)

Located at the Florence Airport, 2000 Airport Way; (541) 991–6822. Operates sunrise to sunset, weather permitting. Half-hour tour, $40 per person, two-person minimum; 15-minute tour, $25 per person, two-person minimum.

The pilot can take up to three passengers at a time on flights overlooking the lakes, coastal forests, and ocean. You might even spot migrating whales.

SANDLAND ADVENTURES FAMILY FUN CENTER (ages 8 and up)

85366 U.S. 101, located less than a mile south of Florence; (541) 997–8087; www.sandland.com. Open daily 9:00 A.M.; closing hours vary according to season. Dune buggy tours $10–$30; self-driven rentals $45 per hour.

While the older members of the family hit the beach in a mini-rail buggy, parents can take turns staying behind with younger ones to play miniature golf or ride in bumper boats or go-carts. The whole family can take a tour in giant open-air dune buggies that seat four to five passengers and the driver.

op Florence Events

MAY

Rhododendron Festival. Florence's yearly event draws thousands who enjoy arts and crafts, floral displays, 5 and 10K runs, parades, and more. (541) 997-3128; www.florencechamber.com.

SEPTEMBER

Florence Fall Festival. This event welcomes fall with a chowder cook-off, live music, arts and crafts, and microbrew tasting. A carnival in Old Town is just the ticket for the kids. (541) 997-3128.

Reedsport

Home to the Oregon Dunes National Recreation Area headquarters, Reedsport is close to several freshwater lakes and often-overlooked campgrounds that are filled with wax myrtle and huckleberry bushes. It might be one of the few areas along the coast that offers a measure of outdoor privacy in the summer.

UMPQUA DISCOVERY CENTER (ages 5 and up)

409 Riverfront Way, off U.S. 101; (541) 271–4816; E-mail: discover@harbor side.com; www.harborside.com/~discover. Open daily 9:00 A.M.–5:00 P.M. in summer, 10:00 A.M.–4:00 P.M. rest of year. $5.00 adults; $3.00 ages 6–15; under 6 **Free***. Family ticket $12 for two adults and up to three children.*

The center opened in 1993, and has in a short time developed an impressive exhibit area designed to educate visitors about the local geography, geology, and relationships between people and the environment. Kids love the periscope and computerized information stations. A new interactive exhibit wing explores the unique cultural history of tidewater towns, where life revolved around whether the tide was coming in or going out. The natural-history wing features area geology and the changing landscape. A working weather station helps kids learn about maritime climates.

LOON LAKE RECREATION AREA (all ages)

Located east on State Highway 38, about 20 miles east of Reedsport; (541) 599–2254 for information; (888) 242–4256 for campground reservations. Call for hours and fees. Always open. **Free***.*

Created by a major landslide about 1,400 years ago, the area is now a popular summertime spot for swimming, camping, waterskiing, and fishing. When it's foggy on the coast in the summer, locals often head here to find the sun. Throughout the summer, park rangers offer interpretive programs and nature walks. **Loon Lake Lodge** (541–599-2244) offers boat rentals, cabin and room rentals, and a boat dock.

UMPQUA LIGHTHOUSE STATE PARK (ages 5 and up)

Located 6 miles south of Reedsport, less than a mile off U.S. 101; (800) 551–6949; (800) 452–5687 for campground reservations; www.oregon stateparks.org. **Free***.*

Here's a gem tucked in a rolling coastal hillside covered with fir, Sitka spruce, and hemlock, with huckleberry and rhododendron creating a lush understory. At the center of the park is tiny **Lake Marie,** with a sandy beach near a picnic area. Hiking trails circle the lake and lead to the beach, passing a viewpoint overlooking the large Punch Bowl area of the Oregon Dunes. Yurts and log cabins are available to rent, in addition to RV and tent camping spaces.

UMPQUA RIVER LIGHTHOUSE (ages 5 and up)
Located 6 miles south of Reedsport, less than a mile off U.S. 101; (800) 551–6949 or (541) 271–4631; www.oregonstateparks.org. Open daily except Tuesday for tours, May through September, 10:00 A.M.–4:00 P.M.; off-season tours by appointment. Free.

Inside is a museum that tells the story of this 1894 lighthouse and of Fort Umpqua, built to protect the lighthouse and settlers from the Umpqua Indians, who didn't welcome either intrusion. The 67-foot tower contains the light, which still shines out on the sea.

 DEAN CREEK ELK VIEWING AREA (ages 5 and up)
Located 3 miles upriver on State Highway 38; (541) 756–0100. Always open. Free.

The excellent interpretive panels at the O.H. Hinsdale Interpretive Center describe the elk and some of the other wildlife you might see. If you don't find any elk here, drive on a bit. They're often sighted next to the road in the early morning or evening hours. Bring your binoculars.

Top Reedsport Events

JULY

Reedsport Ocean Festival. Kite-flying contests, old-time games, arts and crafts booths, and live music in a beer garden are all part of this ocean-side community's summer celebration. A parade on Saturday and a salmon dinner Sunday evening at Winchester Bay round out the festivities. (800) 247–2155 or (541) 271–3495.

AUGUST

Sand Fest. Dune buggy races and all kinds of fun in the sand. (541) 271–9303.

Winchester

This small town at the mouth of Winchester Bay provides the nearest access to the Oregon Dunes National Recreation Area. Restless children will appreciate the chance to walk along the docks that moor mammoth fishing boats.

Dune buggies are a fun way to explore the area. Rentals are available from a variety of sources, including:

- **Winchester Bay Dune Buggy Adventures.** *881 U.S. Highway 101, Winchester Bay; (541) 271–6972; www.dunebuggyadventure.com.* Sandboard, ATV rentals, and tours.

- **Dune Country ATV.** *Located on Salmon Harbor Boulevard; Winchester Bay; (541) 271–9357.*

- **Great Adventures.** *By appointment only. (877) 271–0369.* Guided dune buggy, bicycle, and walking tours.

WILLIAM M. TUGMAN STATE PARK (all ages)

Located next to Eel Lake, 9 miles south of Reedsport; (800) 551–6949 (information); (800) 452–5687 (reservations); www.oregonstateparks.org. Open year-round. Day-use area is **Free**.

On the land side of the highway, the lake has a campground where privacy is protected with wax myrtle and huckleberry bushes. It's closed in winter, but the day-use area remains open year-round. Yurt camping as well as walk-in campsites. Kids will appreciate the playground and designated swimming area.

Oregon's Bay Area

Welcome to Oregon's "Bay Area"—that's how signs greet you as you enter this region of three towns—Coos Bay, Charleston, North Bend—that border Oregon's largest natural deep-water port.

COOS BAY

BAYFRONT BOARDWALK (ages 5 and up)

Located at the Coos Bay waterfront; (541) 269–0215. Always open. **Free**.

The new Coos Bay waterfront project and paved trail is an easy ⅔-mile walk where the kids can view a tiny tug and colorful flag display. Huge ships from all over the world dock here. Several cafes and eateries line nearby avenues.

Money-saving Travel Tip

- Check museums for special children's programs that are offered during the summer months. Some schedule half-day programs that provide a nice respite for families with preschoolers.

un Facts

■ The **Doerner Fir** in Coos Bay is the largest known Douglas fir in the world. You can reach it by driving south on U.S. 101 then heading east on State Highway 42. The kids will be awestruck by the 329-foot-tall, 11½-foot-wide tree. A self-guided tour map is available from the local Bureau of Land Management office (541–756–0100). Take advantage of the **Free** working forest tour offered by Menasha Forest Products Corp. (Call 541–269–0215 for reservations.)

■ **Coos Bay** sits at the midpoint btween Seattle, Washington, and San Francisco, California.

 EGYPTIAN THEATER (ages 5 and up)
229 South Broadway; (541) 267–3456. Call for prices, times.
   If the weather turns foul, you can warm up inside this old theater. It's a classic remnant of the elegant 1920s era.

 COOS ART MUSEUM (ages 8 and up)
235 Anderson Avenue; (541) 267–3901. Open Tuesday through Friday, 10:00 A.M.–4:00 P.M.; Saturday, 1:00–4:00 P.M. Suggested donation: $2.00 adults; $1.00 ages 6–11; under 6 **Free**.
   Here you'll find an impressive collection of both contemporary and historic art. Call ahead to find out about the many children's educational programs offered throughout the year.

 MINGUS PARK (ages 5 and up)
725 North Tenth Avenue, Coos Bay; (541) 267–1360. Call for more information. Always open. **Free**.
   The community swimming pool, open during summer months, will occupy the kids while you walk the trails in the adjacent arboretum and rhododendron gardens. A playground sits next to a pond, where ducks and geese clamor for crumbs.

 EMPIRE LAKES AT JOHN TOPITS PARK (ages 5 and up)
Located on Hull Street next to Southwest Oregon Community College, north of Newmark Avenue; (541) 269–8918. Always open. **Free**.

Two lakes reserved for nonmotorized boating and rimmed with walking and cycling trails make this a nice retreat for the day. A paved walking and biking path circles Lower Empire Lake, which also boasts a swimming beach.

 MILLICOMA MARSH INTERPRETIVE TRAIL (ages 5 and up)
Located on Blossom Gulch, near Blossom Gulch School in Coos Bay; (541) 269–0215. Always open. **Free**.
    This self-guided one-mile trail at Coos Bay leads to an estuary and freshwater marshes and offers a great spot for birdwatching.

NORTH BEND
This community marks the southern edge of the Oregon Dunes National Recreation Area, that giant sandbox stretching 45 miles north to Florence. There are a variety of options for exploring this popular recreation area, including cars, boats, dune buggies, and hiking trails.

PACIFIC COAST RECREATION (ages 8 and up)
68512 Coast Highway 101; (541) 756–7183. Open daily, 9:00 A.M.–5:00 P.M. 4-wheel rentals $30 per hour. Sand dune tours $12 adults, $8 ages 14 and under.
    You and your kids will enjoy these sand dune tours. You can also rent your own four-wheel ATVs, depending on your children's size and ability.

SPINREEL DUNEBUGGY RENTALS (ages 8 and up)
67045 Spinreel Road, 10 miles north on U.S. 101; (541) 759–3313; www. spinreel.com. Open daily, 9:00 A.M.–sunset year-round. Call ahead in winter. Four-wheeler rental $35 first hour, $30 second hour. Dune buggy tour, $12 half hour; $17. Three-person minimum. Children can take out four-wheelers with parental supervision.

*S*uper Shopping The Real Oregon Gift Myrtlewood Factory Tour (ages 5 and up). *Located in North Bend, 3955 Coast Highway 101; (541) 756–2220. Open daily, 9:00 A.M.–4:00 P.M.; shop open until 5:00 P.M. Call first to book a five- to ten-minute tour (summer only).* **Free**. This is a good stop if you're looking for unique gifts to bring home to friends and family.

An Adventure to Remember South Slough National
Estuarine Research Reserve (5 and up). *(P.O. Box 5417, Charleston 97420) located on Seven Devils Road, south of Charleston; (541) 888–5558. Open daily, 8:00 A.M.–4:30 P.M. in summer; Monday through Friday 8:30 A.M.– 4:30 P.M. in winter.* **Free.** This slightly out-of-the-way oasis provides a wonderful environmental learning adventure for the entire family. The 4,400-acre South Slough, reserved for the study of estuarine life and ecosystems, is one of only a few remaining sloughs in the U. S. that do not have a city or town built on their shores. An estuary marks the junction where the river meets the sea, mixing fresh and salt water to create a complex environment that supports a unique variety of plants and animals. This South Slough is the southwestern arm of the larger Coos Estuary. There's a dramatic shift in temperatures as you begin your hike to the marshes. At the trailhead are deciduous trees, which suddenly give way to fragrant, moist ferns and a much cooler terrain—an instant lesson for children about the ways flora and fauna impact climate. At the end of the trail, you're rewarded with a viewing deck from which to marvel at the expanse of fresh and saltwater marshes and mudflats. Be sure to stop by the Interpretive Center at the top of the hillside above the estuary, where you will find detailed trail maps and can view exhibits on the wildlife found in the estuary. An informational video is available at the center for those unable to walk the trail. Write or call ahead for a list of summer educational programs, or visit www.south sloughestuary.com.

COOS COUNTY HISTORICAL SOCIETY MUSEUM (ages 5 and up)

1220 Sherman Avenue (U.S. Highway 101), North Bend; (541) 756–6320 or (541) 756–4847; www.wholeshebang.com/cooshistoricalmuseum.html. Open Tuesday through Saturday, 10:00 A.M.–4:00 P.M. $1.00 adults; 25 cents ages 5–12; under 5 **Free.**

Old Locomotive 104 from the Coos Bay Lumber Company rests outside. Inside your kids will appreciate the miniature boat model and learn about several area shipwrecks.

SIMPSON PARK (all ages)

On Sherman Avenue, adjacent to North Bend Visitors Center and Coos County Historical County Museum; (541) 756–2656. Always open. **Free.**

The park has picnic tables and a "Frisbee golf" course that will have your whole family stepping up to the "tee" to meet the challenge of landing the Frisbee in basket "holes" atop bright poles. Pick up a **free** scorecard from the Visitor Center, next to the museum. If you left your Frisbee at home, **Moe's Bike Shop** (1397 Sherman Avenue; 541–756–7536) across the street has several varieties for sale.

CRANBERRY SWEETS CANDY FACTORY (all ages)

1005 Newmark Avenue, Coos Bay; (541) 888–9824. Open Monday through Saturday; 9:00 A.M.–6:00 P.M.; Sunday, 11:00 A.M.–4:00 P.M.

Your children will enjoy this factory and store where scrumptious chocolate and cranberry confections are made and sold.

op Bay Area Events

JULY

Oregon Coast Music Festival. These concerts, which are held in Shores Acres State Park, in Coos Bay, run the gamut from classical to jazz and folk. A number of events during the festival weeks are geared to introducing children to classical music. (541) 267–0938.

AUGUST

Blackberry Arts Festival. This annual fair features handmade arts and crafts along with food booths and live entertainment. (541) 751–9663.

SEPTEMBER

Bay Area Fun Festival. Held in downtown Coos Bay, this midmonth weekend starts with a parade and includes live entertainment and family-oriented activities. (541) 269–0215; www.oregonsbayareachamber.com.

CHARLESTON AREA

SHORE ACRES STATE PARK (ages 5 and up)

Located four miles southwest of Charleston; (800) 551–6949 or (541) 888–3732; www.oregonstateparks.org. Open daily, 8:00 A.M.–dusk. $3.00 day-use fee.

The dramatic tilt of the layered rock formations, waves crashing over them, lures artists and photographers to the cliff tops. The botanical and Japanese gardens are not, perhaps, your child's idea of a great time, but there are plenty of places for kids to run while the grown-ups appreciate the beauty of exquisitely landscaped gardens. Once the home of lumber baron Louis J. Simpson, the park is open for day use throughout the year. Part of the Oregon Coast Trail winds through the park. During the winter, storm watching is awe-inspiring from the large, glass-enclosed gazebo above the cliffs. In December, visit the park just before dusk, when the garden is transformed with thousands of colored lights.

CAPE ARAGO STATE PARK AND LIGHTHOUSE
(ages 5 and up)

Located 15 miles southwest of Charleston off U.S. 101; (800) 551–6949; www.oregonstateparks.org. Call for hours. **Free**.

The victim of erosion and harsh weather, the lighthouse is not open to the public, but tremendous views are available just south of the lighthouse. For tidepooling, head down the steep trail to South Cove, where the rocky shoreline is bursting with sea life. Watch out for slippery rocks.

Other Things to See and Do in the Bay Area

- **Rockhounding (all ages).** *Best spot is 8 miles south of Charleston at Seven Devils Wayside & Whiskey Run; day-use area.* **Free**. Agates, agatized myrtle, jasper, and other woods can be gathered here.

- **Clamming (ages 5 and up).** *Best locations are the tiny seafront community of Charleston and the Coos Bay estuary. Always open.* **Free** *when you bring your own buckets and digging tools.* Abundant in this area are mussels, softshell, bay, butter, littleneck, cockle, and gaper clams. All local waters are open for clamming. Although clams may be removed without a license, it's unlawful to remove them from their shells before leaving the clamming area.

For more information, call the Bay Area Chamber of Commerce at (541) 269–0215; www.oregonsbayareachamber.com.

Bandon

Bandon-by-the-Sea is such a popular spot, you'll want to make plans well in advance, particularly now that it's home to a new world-class golf course. The local beach, renowned for its majestic rock formations, is also the perfect spot for birdwatching and sandlecastle-building. Rockhounds often find agate, jasper, and petrified wood here.

COQUILLE RIVER MUSEUM, BANDON HISTORICAL SOCIETY (ages 5 and up)

270 Fillmore Street and U.S. Highway 101; (541) 347–2164. Open Monday through Saturday, 10:00 A.M.–4:00 P.M.; Sunday afternoon late May through September (hours vary); $2.00 adults; 12 and under **Free**.

A nice array of exhibits that includes local history, pioneer and maritime life, Native American culture, the Bandon fire, and cranberry-industry memorabilia.

BANDON CHEESE FACTORY (all ages)

680 South Second; (541) 347–2456. Open Monday through Saturday, 8:00 A.M.–5:30 P.M.; Sunday, 9:00 A.M.–5:00 P.M. **Free**.

Taste several local varieties of cheese and watch the "cheddaring" process through picture windows just behind the deli. Enjoy huge and inexpensive scoops of Oregon-made ice cream—watch out, they're a meal in themselves. This is a good place to gather the supplies you need for making a picnic lunch.

BANDON'S OLD TOWN DISTRICT (ages 5 and up)

Located between U.S. 101 and the Bandon Boat Basin; (541) 347–9616. Most shops are open daily year-round, 9:00 A.M.–6:00 P.M.

Take your time strolling in and out of this colorful blend of curio, book, and arts and crafts shops.

Free Things to Do in Bandon

TIDE POOLS (ages 5 and up)

- **Face Rock Wayside.** *Located in Bandon State Park, along Beach Loop Road just south of Bandon; (800) 551–6949; www.oregonstateparks.org. Day use only. Call for hours.* **Free**. The sea stacks along this stretch of beach all have names. **Face Rock,** the most distinctive of these, is named for Ewauna, the beautiful daughter of Chief Siskiyou. She swam alone in the sea and was caught by the evil ocean spirit Seatka, who threw Ewauna's cat and kittens into the sea with her, and turned them all to stone. Ewauna's chin points toward Cat and Kittens Rocks to the north.

BIG WHEEL GENERAL STORE (ages 5 and up)

*Baltimore between First and Second streets; (541) 347–3719; open 9:00 A.M.–
7:00 P.M. daily in summer, 9:00 A.M.–5:30 P.M. rest of year; open at 10:00 A.M.
on Sunday.*

After your fresh shrimp or crab salad, buy a sweet treat at the store's
fudge factory. Check out the 𝐅𝐫𝐞𝐞 "driftwood museum" while you're
there.

CRANBERRY SWEETS (all ages)

*Chicago Avenue and First Street; (541) 347–9475. Monday through Saturday,
9:00 A.M.–6:00 P.M.*

If the fudge wasn't quite enough, satisfy your sweet tooth at this
sweet shop.

Top Bandon Events

MAY

Sandcastle and Sand Sculpture Contest. Build a sandcastle or sculpture
by yourself or team up with other beach artisans.

JULY

Old Fashioned July Fourth Celebration. Join the residents of this
charming coastal community in their Independence Day celebration,
complete with a parade, old-fashioned fireworks, annual fish fry, and
crafts fair.

SEPTEMBER

Cranberry Festival. This lively local event features a street fair, parade,
food booths, dances, and, of course, cranberries. (541) 347–9616.

WINTER

Bandon Storm Watchers. For years this lively group has gathered in
winter to watch nature's own drama play out in the sea. Members serve
as interpretive guides to visitors. (541) 347–4721; www.bandon.com/
storms.

For information on Bandon events, call (541) 347–9616; www.bandon.
com; E-mail: bandoncc@harborside.com.

THE BOAT BASIN (all ages)

Located on First Street at the Old Town dock; (541) 347–9616. ꞙree.

This is a great place to watch the boats or head out on the public pier for fishing or crabbing.

 PORT O' CALL (ages 5 and up)

On the dock in Old Town at 155 First Street; (541) 347–2875. Open daily, 9:00 A.M.–5:00 P.M. Clamming $3.00; crabbing $5.00; fishing $7.00 (includes bait, rod, hooks).

Rent crab rings, fishing rods, and boats here. They'll tell you the best spots for jetty fishing or clamming and even cook your crab. If you don't feel like catching your own, they sell freshly caught seafood retail.

 ADVENTURE KAYAK (ages 10 and up)

315 First Street; (541) 347–3480; www.adventurekayak.com. Open daily in summer, 10:00 A.M.–5:00 P.M.; call for winter hours. $20 single kayak; $30 double kayak for two hours; tours $35–$65 per person, depending on the tour. Reservations required.

Learn about the natural wildlife and estuaries in the area from professional kayak guides. There's no whitewater to worry about, only gorgeous scenery to watch from water level. Tours run for two hours and depart twice daily. Special tours are scheduled as needed.

 COQUILLE RIVER LIGHTHOUSE (ages 5 and up)

Located in Bullard's Beach State Park; (541) 347–2209. Open for tours Wednesday–Sunday in April, daily May through October, 10:00 A.M.–4:00 P.M.; extended hours in summer months. Tours on request, November through March. ꞙree.

The Coquille River Lighthouse, built in 1896, is a popular subject for many a photographer and turns up on many coastal calendars.

 OREGON ISLAND NATIONAL WILDLIFE REFUGE (ages 5 and up)

 Located on Eleventh Street Southwest; (541) 347–3683; www.bandon.com/page37.html. Always open but best time to view wildlife is early morning or late afternoon. ꞙree.

The "islands" are actually large offshore rocks that provide habitat for very large numbers of sea birds and mammals. Coquille Point area presents one of the most spectacular places for viewing puffins, murres, oystercatchers, seals, and other animals who congregate on these off-shore rocks. A group called Seashore Education for Awareness (SEA) often has volunteers here and elsewhere along the coast with spotting scopes to enhance your viewing.

oney-saving Travel Tip

- Consider having your main meal at noon, when restaurants sometimes offer the same menu items at half the cost of dinner entrees.

 ### BANDON MARSH NATIONAL WILDLIFE REFUGE (ages 5 and up)
Located at the mouth of the Coquille River off Riverside Drive; for information call (541) 867–4550. Day-use area. Always open. **Free**.

This estuary at the river mouth contains nearly 300 acres of salt marsh. Some 115 species of migratory birds, 8 species of mammals, 45 species of fish, and other forms of sea life can be found within the refuge. Bring your binoculars for a closer look. SEA (Shoreline Education for Awareness) volunteers are often here with spotting scopes and to show visitors the legal access routes. See www.bandon/com/page37.html.

FREE FLIGHT (ages 5 and up)
1185 Portland Avenue; (541) 347–3882; www.bandon.com/page13.html. Call for reservations. **Free**, *but donations welcome.*

Bandon's bird and mammal rescue and rehabilitation volunteers are happy to talk to visitors about local efforts to return wildlife to their natural habitats. Tours are available by appointment.

 ### BANDON BEACH RIDING STABLES (ages 8 and up)
Along Beach Loop Road; (541) 347–3423. Rides depart every two hours beginning at 10:00 A.M. year-round. Call for reservations. $30 per hour.

Guided horse rides with gentle horses are available for all ages.

 ### WEST COAST GAME PARK (all ages)
Located 7 miles south of Bandon on U.S. 101; (541) 347–3106; www.game parksafari.com. Open daily in summer, weather permitting, 9:00 A.M.; check for

closing times. $8.50 age 13 and older; $8.00 ages 7–12; $5.00 ages 2–6; 5 and under **Free**.

If your kids are fond of animals, this will be a sure winner. A walk-through safari covering ten acres of the twenty-one-acre preserve brings you up close and personal with seventy-five different species of wildlife. Children might pet bear cubs, tiger cubs, or baby leopards. The many hoofed animals—deer, goats, caribou, and others—swarm around you as you feed them from ice cream cones filled with animal ambrosia.

FABER FARMS & THE OREGON CRANBERRY COMPANY

519 Morrison Road; (541) 347–1166. Open daily 10:00 A.M.–4:00 P.M.; extended hours during October, which is harvest time. **Free**.

Take a tour of this working cranberry farm, which welcomes private parties and large groups.

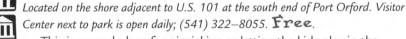

Fun Facts Oregon is among the five states in the country where tart and tangy **cranberries** are grown. Buy them in candy form in several of the local shops, celebrate them at the community's fall festival, or view them along the highway in late September and October.

Port Orford

The westernmost town in the lower forty-eight states, Port Orford is perched on the headland in the shadow of Humbug Mountain. The picturesque commercial harbor is unique in that it opens directly to the sea, without a river bar.

BATTLE ROCK CITY PARK (all ages)

Located on the shore adjacent to U.S. 101 at the south end of Port Orford. Visitor Center next to park is open daily; (541) 322–8055. **Free**.

This is a good place for picnicking or letting the kids play in the sand. It was the scene of a fierce Native American battle in 1851. After lunch, take advantage of an obliging hiking trail.

BUFFINGTON MEMORIAL PARK (ages 5 and up)

Located off Fourteenth Street and Lakeshore Drive; (541) 331–8055. Always open. **Free**.

Sit in the shade while your kids run off energy or swing from the playground equipment. The park provides picnic facilities, tennis and handball courts, basketball courts, and a nature jogging trail.

CAPE BLANCO STATE PARK AND LIGHTHOUSE (ages 5 and up)

Located nine miles north off U.S. 101; (800) 551–6949; www.oregonstate parks.org. Lighthouse open April 1 through October 31, Thursday through Monday 10:00 A.M.–3:30 P.M. Park open year-round. **Free**.

The 1870 Cape Blanco Lighthouse, the oldest continuously operating lighthouse in Oregon, is located on the westernmost point in the forty-eight contiguous states. The campground, on a bluff adjacent to the lighthouse area, provides electrical sites with picnic tables, fire rings, and water. Bushes of huckleberry, salal, salmonberry, and thimbleberry lend privacy to the individual campsites. Several trails take off from the campground. Within the park is the 1898 **Hughes House,** which visitors can explore during the summer months Thursdays through Sundays.

HUMBUG MOUNTAIN STATE PARK (ages 5 and up)

Six miles south of Port Orford on U.S. 101; (800) 551–6949; www.oregon stateparks.org. Open daily year-round. **Free**.

From the campground, a fairly strenuous trail leads 3 miles to the summit of Humbug Mountain where, if the weather is clear, you'll enjoy an amazing 360-degree view. If the children are not up for climbing, try the lesser-known 2.6-mile hike north from the campground along the old coast highway. The trail ends at the highway just south of Rocky Point, which is a terrific spot for exploring tide pools.

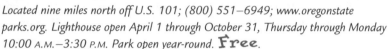

*B*erry Interesting In late September and throughout October you will see farmers harvesting cranberries along U.S. 101 in Port Orford. Watch them gathering these round, red berries with a "beater" that churns the bog water, and loosens them from their vines.

PREHISTORIC GARDENS (ages 5 and up)

About 12 miles south of Port Orford; (541) 332–4463; www.prehistoric gardens.com; E-mail: info@prehistoricgardens.com. Open daily year-round, 8:00 A.M.–dusk. $6.00 adults; $5.00 ages 12–18; $4.00 ages 4–11; 3 and under **Free**.

Wander through dense coastal rainforests where life-size models of prehistoric dinosaurs and other creatures lurk. Jurassic Park? Well, no, but young children will be captivated by the huge, brightly colored creatures they've read about. Parents will appreciate the luxuriant foliage of ferns and mosses that keep the forest looking green and lush year-round. The giant Tyrannosaurus Rex standing alongside the highway lets you know you've arrived. Some visitors say winter is the best time to visit the gardens because Oregon's misty weather provides just the right prehistoric ambiance.

Top Port Orford Events

SEPTEMBER

Port Orford Seafood Festival. You'll find junk art, beach games, dock walks, and music here, plus a scrumptious albacore barbecue. (541) 332–8055.

DECEMBER

Hughes House Christmas Tours. The whole community gets involved in decorating this resplendent 1898 Victorian house, which is nestled in Cape Blanco State Park. (541) 332–8055.

Gold Beach

Nestled on the shores of the Rogue River is Gold Beach. Early prospectors literally scooped up gold off the beaches. Later the area attracted sport fishermen. It was here that author Zane Grey wrote his novel *The Rogue River Feud*. Now Gold Beach is the launching spot for a variety of jet boat tours.

ROGUE WILDERNESS WHITEWATER TRIPS (ages 8 and up)

For reservations and information, (541) 336–1647; www.wildrogue.com/water. htm; E-mail: rwi@wildrogue.com. Operates May through September. Trips begin at 9:00 A.M. and noon. Advance reservations required. $50 half day, $70 full day.

Rafting presents another way for the family to take in river sites. This company offers four-hour whitewater rides.

HAWK'S REST RANCH STABLES AND TRAIL RIDES (ages 8 and up)

Located 11 miles south of Gold Beach at the Siskiyou West Day Lodge, east at Pistol River junction; (541) 247–6423; www.siskiyouwest.com/Hawks.htm. Open daily year-round, 8:00 A.M.–6:00 P.M. $25 for one-and-a-half hour rides. 60-minute ride $20 each; 90-minute walking ride $25 on beach or ranch; pony rides $10 for 15 minutes. Surrey ride $15 per person.

Experience the old-fashioned way of exploration, beginning your day with a ride up an alder-lined creek or ending it with a sunset ride on the beach. They'll also take you on a half-hour surrey ride.

JERRY'S JET BOATS ROGUE RIVER MUSEUM (ages 6 and up)

Port of Gold Beach off Port Drive Mail; (541) 247–4571. Open daily year-round. **Free**.

This family-run jet-boat tour company has collected river memorabilia and geological exhibits that follow the formation of the Rogue River Canyon.

Jet Boating the Rogue River

One of the most popular experiences in Gold Beach is a jet boat trip up the Wild and Scenic Rogue River. Several tour companies operate full- and half-day trips on the river, stopping for lunch at one of several resort lodges upriver. Tours start the first of May, and usually end in late October. There's no age limit for either of the following trips.

- **Jerry's Jet Boats.** *Port of Gold Beach off Port Drive Mail; (800) 451–3645 or (541) 247–4571; www.Roguejets.com. Open May 1 through October 30. Tours depart daily at 8:00 A.M. May through October and 8:30 A.M., noon, and 2:30 P.M. July through Labor Day. $30 adults; $12 ages 4–11; under 4* **Free**, *for 64-mile "short trip"; prices vary for longer trips.*

- **Mail Boat Hydro Jets.** *Take Rogue River Road east from U.S. 101 at the Wedderburn Store, just north of Gold Beach. (800) 458–3511 for reservations; (541) 247–7033 for brochure or information; info@mailboat.com; www. mailboat.com. Open May through October. Tours depart 8:30 A.M. and 2:30 P.M. July through Labor Day; 8:30 A.M. only May through October.* Take the 64-mile Original Postman's Run, and learn how the area's first postmen delivered mail to the remote community of Agness. *$30 adults; $12 ages 4–11; under 4* **Free**. Expect to get splashed a bit on the longer trips (84-mile and 104-mile), which surge through river rapids.

CURRY COUNTY HISTORICAL MUSEUM (ages 5 and up)
Located at the Curry County Fairgrounds, 29410 Ellensburg Avenue; (541) 247–6113. Open Tuesday through Saturday, noon–4:00 P.M. June through September; Saturday noon–4:00 P.M. rest of year. **Free** *but donations welcome.*
   You'll see exhibits of old-time logging equipment, and Native American arrowheads, petroglyphs, a canoe, baskets, and other artifacts. A maritime display shows old photographs of shipwrecks that occurred along the Pacific Coast. Call to find out about the free monthly programs offered September through May.

op Gold Beach Event

JULY

Curry County Fair. One of Oregon's largest flower shows plus a parade, rodeo, and lamb barbecue are featured in this annual county-sponsored event. (541) 247–4541; E-mail: curryfair@harborside.com.

kings

Brookings is known as Oregon's "Banana Belt," where the weather is warm and sunny more often than anywhere else on the Oregon Coast, and sometimes in the entire state! Coming into Brookings from Gold Beach, you'll cross Thomas Creek Bridge, which is 345 feet high and the highest bridge in Oregon. Less than 10 minutes from the California border, Brookings is within easy reach of the Golden State's majestic redwoods.

 TIDEWIND SPORTFISHING (ages 8 and up)
16368 Lower Harbor Road, Brookings Harbor; (541) 469–0337 or (800) 799–0337; www.tidewindsportfishing.com; E-mail: tidewinds@harborside.com. Open daily, 6:00 A.M.–5:00 P.M. Fishing charters: $60 adults; $50 ages 14–18; $45 ages 13 and under. Scenic tour: $18 adults, $9 children.
   Tidewind offers fishing and scenic tour charters as well as whale-watching trips. Costs include tackle and gear. Just bring a lunch.

 KID TOWN IN AZALEA PARK (all ages)
Follow the signs at the north end of harbor bridge; park entrance is on the right. Located on North Bank Chetco River Road. (541) 469–3181 or (800) 535–9469. Day use only. **Free**.

Younger children love it here. It's a child-size fortress, complete with turrets and towers, slides and tunnels. Parents will enjoy wandering among the park's many azalea bushes—some 300 years old—when the spring bloom is on.

SAMUEL H. BOARDMAN STATE PARK (all ages)

Located four miles north on U.S. 101; (800) 551–6949; www.oregonstateparks. org. Closes at dusk; open year-round. **Free.**

Named for the first Oregon parks superintendent, who believed Oregon's shining coastline should be saved for the public, the park covers 11 miles of coastline, beginning 4 miles north of Brookings. All along this stretch are fascinating and picturesque rock formations and tide pools to explore. You can gain access to the beach at both Whalehead Cove Viewpoint, overlooking Whalehead Island, and at Indian Sands Wayside. At the south end of Indian Sands beach, look for the Indian midden, an area with huge piles of shells and bones left behind after many feasts. This is a look-but-don't-touch situation—disturbing the midden is against federal law. The park offers several interpretive events and nature programs in the summer.

NATURAL BRIDGE VIEWPOINT (ages 5 and up)

Located about 9 miles north of Brookings near the beach access point at Miner Creek; (541) 378–6305. Always open. **Free.**

From the parking area, walk south along the trail to a viewing platform to see the remains of ancient sea caves that collapsed eons ago. It's a short but often steep walk to the beach. For trail maps, write to the Trails Coordinator, Oregon State Parks, 1115 Commercial Street NE, Salem 97310. The 27-mile Oregon Coast Trail winds through the park.

ALFRED A. LOEB STATE PARK (all ages)

North Chetco River Road, 8 miles northeast of Brookings; (800) 551–6949; www.oregonstateparks.org. **Free.**

Loeb State Park sits in a grove of old-growth myrtlewood. You can camp and picnic here, take a swim in the Chetco River, throw a fishing line into one of the best salmon streams in the area (**Emily Creek**), or walk a 1¼-mile nature loop trail through a redwood forest. Yes, redwoods in Oregon! The most

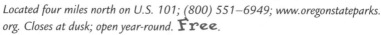

Fun Facts Loeb State Park protects 320 acres of **myrtlewood,** a tree found only in the state of Oregon and in the Middle East.

impressive of the trees you'll pass are between 300 and 800 years old. A self-guiding brochure with a map is available at the trailhead in the day-use area of the park along the Chetco River. In addition to campsites, log cabins are available to rent.

CHETCO VALLEY HISTORICAL SOCIETY MUSEUM (ages 6 and up)
15461 Museum Road; (541) 469–6651. Open Thursday–Sunday, noon–4:00 P.M. mid-March to October; extended days and hours in the summer. **Free**, *but donations welcome.*

This pioneer museum is housed in the historic Blacke House. The largest Monterey cypress tree in the United States is on the grounds.

Top Brookings Events

MAY

Azalea Festival. This week of special events celebrates the glories of springtime on the coast. (800) 877-9741 or (541) 469-9741.

JULY

Southern Oregon Kite Festival. Fly your own kite or watch others launch theirs at the Port of Brookings-Harbor. (541) 469-2218.

Where to Eat

IN BANDON
Bandon Gourmet. *92 Second Street; (541) 347-3237.* Specializes in artisan breads, wood-fired pizzas, and gourmet desserts. Breakfast and lunch served daily. $-$$

The Station Restaurant. *635 Second Street Southeast; (541) 347-9615.* In the gift shop next door, kids enjoy watching the German-made LGB model trains, and the glass hive full of live honeybees. Breakfast, lunch, dinner. $$-$$$

IN BROOKINGS
Slugs and Stones and Ice Cream Cones. *Lower Harbor Road; (541) 469-7584.* You can bribe your children to let you peacefully enjoy the stunning viewpoints along the way with a promise of an ice cream cone. The "For Kids Only" menu offers "Slyme Sundae" and "Baby Pickles Gummy Worm Sundae." $

Wharfside Restaurant. *16362 Lower Harbor Road; (541) 469-7316.* Kids enjoy the old boat incorporated into the restaurant's structure. There's also window service for the covered picnic tables outside in addition to indoor seating. Seafood and vegetarian entrees. $$

IN COOS BAY

Blue Heron Bistro. *100 Commercial Street; (541) 267–3933.* It has a European feel and serves somewhat upscale food with all fresh ingredients, but the atmosphere is definitely casual. $$-$$$

IN FLORENCE

Blue Hen Cafe. *1675 U.S. 101; (541) 997–3907; www.bluehencafe.com.* The whole family will enjoy the extensive breakfast menu. Huge portions at all meals make this a best buy. Oregon's People's Choice and *Oregon Coast* magazine winner for best chowders. $-$$

Bridgewater Restaurant. *1297 Bay Street; (541) 997–9405; www.bridgewater. oldtownflorence.com.* Seafood entrees are offered in a tropical-like setting that supplies crayons and colorable children's menus. $$-$$$

Mo's Restaurant. *1436 Bay Street; (541) 997–2185; www.moschowder.com.* Here's another chance to stop by the state's legendary chowder chain for a bowl of hearty clam chowder. The kids will have fun watching the boats go by. $-$$

Clawson's Windward Inn Restaurant. *3787 North U.S. 101 in the north end of town; (541) 997–8243.* Local seafood, steaks, homemade bread and pastries are served. It also offers bistro dinners for the budget conscious. $$-$$$

IN GOLD BEACH

Gold Beach House. *29212 Ellensburg Avenue (U.S. 101); (541) 247–0825.* Seafood, steaks, and Italian cuisine for lunch or dinner. Ocean-view dining. $$-$$$

Savory Natural Foods. *29441 Ellensburg Avenue on U.S. 101; (541) 247–0297.* This natural grocery deli has organic produce, bulk foods, a juice bar, and a small cafe. $

Spada's Family Restaurant. *29374 Ellensburg Avenue (U.S. 101); (541) 247–7732.* Seafood, steaks, Italian dinners, sandwiches, and New York pizza round out an extensive menu. Breakfast, lunch, dinner, and Sunday buffet. $$-$$$

IN REEDSPORT

Don's Main Street Family Restaurant. *2115 Winchester Avenue; (541) 271–2032.* Here's a casual dining establishment for breakfast, lunch, or dinner, with ice cream treats for the kids. $-$$

Where to Stay

IN BANDON

Sunset Oceanfront Accommodations. *1865 Beach Loop Road; (800) 842–2407 or (541) 347–2453; www. sunsetmotel.com.* Sixty-six units. Kitchenettes, pets allowed, spa pool, and

easy access to Bandon's famous beach. $-$$$$

Table Rock Motel. *840 Beach Loop Road; (541) 347–2700.* Fifteen units. Simple but clean rooms. Kitchenettes. Pets allowed. Just behind the building is the Oregon Island Bird Sanctuary. $-$$$

Bullards Beach State Park. *Located 2 miles north of Bandon; (800) 452–5687 for reservations; www.oregonstateparks.org.* Campsites and yurt camping are available here year-round. Beach access. In the summer, state rangers provide educational activities for children. $

IN BROOKINGS

Best Western Beachfront Inn. *16008 Boat Basin Road; (800) 468–4081 or (541) 469–7779.* One hundred two guest rooms, many of which are within 50 feet of the ocean. Kitchenettes, heated pool, spa. All rooms have ocean view with microwave, fridge, and coffeemaker. Easy beach access. $$-$$$$

Westward Motel. *1026 Chetco Avenue; (541) 469–7471.* Thirty-one units. Small pets OK, downtown location, walking distance to shops. $$

Harris Beach State Park. *1655 U.S. 101 North, 2 miles north of Brookings; (800) 452–5687 for reservations; www.oregonstateparks.org.* Tent and yurt camping. Five RV spaces. $

IN FLORENCE

Driftwood Shores Resort. *88416 First Avenue; (800) 422–5091 or (541) 997–8263.* One hundred thirty-six units. Restaurant, indoor pool, spa. All rooms have ocean views. $$$

Holiday Inn Express. *2475 U.S. 101; (541) 997–7797; (800)–HOLIDAY.* Fifty-one units. Continental breakfast. Spa and exercise room. Laundry facilities. $$-$$$

Lighthouse Inn. *155 U.S. 101; (541) 997–3221; www.lighthouseinn.tripod.com.* Thirty units. A traditional motel with

recently refurbished family units and a large suite that accommodates families of six, it sits a block off the river near Old Town. Pets allowed. $-$$$

Siltcoos Lake Resort. *82855 Fir Street; located at Westlake junction on the coast highway; (541) 997–3741.* Rents eight small units with kitchenettes, as well as twelve RV spaces. Children's playground, picnic and barbecue areas, boat moorage and rentals, and a tackle shop complete the amenities. $-$$

Jessie Honeyman Memorial State Park. *84505 U.S. 101 South; (800) 452–5687 for reservations; www.oregon stateparks.org.* Lodge open daily from mid-March through the summer. Reserve one of the 240 campsites and RV spaces in the park well in advance. Canoe and paddle boat rentals available. Three sparkling freshwater lakes make this a vacation favorite of locals and visitors. $

Fish Mill Lodge and RV Park. *4484 Fish Mill Way; (541) 997–2511.* Fully-equipped kitchen rooms overlooking Siltcoos Lake. $-$$$

IN THE BAY AREA

Best Western Holiday Motel. *411 North Bayshore Drive, Coos Bay; (541) 269–5111 or (800) 228–8655.* Seventy-seven units. Kitchenettes, spa pool, fitness center; pets allowed. $$

Red Lion Inn. *1313 North Bayshore Drive, Coos Bay; (541) 267–4141 or (800) 733–5466.* One hundred forty-three rooms. Dining room, swimming pool, spa, and large rooms make this a favorite central spot for families. $$-$$$

Sunset Bay State Park. *Located three miles south of Charleston on Cape Arago Highway; (800) 452–5687; www.oregon*

stateparks.org. One of the most beautiful state parks in Oregon, nestled in a snug cove at the base of coastal hills with easy access to the beach and hiking trails. $

IN GOLD BEACH

Azalea Lodge. *29481 Ellensburg Avenue (U.S. 101); (800) 381–6635 or (541) 247–6635.* Seventeen units. Laundry facilities. $$

Inn of the Beachcomber. *29266 Ellensburg Avenue (U.S. 101); (800) 690–2378 or (541) 247–6691.* Forty-nine units. Ocean views, beach access, fireplaces, kitchenettes, pool, and spa. $$–$$$$

Gold Beach Resort and Condominiums. *29232 South Ellensburg Avenue (U.S. 101); (541) 247–7066 or (800) 541–0947; www.gbresort.com.* Thirty-nine rooms; four condos. One of the only beachfront accommodations in the area. Indoor swimming pool, hot tub. Microwave, refrigerator, coffeemaker in each room. All rooms have ocean view. Restaurant just across the parking lot. $$–$$$$

Ireland's Rustic Lodges. *1220 South Ellensburg Avenue (U.S. 101); (541) 247–7718; www.irelandrusticlodges.com.* Seven log cabins, thirty-three lodge rooms, some with kitchens and fireplaces. Shaded parklike setting. $$

For More Information

Bandon Chamber of Commerce. *300 S.E. Second Street, P.O. Box 1515, Bandon, OR 97411; (541) 347–9616; www.bandon.com.*

Bay Area Chamber of Commerce. *50 E. Central Avenue, Coos Bay, OR 97420; (800) 824–8486 or (541) 269–0215; www.oregonsbayareachamber.com; E-mail: bacc@oregonsbayareachamber.com.*

Brookings-Harbor Chamber of Commerce. *P.O. Box 940, 16330 Lower Harbor Road, Brookings, OR 97415; (800) 535–9469 or (541) 469–3181; www.brookingsor.com; E-mail: chamber@wave.net.*

Charleston Information Center. *P.O. Box 5735, Charleston, OR 97420; (800) 824–8486 or (541) 888–2311 (May to September).*

Coquille Chamber of Commerce. *119 North Birch Street, Coquille, OR 97423; (541) 396–3414; www.harborside.com/~chamber2000.*

Florence Area Chamber of Commerce. *P.O. Box 26000, 270 U.S. 101, Florence, OR 97439; (541) 997–3128 or (800) 524–4864; www.florencechamber.com; E-mail: florence@harborside.com.*

Gold Beach Chamber of Commerce Visitor Center. *29279 Ellensburg, Gold Beach, OR 97444; (800) 525–2334 or (541) 247–7526; www.goldbeachchamber.com; E-mail: info@goldbeachchamber.com. See also www.goldbeach.org.*

Port Orford Chamber of Commerce. *P.O. Box 637, Battle Rock Park, Highway 101 South, Port Orford, 97465; (541) 332–8055; www.portorfordoregon.com; E-mail: pochamb@harborside.com.*

Oregon Dunes National Recreation Area Visitor Center. *855 Highway Avenue, Reedsport, OR; (541) 271–3611; www.fs.fed.us/r6/siuslaw/odnra.htm.*

Portland and the Columbia Gorge

The confluence of the Willamette River and the mighty Columbia seemed a natural place to establish a port city that would serve as a shipping center for getting goods to settlers along both rivers. Portland, named after Portland, Maine, on the toss of a coin, has a population of more than 450,000 in the city and one and a half million in the larger metropolitan area.

Now known as the City of Roses, Portland grew from the pioneer spirit that brought hundreds of thousands of settlers along the Oregon Trail despite often heartbreaking hardships. The Columbia River was perhaps the most formidable challenge they faced, and many decided to take the longer, more strenuous overland route rather than risk all on the churning waters of the Columbia. To look at it today, with its wide, calm waters tamed by a series of dams, you'd think no river could be more placid. For many pioneers it wasn't until the river stretched wide beyond the Columbia River Gorge that it calmed enough for them to think of settling along its banks.

Central Portland

PIONEER COURTHOUSE SQUARE (all ages)

Located in the block between Broadway and Fifth, and Southwest Morrison and Yamhill; (800) 962–3700 or (503) 823–2223 or (503) 275–8355; www. travelportland.com or www.parks.ci.portland.or.us. Always open. Free.

Kids enjoy splashing in the fountain or trying to get a smile from the "umbrella man"—a lifelike bronze sculpture. The **Weather Machine** is another kid favorite. At noon each day, the machine plays a musical fanfare and sprays mist, out of which comes the symbol for the day's weather—a stylized sun, a dragon for storms, or a great blue heron for Oregon's perennial drizzle. In summertime the square comes alive with

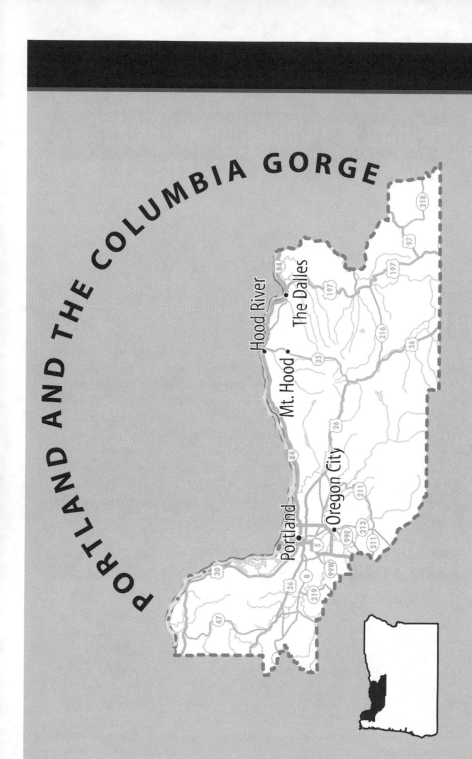

PORTLAND AND THE COLUMBIA GORGE

Hood River

The Dalles

Mt. Hood

Portland

Oregon City

concerts, some planned and some impromptu, from sometimes very talented buskers (street musicians). The square is also home to the Portland Visitors Association and the Tri-Met offices, where you can get information on bus and light rail services in the city.

PORTLAND CLASSICAL CHINESE GARDEN (ages 3 and up)

Northwest Third Avenue and Everett Street; (503) 228–8131; www.portland chinesegarden.org. Open daily, November through March 10:00 A.M.–5:00 P.M., April through October 9:00 A.M.–6:00 P.M. Hours extended to 8:30 P.M. first Thursday of every month. Tours offered daily at noon and 1:00 P.M. $6.00 adults, $5.00 students, under 5 **Free**.

Created to mimic a Ming dynasty garden, Portland's authentic Suzhou-style garden was designed by architects and artisans from China to convey artistic beauty and symbolic meaning, embodying the balance and harmony of nature. The 40,000-square-foot walled garden encloses a full city block and includes an 8,000-square-foot lake, a teahouse, nine restful pavilions, and nearly one hundred specimen trees, water plants, bamboo, and orchids. The standing Taihu rocks were mined from Lake Tai, a freshwater lake near Suzhou in China. More than 500 tons of rocks were shipped to Portland along with the fir, gingko, and nanmu woods used for columns and beams in the pavilions. This is an amazing oasis of tranquility in the heart of Portland's bustling downtown.

LLOYD CENTER (all ages)

2201 Lloyd Center; (503) 282–2511. Call for hours.

The completely refurbished mall is a favorite teen spot, but kids of all ages love the **Lloyd Center Ice Chalet** (503–288–6073), which has been entertaining families for more than thirty years.

NIKE TOWN (all ages)

930 Southwest Sixth at Sixth Avenue and Salmon Street; (503) 221–6453. Open Monday through Thursday and Saturday, 10:00 A.M.–7:00 P.M., Friday 10:00 A.M.–8:00 P.M.; Sunday, 11:30 A.M.–6:30 P.M.

For sports enthusiasts, this is a must. Enter through sliding doors reminiscent of Star Trek, and tour the two-story museum and gallery that contains memorabilia from some of the greatest professional sports stars. Of course, the retail store is here, too, but you can enjoy the museum without buying anything.

POWELL'S CITY OF BOOKS (all ages)

1005 West Burnside; (800) 878–7323 or (503) 228–4651; www.powells.com. Open daily, 9:00 A.M.–11:00 P.M.

Here's a bookstore that's very close to being a city within a city—it takes a map to find your way through the stacks and stacks of books in room after room. Families will want to head to the "rose" room for children's books. Both new and used books are available. There's a coffee house–style cafe upstairs that serves espresso drinks for weary moms and dads and cookies and pastries to kids. Powell's is the largest new and used bookstore in the world, with more than a million books.

OREGON ZOO (all ages)

4001 Southwest Canyon Road, 2 miles west of Portland off U.S. 26; (503) 226–1561; www.oregonzoo.org. Open daily year-round, 9:00 A.M.–5:00 P.M. (last entry at 4:00 P.M.) $6.00 adults; $4.00 ages 3–11; ages 2 and under Free. Free *Zoo Day is the second Tuesday of every month after 1:00 P.M.*

From a thunder-and-lightening storm in the West African rainforest to the underwater viewing areas in the Penguinarium and the Arctic Tundra where the polar bears roam, the zoo takes your family into strange and wonderful new worlds. Visit Packy, the "baby" elephant that made international headlines on April 14, 1962, as the first elephant born in captivity. Every year there's a birthday celebration for the now ponderous pachyderm. Have a snack or lunch in the Africafe while you watch exotic birds flying in the aviary. The Amazon Flooded Forest exhibit opened recently, offering above- and below-water viewing. You'll feel as if you're exploring a remote South American jungle.

INTERNATIONAL ROSE TEST GARDENS (ages 5 and up)

400 Southwest Kingston Avenue; (503) 823–3636. Open daily, 7:30 A.M.–9:00 P.M. Free.

Roses begin blooming in late May and continue through September in this 4.5-acre sanctuary. The many rhododendrons and azaleas start the blazing show off early in March or April. In summer months, Free concerts are held in the amphitheater, and you can spread out a picnic lunch just about anywhere. This is one of the largest and oldest rose test gardens in the United States. The **Zoo Train** skirts the zoo perimeter and travels through the arboretum. Proceeds from the gift shop support the gardens.

HOYT ARBORETUM (ages 5 and up)
4000 Fairview Boulevard, adjacent to the Oregon Zoo and International Rose Test Gardens; (503) 228–8733; www.hoytarboretum.org; E-mail: haffdir@ci.portland. or.us. Open daily, 6:00 A.M.–10:00 P.M. Visitor Center open daily 9:00 A.M.– 4:00 P.M. Free.

Laced with 10 miles of trails that wind through the largest selection of conifer species in the United States, as well as a huge variety of deciduous trees and shrubs, the arboretum is a quiet respite from the lively zoo. Markers identify the various species. In the fall take a self-guided "autumn color" walk through 1½ miles of vibrant maple, persimmon, dogwood, and photinia. New plantings include a bamboo garden, a magnolia area that blooms April through June, and a holly area with hollies from all over the world.

 JAPANESE GARDENS (ages 5 and up)
Just up the hill from the International Rose Test Gardens; (503) 223–1321; www.japanesegardens.com. Call for hours, which vary seasonally. $6.00 adults; $3.50 students; children 5 and under Free.

Take a breather from the busier pace at the zoo and stroll through these soothing and peaceful gardens. In May there's a special Children's Day.

 WORLD FORESTRY CENTER (ages 5 and up)
4033 Southwest Canyon Road; across the large parking lot from the zoo; (503) 228–1367; www.worldforest.org. Open daily, 10:00 A.M.–5:00 P.M. in winter; 9:00 A.M.–5:00 P.M., rest of year. $3.50 adults, $2.50 ages 6–18, children 5 and under Free.

Families have a chance to see petrified wood and view exhibits on old-growth and rainforests, and participate in a wide range of activities directed at both children and adults.

  TRYON CREEK STATE NATURAL AREA (ages 5 and up)
11321 Southwest Terwilliger Boulevard; (503) 636–4398, (503) 636–9886, or (800) 551–6949; www.oregonstateparks.org. Open dawn to dusk. Free.

More than a dozen miles of walking and cycling trails are available here, including trails with handicapped access. The **Nature Center** presents exhibits and programs for kids and adults throughout the year.

FOREST PARK (ages 5 and up)

Stretches 8 miles through the hills of northwest Portland; (800) 962–3700 or (503) 823–2223; www.parks.ci.portland.or.us. Open daily, dawn to dusk. **Free**.

With nearly 5,000 acres, this is the largest forested municipal park in the nation. Its amazing network of more than 70 miles of hiking and biking trails through tall timber allows city dwellers to escape into a wilderness experience right in their back yard. Elk, black bears, and deer live in this virtually untouched municipal park. For a map of Wildwood Trail and others in Forest Park, stop at Hoyt Arboretum Visitor Center, 4000 Fairview Boulevard.

AUDUBON HOUSE (ages 5 and up)

Located next to Portland's Forest Park, 5151 Northwest Cornell Road; (503) 292–6855; www.audubonportland.org. Park open dawn to dusk; house open 10:00 A.M.–6:00 P.M. Monday through Saturday; 10:00 A.M.–5:00 P.M. Sunday. **Free**.

Resting at the edge of its own extensive park, your kids can stroll in search of the many bird species attracted by the nesting and feeding stations. The Audubon Society frequently offers nature walks, birdhouse-building workshops, and other events to entertain and educate your youngsters. While you're there, pick up a **Free** pamphlet, "North Portland Naturally," which gives you several other ideas of where to experience nature in the city.

PORTLAND'S PITTOCK MANSION (ages 8 and up)

3229 Northwest Pittock Drive; (503) 823–3624; www.mediaforte.com/pittock. The house is open daily, noon–4:00 P.M.; the park is open 7:00–9:00 P.M. year-round. Closed major holidays and the month of January. $4.50 adults; $2.00 ages 6–18; 5 and under **Free**.

Take a guided tour of this 1914 mansion and grounds, which are open to the public. On site, you can picnic on the lawn of this forty-six-acre park, which connects with Forest Park and its many walking trails.

CM2: CHILDREN'S MUSEUM-SECOND GENERATION (ages 6 months and up)

4015 Southwest Canyon Road; (503) 223–6500; www.pdxchildrensmuseum.org. Open Tuesday through Saturday, 10:00 A.M.–5:00 P.M.; Friday 9:00 A.M.–8:00 P.M.; Sunday, 11:00 A.M.–5:00 P.M. General admission $5.00; children under 1 **Free**.

Plan on spending an afternoon in this wonderland for kids, which has three floors of exploratory, hands-on exhibits and fun centers. The Clay Shop gives budding sculptors a chance to create, and the carpeted Baby Room challenges babies from infancy to two years with all kinds of visual and physical stimuli. The latest area, Kid City Medical Center, gives kids a chance to play doctor with parental supervision in a realistic setting.

 ### PORTLAND ART MUSEUM (ages 5 and up)

1219 Southwest Park Avenue; (503) 226–2811; www.pam.org. Open Tuesday through Saturday, 10:00 A.M.–5:00 P.M.; Sunday, noon–5:00 P.M.; Wednesday and first Thursday of each month open until 8:00 P.M. $7.50 adults; $6.00 students 19 and over, $4.00 ages 5–18.

The kids will love seeing one of the premier collections of Northwest Indian art in the country, especially the ceremonial masks used in dances and potlatch celebrations. The museum also hosts many distinguished traveling exhibits that have included such works as M.C. Escher, Gauguin, and Monet.

Ticket Central Like several of the world's major cities, Portland now has a central location for purchasing day-of-show discount theater tickets. Located in the **Pioneer Courthouse Square** at 701 Southwest Sixth Avenue, Ticket Central lets you book all your tickets in advance or take advantage of last-minute deals. For information call (503) 275-8352.

 ### COLUMBIA GORGE (all ages)

1200 Northwest Front Avenue, Suite 110, Portland 97209 (for reservations); (503) 223–3928; www.sternwheeler.com. Call for prices, schedules.

This 599-passenger sternwheeler is one way to experience the Willamette River from the water, when it runs from Portland and Cascade Locks, October until mid-June. It offers harbor cruises every month of the year (although only on Christmas Eve and New Year's Eve in December). Lunch cruises are available weekdays, dinner cruises on Saturday nights, and brunch cruises on Sundays from April to November.

 ### THE ROSE (all ages)

6211 North Ensign Street, Docks at RiverPlace Marina; (503) 286–7673; www.sternwheelerrose.com. Call for hours, prices, and reservations.

The 130-passenger sternwheeler offers programs similar to the *Columbia Gorge* on a more intimate scale year-round.

WILLAMETTE SHORE TROLLEY (all ages)

(503) 222–2226 or (503) 640–1434. Call for hours, fares, and departure times.

Operates March through September between Portland's RiverPlace and Lake Oswego, passing through a warehouse district to the river's shore, then past Willamette Park and through the S-shaped Elk Rock Tunnel. At Lake Oswego the Tillamook Ice-Creamery, about a block from the train stop at 37 Southwest A Street, is the only place—along with a sister store in Beaverton—to sell the coastal product outside the factory in Tillamook.

GOV. TOM MCCALL WATERFRONT PARK (all ages)

Located in downtown Portland, stretching 2 miles along the Willamette River; (800) 962–3700 or (503) 823–2223; www.parks.ci.portland.or.us. Always open. Free.

A terrific place for walking, jogging, and cycling, here you also can rent in-line and roller skates, and the necessary safety equipment, from **ICU Skate Company,** 133 Southwest Ash Street, in the New Market Theater near the Saturday Market. From there you can skate to the park, then south along the river to the **RiverPlace Promenade,** where you can get ice cream cones or espresso from sidewalk vendors or grab a curbside cafe table for a bite of lunch. Horse-drawn carriages take off from River-Place and are fun to watch even if you don't want to splurge for your own ride.

OREGON MARITIME CENTER AND MUSEUM (ages 5 and up)

113 Southwest Naito Parkway; (503) 224–7724. Open Friday, Saturday, Sunday 11:00 A.M.–4:00 P.M. $4.00 adults; $2.00 ages 8–17; under 8 Free.

Young and old alike are intrigued with the many scale-model ships and nautical artifacts on display. The most fascinating part of the museum is listening to the "watch-standers," volunteer docents who provide living history programs—each one an "old salt" with many years at sea. You'll also tour the historic steam sternwheeler *Portland.*

OREGON HISTORICAL SOCIETY (ages 5 and up)

1200 Southwest Park Avenue; (503) 222–1741; www.ohs.org. Open Tuesday through Saturday, 10:00 A.M.–5:00 P.M.; Sunday, noon–5:00 P.M.; until 8:00

P.M. Thursday. $6.00 adults; $3.00 students; $1.50 ages 6–12; 5 and under ℱree.

Many kid-centered exhibits and programs are shown here. Children also enjoy the larger-than-life-size murals outside, bordering the Portland Park Blocks.

OREGON MUSEUM OF SCIENCE AND INDUSTRY (OMSI) (ages 5 and up)

1945 Southeast Water Avenue; (800) 955–6674 or (503) 797–4000; www.omsi.edu. Summer hours, 9:30 A.M.–7:00 P.M.; winter hours, 9:30 A.M.–5:30 P.M.; closed Mondays. $6.50 ages 14 and up; $5.00 ages 4–13; 3 and under ℱree.

Let your kids experience interactive exhibits that teach as well as entertain. Hands-on fun ranges from computer games to earthquake and tornado simulations. The **OMNIMAX Theater** here is the first of its kind in Oregon, with a five-story domed screen and complete surround sound, light, and motion that let you experience changing exhibitions, from earthquakes to volcanic eruptions, or journeys, such as exploring the Grand Canyon from top to bottom. The **Murdock Sky Theater** presents amazing laser light shows and astronomy. The Omnimax shows change periodically, and hours vary, so call first.

WILLAMETTE JET BOAT EXCURSIONS (ages 6 and up)

1945 Southeast Water Avenue, adjacent to the Oregon Museum of Science and Industry (OMSIU); (800) 538–2628 or (503) 231–1532; www.jetboatpdx. com. Reservations recommended. Daily departures April through mid-October at 10:45 A.M. and 2:45 P.M.; July and August departures at 10:45 A.M., 1:45 P.M., and 5:45 P.M. $25 adults; $15 ages 4–11; 3 and under ℱree.

This is an exciting way to view the Portland skyline, waterfront activity, and bird life on the 37-mile round-trip excursion from the docks next to OMSI to the base of Willamette Falls in Oregon City.

EASTBANK ESPLANADE (all ages)

Stretches from the Steel Bridge to the Hawthorne Bridge on the east side of the Willamette River; (503) 823–2223; Open daily year-round. ℱree.

The mile-long esplanade features a 1,200-foot floating walkway—the longest in the United States—public boat docks, river overlooks and cantilevered walkways, plazas, urban markers and interpretive panels, public art, and access to the **Steel Bridge Walkway,** built for bicyclists and pedestrians on the lower deck of the Steel Bridge. Fully accessible, the walkway gives pedestrians a safe connection to the Convention Center, Lloyd District, and Old Town/Downtown. The Steel Bridge is on the National Historic Register and is the only telescoping vertical lift span truss bridge in operation in America.

SAMTRAK, OPEN-AIR TRAIN (all ages)

(503) 653–2380. Operating daily except Mondays and Tuesdays, May through October. $5.00 ages 13 and over; $3.00 ages 2–12; under 2 **Free**.

Hop on this open-air train that travels along the banks of the Willamette River to Oaks Amusement Park, a 3-mile route that runs along the **Oaks Bottom Wildlife Refuge** and the river. The round-trip takes an hour, but you can stop off at either end of the line to enjoy the museum or the park.

OAKS AMUSEMENT PARK (ages 5 and up)

Located alongside the Willamette River, just east of the Sellwood Bridge; (503) 233–5777; www.oakspark.com. Open Memorial Day through Labor Day. Call for times. **Free** *entry. Charge for individual rides.*

Considered the oldest continuously running amusement park in the country, this park has been delighting kids of all ages since 1904. The fun includes a roller skating rink complete with 1923 Wurlitzer organ open year round, amusement rides that range from toddler swings and an antique carousel to the Looping Thunder roller coaster and the Screaming Eagle ride. There's also a beautiful, shady picnic area, and a sandy beach.

LADYBUG THEATER (ages 3 and up)

Located at Smile Station, 8210 SE Thirteenth, at the foot of Southeast Spokane Street; (503) 232–2346. Call for hours, prices.

Oregon's premier children's theater offers a wonderful introduction to live performing arts for kids two and a half and older.

MT. TABOR PARK (ages 5 and up)

Southeast Salmon and Sixtieth; (800) 962–3700 or (503) 823–2223; www. parks.ci.portland.or.us. Call for hours. **Free**.

This 195-acre park frames the only extinct volcano within the limits of any U.S. metropolitan area. The park now contains a permanent exhibit of the volcanic cone. Hiking trails take you to the top, where the view of Portland is terrific.

THE GROTTO (all ages)

Sandy Boulevard at Eighty-fifth Street; (503) 245–7371; www.thegrotto.org. Gardens and gift shop are open daily, year-round. Call for hours and admission price.

You will find respite at this sixty-two-acre garden that includes a natural stone grotto in the side of the cliff. The lands of this meditative setting are owned by the Roman Catholic Church, but people of all faiths are welcome. Regular church services are held outdoors at the Grotto during spring and summer, weather permitting. Two annual events, the Christmas Festival of Lights and Gallery in the Woods, are held here in December and June.

 SAUVIE ISLAND (all ages)

 18330 Northwest Sauvie Island Road (for trail maps), about 10 miles north of downtown Portland off U.S. 30; (503) 621–3488. Call for hours. Parking $3.50 per day, $11.00 annually.

 If you are looking for a wonderful retreat, whether it be a beach picnic and swim in August, a trip to island farms to select jack-o'-lanterns, or birdwatching for sandhill cranes in March, Sauvie Island has it all. It's home to farmers as well as to the **Sauvie Island Wildlife Area,** which is open daily. However, during waterfowl season much of the area is closed to protect migrating geese, ducks, and swans. Hiking trails wind through the 12,000-acre wildlife area, which covers half of the island. Handicapped-accessible fishing docks are available at Big Eddy and Gilbert River boat ramps in the wildlife area.

 WALTON BEACH (all ages)

Located about 10 miles north of the Sauvie Island Wildlife Office off Reeder Road; (800) 962–3700 or (503) 275–8355. Always open. **Free**.

This stretch of sandy beach along 3 miles of the Columbia River is a favorite spot for swimming, fishing, and picnicking (no tables, but you can spread your blanket on the sand). Stop by the Cracker Barrel Grocery Store for provisions on the way.

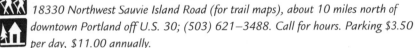 **BYBEE-HOWELL HOUSE (ages 5 and up)**

13901 Northwest Howell Road; (503) 621–3344; www.ohs.org. Open Saturday and Sunday, 11:00 A.M.–5:00 P.M., Memorial Day through Labor Day. Recommended donation $3.00 adults, $2.00 children.

This museum is located in an old colonial-style farmhouse operated by the Oregon Historical Society. Next door, stop in to view farm tools from the 1840s to the turn of the century, before the introduction of gasoline-powered farm equipment. They'll also enjoy looking at the old farm photographs. They can climb on some of the larger pieces of equipment.

WEST SIDE

Portland's western hills are a popular spot in the summer and fall for appreciating the bounty of the harvest. U-pick farms abound, for everything from Oregon's own marionberries (grown in very few places in the country), delicious peaches, and tasty hazelnuts to bright orange pumpkins and juicy wine grapes. For a display of fall colors, take a drive from Beaverton along Farmington Road.

ENKINS ESTATE (all ages)

Grabhorn Road, off Farmington and 209th, continue along Grabhorn to its junction with Scholls Ferry Road, then return on the loop to Beaverton; (503) 642–3855; www.thprd.org. Grounds open daily, 8:00 A.M.–8:00 P.M. in summer; 8:00 A.M.–5:00 P.M. October through May. Call for information about touring building. **Free.**

Once a private residence and now a public park, the estate has lovely gardens for a walk or a picnic. You'll pass a number of farms before you get there, many of which produce, in September and October, the most spicily refreshing apple cider you've ever tasted. You will also find U-pick walnut and hazelnut farms. For adults, a stop at one of several wineries along the way is especially fun.

Family Favorites in Portland and the Columbia Gorge

1. Saturday Market
2. Portland's Metro Washington Park Zoo
3. Japanese Gardens
4. Oregon Museum of Science and Industry
5. Children's Museum
6. Oaks Amusement Park
7. Powell's City of Books
8. Columbia River Gorge National Scenic Area
9. Mt. Hood Scenic Railroad
10. Ramona Falls, near Sandy

GREENWAY PARK (all ages)

Located in Beaverton, it's a narrow stretch of parkland between Scholls Ferry Road and Hall Boulevard; (800) 962–3700 or (503) 823–2223; www.parks.ci. portland.or.us. Call for hours. **Free.**

A small stream flows along one side, and more than 3 miles of paved walking and cycling paths wind from one playground area to the next—five in all. The level ground and wide paths are ideal for little ones to pedal or for the whole family to roller-skate.

MALIBU GRAND PRIX (see height requirement)

9405 Southwest Cascade Avenue; (503) 641–8122. Open Monday through Thursday, 11:00 A.M.–10:00 P.M.; Friday and Saturday, 11:00 A.M.–11:00 P.M.; Sunday, 11:00 A.M.–9:00 P.M. Call for prices.

For fast-paced family fun, primarily for families with kids who are at least 4 feet, 6 inches tall, you'll find adult- and kid-size "Indy-500" cars to put to the test on the racetrack.

JACKSON BOTTOM WETLANDS (all ages)

Trailhead is located off State Highway 219 south of Hillsboro; (503) 681–6206; www.jacksonbottom.org. Open dawn to dusk. **Free.**

The preserve has developed a number of educational programs that you and your kids can appreciate together. One of the simplest ways to get a sense of the wetlands environment is to walk the **Kingfisher Marsh Interpretive Trail,** which takes you on a 3-mile-long walk along the Tualatin River and into the Kingfisher Marsh.

EAST SIDE

Troutdale is the home of a large factory outlet shopping center and of **Lewis & Clark State Park** on the Sandy River, just south of where it empties into the Columbia.

TROUTDALE RAIL MUSEUM (ages 5 and up)

473 East Historic Columbia River Highway, located at the edge of town toward the Sandy River; (503) 661–2164. Open Sunday, Monday, and Thursday 10:00 A.M.–6:00 P.M., Friday–Saturday 10:00 A.M.–8:00 P.M., May through September but call first. $2.00 admission, children under 12 **Free.**

It's an original 1882 rail depot, and one of the earliest stations along the Columbia.

BLUE LAKE PARK (ages 5 and up)

Located on Marine Drive, off 205th Avenue; (800) 962–3700 or (503) 275–8355. Call for hours. Free.

Concrete-bordered swimming areas line the sandy north shore. The inventive dragon slide and other playground equipment keep kids busy between stops at the snack bar. You can rent paddleboats, canoes, and rowboats.

CANDY BASKET (ages 5 and up)

1924 Northeast 181st; (800) 864–1924 or (503) 666–2000. Open 9:30 A.M.–5:30 P.M. Monday through Friday; 10:00 A.M.–5:00 P.M. Saturday.

A stream of warm, luscious chocolate cascades over 20 feet, 3 inches of sculpted marble and bronze in this will-bending store. The fountain circulates 2,700 pounds of chocolate, and the aroma is scrumptious. The one-of-a-kind cascade is part of a tour through the candy factory.

FAMILY FUN CENTER AND BULLWINKLE'S RESTAURANT (ages 1–12)

29111 Southwest Town Center Loop, Wilsonville; located off Interstate 5 at exit 283, 20 miles south of Portland; (503) 685–5000; www.fun-center.com. Open Sunday through Thursday, 11:00 A.M.–9:00 P.M., Friday and Saturday, 9:00 A.M.–11:00 P.M. Call for prices.

A variety of play areas for kids twelve months to twelve years old makes this a welcome stop for the whole family. Socks are required, and shoes are left behind when you venture into the "soft" playgrounds. There are forty events covering three levels, including a cafeteria, a video game room, go carts, bumper cars, a climbing wall, and a miniature golf course.

SOUTH SIDE

Oregon City was founded by the Hudson's Bay Company, which had been founded on the fur trade and had its western headquarters at Fort Vancouver, Washington, just across from the Columbia River. This community is considered by many to be the end of the Oregon Trail.

OREGON TRAIL INTERPRETIVE CENTER (ages 5 and up)

Take Interstate 205 to Exit 10. Turn right at the first stop light; you can't miss the center's enormous covered wagons. (503) 557–1151; www.endoftheoregontrail. org. Open Monday through Saturday, 9:00 A.M.–5:00 P.M.; Sunday, 10:00 A.M.–5:00 P.M. $6.50 adults; $4.00 ages 5–12; under 5 Free.

The center consists of a complex of three 50-foot-tall Conestoga wagon–shaped buildings commemorating the importance of the trail to our nation's growth. One building contains living-history programs and an audiovisual presentation to acquaint visitors with the history of the Oregon Trail. Another is designed in the style of a Missouri provisioner's store—sort of a mid-19th-century superstore, according to one of the organizers. The third building offers exhibits, living-history demonstration areas, and a gift shop.

 CLACKAMAS COUNTY HISTORY MUSEUM (ages 5 and up)
211 Tumwater Drive located on the bluff above the river; (503) 655–5574; www.orcity.com/museum. Open Monday through Friday, 10:00 A.M.–4:00 P.M.; weekends, 1:00 P.M.–5:00 P.M. $4.00 adults; $2.00 children; family admission (up to 5) $10.00.

One of the treasures among small-town history museums, these exhibits cover the course of local history, from Native American life and culture to the fur trading days of the Hudson's Bay Company and the settlement of early pioneers.

An Adventure to Remember We've been to the Oregon Museum of Science and Industry (OMSI) a number of times, both as a family and with out-of-town visitors. Newly relocated in a gorgeous waterfront location, the museum is a bit out of the main traffic stream now but well worth a visit. There's an extensive gift shop, restaurant, IMAX Theater, and numerous hands-on exhibit rooms; you will find that several hours pass with nary a "When are we leaving?" inquiry from the little ones. Send away for a brochure because the museum schedules well in advance classes and exhibits that not only educate but intrigue. You can spend hours looking at hands-on exhibits that give a look at human body systems; dioramas that depict the evolution of man; and look-and-touch displays that examine, through superheroes such as Superman, Wonder Woman, and Batman, the marvels of movement, speed, and space. The IMAX Theater blends the wonders of nature and technology with explorations of the most intrepid human adventures, such as the climb to Mt. Everest, a river rafting trip along the Colorado, and an airplane ride over the Grand Canyon. The images on the massive screen quite literally envelop the viewer and force the squeamish of stomach to hold onto their seats.

un Facts

- **Matt Groening**, creator of the popular TV show, *The Simpsons*, got his start in Portland.

- Portland's **Mt. Tabor** is the only extinct volcano located within a city's limits in the United States.

- **Mill Ends Park** is 24 inches in diameter and the world's smallest dedicated park. Portland also has Forest Park, the largest forested municipal park in the nation.

- **Powell's Bookstore** is the largest new and used bookstore in the world, with more than 1 million books in a store that takes up a full city block.

 ### MCLOUGHLIN HOUSE (ages 5 and up)
713 Center Street; (503) 656–5146. Open Tuesday through Saturday, 10:00 A.M.–4:00 P.M.; Sunday, 1:00–4:00 P.M., closed on Mondays, holidays, and the month of January. $4.00 adults; $2.00 children.

Take a guided tour of the home in which Dr. John McLoughlin of the Hudson's Bay Company retired in 1846. The furnishings have been fully restored and are authentic to the mid-nineteenth century.

OREGON CITY TOWER (ages 5 and up)
Located near the McLoughlin House; (800) 962–3700 or (503) 275–8355. Call for hours. **Free**.

Take a **Free** elevator or stairs from the top of the bluff down to river level; from the observation deck at the top you have a great view of the Oregon City Falls.

 ### YAMHILL MARKET PLACE (all ages)
Second and Taylor in downtown Portland; (800) 962–3700 or (503) 275–8355. Call for hours. **Free**.

At Pioneer Courthouse Square you can hop aboard the eastbound **Max** light rail train and take it to this popular downtown fresh produce and seafood market, which bustles with activity in the early morning hours as vendors unload their stock.

op Portland Events

MAY

Rock Creek Campus. Hayrides for the kids and plenty of country music are all part of this lively program. (800) 962–3700 or (503) 222–2223.

SUMMER

"Your Zoo and All That Jazz" concerts are held on the lawn outside the Africafe at the Portland Zoo every Wednesday night in summer; Thursdays bring **"Rhythm and Blues Zoo Concerts."** Pack a picnic lunch and wind down here for the day. (800) 962–3700 or (503) 222–2223.

JUNE

Hot Air Balloon Classic. Head for Beaverton to see the sky filled with colorful hot-air balloons during three days of festivities. (800) 962–3700 or (503) 222–2223.

Junior Rose Festival Parade. The largest children's parade in the world, which takes places at Tom McCall Waterfront Park, usually involves more than 10,000 children.

Portland Rose Festival. This yearly mega event includes parades, carnivals, concerts, boat and Indy car races, an airshow, and fireworks. (503) 227–2681.

AUGUST

Homowo Festival. Originating in Ghana, the festival features music, dance, African and Caribbean food, arts and crafts, and storytelling for the kids. (503) 288–3025.

LABOR DAY WEEKEND

Artquake. Meander through this celebration of visual and performing arts, and literature. The **Children's Park** draws thousands of youngsters and their parents to performances, crafts activities, and general fun in the South Park Blocks, near the Portland Art Museum on Park Avenue. (800) 962–3700 or (503) 222–2223.

OCTOBER

Haunted Caves. The Washington County Fairplex annually houses this 20-year-old event that benefits local charities. (800) 537–3149 or (503) 644–5555.

PORTLAND SATURDAY MARKET (all ages)

Second Avenue and Burnside under the Burnside Bridge; (503) 222–6072; www.portlandsaturdaymarket.com. Rain or shine, open Saturday 10:00 A.M.–5:00 P.M., Sunday 11:00 A.M.–4:30 P.M., March through December 24. **Free** *entry.*

About 450 crafts and food booths transform this asphalt area from April through December every Saturday and Sunday. Most weekends, there's nonstop entertainment that aims to please the whole family. Clowns with balloons and vendors who paint faces attract the kids like magnets.

 LAURELHURST PARK (all ages)

Southeast Thirty-ninth and Stark; (503) 823–2223; www.parks.ci.portland.or.us; E-mail: pkweb@ci.portland.us. Open daily dawn to dusk. **Free**.

When I was a child, this was my favorite Portland park. Its natural beauty, towering trees, lush rhododendrons, and the noisy ducks who clamored for crumbs on Laurelhurst Lake all reside vividly in my memory. Therefore, it's truly enchanting to return here and find little changed, except for the addition of lighted tennis courts, volleyball courts, and a bigger playground.

ART FOR KIDS (all ages)

Located along the Transit Mall, easily identified by the brick streets and wide sidewalks at Southwest Fifth and Sixth Avenues; (800) 962–3700 or (503) 275–8355. Always open. **Free**.

Look for the animals—large bronze, cement, or marble structures that invite climbing and touching (it's okay, that was the artists' intent). In the park blocks, between Park and Ninth, stretching from Burnside to Portland State University, you'll also find a variety of sculptures, ranging from traditional to contemporary.

IRA KELLER MEMORIAL FOUNTAIN (all ages)

At Third Avenue between Clay and Market Streets, across from the Civic Auditorium; (800) 962–3700 or (503) 275–8355.

You'll see this fountain is alive with kids and families cooling off in the summer or just enjoying the sound of cascading water in this city-block-size water park.

Molalla

To reach Molalla, take State Highway 213 south from Oregon City. Signs in town point to Feyrer Park and Shady Dell; both are highly recommended locations.

FEYRER PARK (all ages)

Located on the Molalla River; (503) 829–6941. Open dawn to dusk. **Free**.
Swimming holes, picnic tables, and playground equipment make a summertime visit worthwhile for families with energetic kids who have been in the car all day. Camping is available May through September for a fee.

SHADY DELL PACIFIC NORTHWEST LIVE STEAMERS (all ages)

Follow signs in town; (503) 829–6866. Open Sunday afternoons between Memorial Day and Labor Day, weather permitting.
Train rides are **Free**, although donations are gratefully received. The kids will love the electric, steam, and diesel trains this group runs on small-scale tracks along a placid stream, around a pond, over trestles, and through the forest in the Molalla Train Park.

CANBY FERRY (all ages)

To reach the ferry, drive from Feyrer Park Drive along the Willamette River on State Highway 99E; (503) 650–3030. Call for hours, rates.
The ferry has operated since 1914. The ride across the river takes only five minutes, and you can either continue your journey on the opposite side or just ride the ferry back across the river.

MOLALLA RIVER STATE PARK (all ages)

Located downriver from the Canby ferry; (800) 551–6949; www.oregonstate parks.org. Day use area. **Free**.
A gem of a park, this beautiful spot has paved walking trails, lots of ducks, frogs, great blue herons, and other marsh-loving critters, as well as two picnic areas. In summer, locals often bring radio-controlled planes to fly in the open field between the two picnic areas.

op Molalla Event

JULY

Molalla Buckaroo Rodeo. Attend a rodeo for some good old-fashioned fun at the **Buckaroo Rodeo and Fun Center.** It's close to town, and the fun center offers rides and carnival games for all ages. The rodeo has two performances daily, with fireworks. (503) 829–8388.

Canby

Canby is a small agricultural community that grows everything from vegetables, berries and grains to Christmas trees and ornamental shrubs. Close by is the largest dahlia farm in the United States.

 HART'S REPTILE WORLD (ages 10 and up)
11264 South Macksburg Road; (503) 266–7236; www.hartsreptileworld.com. Open daily, 11:00 A.M.–5:00 P.M. $5.00 adults; $4.00 children; under 2 Free.

> With more than 350 reptiles Hart's Reptile World delights kids with the questionable thrill of petting a coiling 22-foot-long python or letting a lizard slither up a sleeve.

 GEORGE ROGERS PARK (ages 5 and up)
Located at the south end of State Street; (503) 266–4600. Call for hours.
 Free.

> One of the most complete family-fun parks in the metro area in Lake Oswego, George Rogers Park offers swimming areas, sandy beaches, a wading stream for kids to splash around in, a waterfall that adds a lilting cascade of sound, great playground structures, and a walking trail that connects with **Mary Young State Park,** about 5 miles upriver. More trails take you to Oswego Creek, and there's even a bit of intriguing local history left in the park—a large chimney that's the last remnant of Oregon's first iron smelter.

Sandy

A quiet community on the foothills of the mountain, Sandy is the gateway to Mt. Hood from the west. Here you'll find a variety of restaurants and lodging options, often less expensive than those on the mountain.

RAINBOW TROUT FARM (all ages)

 Located 7½ miles east of Sandy off Sylvan Drive; (503) 622–5223. Open daily, 8:00 A.M.–dusk, March 1 through October 15. Price based on size of fish caught.
Kids will have fun reeling in their very own fish at this U-catch pond.

OREGON CANDY FARM (all ages)

48620 Highway 26, 5½ miles east of Sandy; (503) 668–5066. Open Monday through Friday 9:00 A.M.–5:00 P.M.; Saturday and Sunday, noon–5:00 P.M. Closed all major holidays.

A viewing window lets your kids watch the candymaking process in the factory, and you can purchase some of the more than 100 chocolate and nonchocolate confections in the "candy room" shop to take home for gifts or munch on in the car.

LOST LAKE (all ages)

Located 20 miles southwest of Hood River on Lost Lake Road; (541) 352–6002
 (Forest Service) or (541) 386–6366 (resort). Call for hours, campground fees.
This is one of the most photographed lakes in the nation, because of the snowcapped peak of Mt. Hood which rises above and often casts its reflection upon the lake's pristine waters. Rent a rowboat, drop a line in the water to catch one of the German brown or rainbow trout lurking beneath the surface of this 231-acre lake, or hike the trail surrounding the lake. Native Americans called the lake E-e-kwahl-a-mat-yan-ishkt, which means "heart of the mountains." It was a favored camping ground, and according to legend, during a potlatch, wolves pursued a snow-white doe that jumped into the lake, swam to the middle, and disappeared. Medicine men called this a bad omen, and the Native Americans left the camp immediately and never returned.

RAMONA FALLS (all ages)

65000 Highway 26 in Welches, located off Lolo Pass Road and Forest Road 1825; (503) 668–1704 or (503) 622–3191. Call about hours, fees.

During the summer take the 4½-mile loop trail leading into the falls. It's one of the most popular day hikes on the mountain, both because it's easy enough for young children and because of the stunningly beautiful falls awaiting you.

  COLUMBIA RIVER HIGHWAY NATIONAL HISTORIC LANDMARK (all ages)

 Crossing the bridge from Troutdale over the Sandy River leads you along the Columbia River Scenic Highway (U.S. 30); (888) 275–6368 or (541) 386–2333; www.odot.state.or.us/hcrh or www.fs.fed.us/r6/columbia. Always open. **Free**.

An engineering feat when it was built between 1913 and 1922, this 55-mile old highway winds through rich agricultural land and deep forests, and cuts through the sides of steep basalt cliffs to a series of waterfalls that pour over the edge on their way to the Columbia. Designated a National Historic Landmark, it was the first modern highway in the Northwest. Several waterfalls here are worth driving many miles to see. Hiking trails take you between falls or to the point where the falls cascade over the cliff tops. Paths at Latourel Falls, Bridal Veil Falls, Wahkeena Falls, Multnomah Falls, Oneonta Gorge, Horsetail Falls, and Elowah Falls are all under a mile.

CROWN POINT VISTA HOUSE (ages 5 and up)

(503) 695–2230. Open to the public mid-April through mid-October 8:30 A.M.–6:00 P.M. daily. **Free**, *but donations welcome*.

One of the first stops along the way on the Columbia River Scenic Highway, the 1917 house gives you a perfect viewpoint from which to see the rugged gorge and the river that carved it. A small gallery and interpretive center, open mid-April to mid-October, offer information on the area. On Saturdays during the summer months the whole family can enjoy folk art demonstrations or historical and cultural programs.

Top Sandy Event

JULY

Music Fair & Feast. Four days of live music, a talent show, food, microbrews and wine from the local winery make this a fun event for the whole family. (503) 668–4006.

MULTNOMAH FALLS (ages 8 and up)

Located in the Columbia Gorge on Interstate 84; (503) 695–2376 (lodge); (503) 695–2372 (Visitor Center); www.fs.fed.us/r6/columbia. Visitor Center open daily, year-round, 9:00 A.M.–5:00 P.M. **Free**.

At 620 feet high, Multnomah Falls is the second highest waterfall in the United States. If you have the time and your kids have the energy, walk the trail to the top of the upper falls, about a mile of fairly steep climbing on a paved path. At the top, follow the creek upstream to some beautiful shaded dells where children can dabble their feet in the water or search for crawdads.

ONEONTA FALLS (ages 10 and up)

Located on the Columbia River National Scenic Highway east of Multnomah Falls; (541) 385–2333; www.fs.fed.us/r6/columbia. **Free**.

Oneonta Falls isn't the tallest or most beautiful of the falls but is a favorite because it's the most fun to get to. Not appropriate for very young children, Oneonta Falls is at the end of a tall, narrow slit carved by Oneonta Creek. The walls rise a sheer 150 feet above the creek bed. The most kid-satisfying route to the falls and the most direct is ¼ mile and gives the kids a chance to hop rocks in the creek and get delightfully damp in the process. Oneonta means "place of peace," and that sense of peace pervades this gorge.

SHEPHERD'S DELL STATE PARK (all ages)

On the Columbia River Gorge on Interstate 84; (800) 551–6949; www.oregon stateparks.org. Call for hours, fees.

Look for a short trail that takes you to two more waterfalls in a small grotto. All of these spots have places for picnicking.

ROOSTER ROCK STATE PARK (all ages)

Accessible only from Interstate 84; (800) 551–6949 or (503) 695–2261. Open daily, 7:00 A.M.–dusk. $3.00 admission fee.

You won't have a hard time finding this park because the large basalt "rooster tail" rock that rises above it makes the site easy to spot. The park has shaded picnic groves, a protected moorage area, and sandy beaches. You may want to be forewarned that at the far east end of the park, a stairway leads to secluded beaches where nude sun bathing is allowed beyond a point 100 yards farther east.

BONNEVILLE LOCKS AND DAM AND FISH HATCHERY (ages 5 and up)

From Portland take Interstate 84 east to exit 40; (541) 374–8442; www.nwp. usace.army.mil/op/b. Call for hours. **Free.**

The visitor center at the dam has some very impressive educational exhibits on river history, the production of electricity, and a Native American sacred burial ground. The viewing windows looking into the fish ladder in the Underwater Observatory give you an up-close look at fish that are bigger than some children. The sturgeon pond, where these ancient giants cruised through ponds rimmed with lilypads, always was my favorite part of the fish hatchery. These prehistoric fish, which thrive in the Columbia River, have been around for 200 million years and grow to lengths of 10 feet and more. Your kids get the whole picture of the salmon life cycle in several areas of the hatchery, and depending on the time of year, they can view fish culturists removing eggs from spawning females, the incubation room where millions of bright red eggs in trays become tiny salmon fry, or the outdoor pools where fry grow big enough to be released into Tanner Creek.

Grounds at the hatchery. *(541) 374–8393. Open daily, 7:30 A.M.– dusk.* Enjoy a picnic dinner on the attractive grounds while your kids enjoy feeding the brooder rainbow trout or climbing on the playground equipment.

EAGLE CREEK (all ages)

Just east of Bonneville Dam; (503) 695–2261. Call for hours, fees.

At **Eagle Creek Park** you'll find a campground, a picnic area, and walking trails as well as some nice swimming holes on the creek. Eagle Creek Scenic Trail, Number 440, takes you past Metlako, Punchbowl, Loowit, and Tunnel Falls in just 6 miles on the way into the **Columbia Wilderness Area.** With kids you'll probably want to walk only the 2 miles to **Punchbowl Falls,** truly one of the most impressive around.

Hood River

The Hood River Valley is Oregon's largest producer of fruit, yielding apples and pears that are valued across the United States. A loop drive, best in late August and early September, takes you past a number of fruit stands where you can buy direct from the growers.

SCENIC MT. HOOD RAILROAD (all ages)

110 Railroad Avenue; (800) 872–4661 or (503) 386–3556; www.mthoodrr. com. Morning excursions weekdays, morning and afternoon excursions weekends; dinner train. Call for hours, fees.

The 1906 train, which departs from the Mt. Hood Railroad Depot, is a link between the Columbia River Gorge and the foothills of this area's other natural wonder, Mt. Hood, the state's highest peak. The Timberline car has snacks and beverages to enjoy along the way.

Fun Facts Hood River is the windsurfing capital of the world.

RHONDA SMITH WINDSURFING CENTER (ages 10 and up)

(541) 386–9463; www.windsurf.gorge.net/rhondas. Open daily; call for hours and fees.

Want to test your might against the famous Columbia Gorge winds? This is one of many surf shops in town, but it offers special kids' programs and rental equipment.

 ### JACKSON PARK (all ages)

Thirteenth and May Streets; (800) 366–3530. Open dawn to dusk. Free.

Families are the center of the fun every Thursday evening in August, with the Families in the Park entertainment series. Bring a picnic and enjoy the program.

 ### SATURDAY FARMER'S MARKET (all ages)

Parking lot between Fifth and Seventh and Cascade and Columbia; (800) 366–3530. Open Saturdays, 9:00 A.M.–3:00 P.M. until mid-October. Free.

Pick up luscious fruit for snacks from local growers at this open air market.

 ### VIENTO STATE PARK (all ages)

Located about eight miles west of Hood River; (800) 551–6949; www.oregon stateparks.org.

Viento State Park is one of several state parks that sit alongside the Columbia. A mix of maple, fir, willow, and pine nestle with tent and trailer sites, making this a pretty place to plunk down for a night's rest. There's a ¼-mile nature trail to Viento Lake, where the wetlands surrounding it provide a good spot for birdwatching.

CASCADE LOCKS AND CASCADE LOCKS HISTORICAL MUSEUM (ages 5 and up)

Located in Cascade Locks Marine Park, west of Hood River; (541) 374–8535. Open daily, noon–5:00 P.M. May through September.

The word Cascade refers not to the mountain range to the east but to the cascading waters once in this part of the Columbia's journey to the sea. Located in the park are displays that describe the river's history. An outdoor barn contains a variety of wagons, and a small building houses the first steam locomotive in the Northwest.

MARINE PARK (all ages)

355 Wanapa, Cascade Locks; just follow Main Street to the park; (541) 374–8619. Open daily, dawn–10:00 P.M.

The story of Lewis and Clark and their trip with Sacajawea and her papoose, and how they navigated the treacherous Columbia with its many chutes comes alive here. Now several dams have tamed the once-wild river. Native Americans sometimes fish here in the traditional manner.

Top Hood River Events

APRIL

Hood River Blossom Festival. Blossoming pear and apple orchards create an exquisite backdrop for Hood River's springtime festival. (800) 366–3530 or (541) 386–2000.

JUNE

Sternwheeler Days. Cascade Locks. Join in a playful event that has plenty of good food and local crafts. (800) 366–3530 or (541) 374–8619.

AUGUST

Gravenstein Apple Fair. With—you guessed it—plenty of apples and apple-inspired goodies to sample, this might be just the pick for a lunch stop. (800) 366–3530 or (541) 386–2000.

OCTOBER

Hood River Valley Harvest Fest. An annual celebration that expresses appreciation for the bounty of fall harvest with food booths, arts and crafts, and pumpkin carving. (800) 366–3530 or (541) 386–2000.

HOOD RIVER FRUIT LOOP (ages 5 and up)

A 45-mile loop drive; (541) 386–7697; http://business.gorge.net/fruitloop. Hours vary at farmstands and farms along the route. See printable map and list of vendors on Web site or call for brochure. **Free.**

During harvest season there's no richer place for tasting the fruits of nature than the Hood River Valley. Thousands of acres of lush orchards and rich farmland form the foreground, with Mount Hood in the background—it's definitely an opportunity for photographs! Some twenty-seven vendors are open along the route for produce and the delicious products made from local fruits and berries. The produce changes through the season: strawberries and raspberries in June, cherries, apricots, and blueberries in July, peaches in August, apples and pears in August and September. October brings chestnuts and sunny orange pumpkins.

 HOOD RIVER COUNTY HISTORICAL MUSEUM (ages 5 and up)

Located in Port Marina Park; (541) 386–6772; E-mail: hrchm@gorge.net. April through October, open Monday through Saturday, 10:00 A.M.–4:00 P.M.; Sunday, noon–4:00 P.M.; September and October, open daily, noon–4:00 P.M. Closed November through March. **Free.**

Native American artifacts and pioneer relics, as well as displays on the development of lumber and fruit-growing industries in the region, make this museum a worthwhile stop.

 HOOD RIVER INTERNATIONAL MUSEUM OF CAROUSEL ART (ages 3 and up)

304 Oak Street; (541) 387–4622; www.carouselmuseum.com; E-mail: mail@ carouselmuseum.com. Open daily, 8:30 A.M.–4:00 P.M. $5.00 adults; $4.00 students; $2.00 under 10.

Billed as having "the world's largest collection of antique carousel art," this museum includes around 140 carousel animals and chariots, an antique steam engine, and a fully operational 1917 Wurlitzer band organ.

 PHOENIX PHARMS U-CATCH TROUT FARM (ages 3 and up)

4349 Baldwin Creek Road, 12 miles south of Hood River off Highway 35; (541) 352–6090; summer hours, Wednesday through Saturday, 10:00 A.M.–5:30 P.M., Sunday 11:00 A.M.–5:30 P.M. Call for prices and off-season hours.

Let your little one get the joy of reeling in a "big one" at this well-stocked pond. There's no license required, and bait and pole are provided. You're also welcome to picnic on the grounds after your angling adventure.

Mt. Hood

Winter isn't the only season for enjoying this majestic mountain, which at 11,235 feet is Oregon's tallest peak. Summer brings hikers, mountain climbers, anglers, boaters, and birdwatchers to the slopes. The winter recreation activities usually extend from late fall through early spring, with year-round skiing available at Timberline Lodge. Several ski resorts on the mountain offer everything from beginner hills to steep, mogul-covered slopes. Night skiing, ski and snowboard rentals, and lessons are available at each site. Snow passes are required November 15 through April 30 and are available at Hood River or Zigzag ranger stations located on U.S. 30 beyond Mt. Hood Meadows or at the Forest Service's information center at Mt. Hood RV Village, 13 miles east of Sandy on U.S. Highway 26.

 ### MT. HOOD MEADOWS (ages 5 and up)

Located on Highway 35; (503) 337–2217; (503) 227–SNOW (snow report); www.skihood.com; E-mail: info@skihood.com. Call for snow levels, prices, and opening hours.

The largest resort on the mountain, the "Meadows" usually opens after mid-November, depending on snow levels, of course.

Top Mt. Hood Events

OCTOBER

Mt. Hood Holiday Spook Train. Ghosts, goblins, witches, and warlocks will be among your fellow passengers on this train. (800)–TRAIN–61.

DECEMBER

Mt. Hood Railroad Christmas Tree Train. If you're traveling through here during the winter, this magical train ride will make your holiday special with carolers, a country-style holiday meal, and, if you're not far from home, the chance to pick up a Christmas tree. (800)–TRAIN–61.

MT. HOOD SKIBOWL (ages 5 and up)

P.O. Box 280, Government Camp 97028; (503) 272–3206; www.skibowl.com. Open daily in winter, weekends only in summer.

You'll find skiing, snowboarding, and tubing hills in winter. In the summer your kids will be thrilled by a ride on Mt. Hood Skibowl's half-mile-long slide, a mountain-hugging luge that takes you down S-curves in sleds complete with brake levers that even young children can control—you go as fast or slow as you like. A racecourse for fancy go-carts, and a "sky chair" that takes hikers and mountain bikers to the top of the lift so they can walk or ride down make this an unforgettable family fun spot.

 ### SUMMIT SKI AREA (ages 5 and up)

Located at the east end of Government Camp on Highway 26; (503) 272–0256. Open weekends and holidays 8:30 A.M.–4:00 P.M. Call for snow levels, prices.

You'll find a great slope for kids to slide down on sleds, inner tubes, plastic bags, or cardboard boxes—anything works to bring giggles and squeals on the slippery slope. Inner-tube rentals for snow play on the hill are available here, along with snowboarding and alpine skiing.

 ### TEACUP LAKE and HOOD RIVER MEADOWS

All are located on U.S. Highway 35; (503) 337–2222. Call for hours, fees.

Groomed cross-country trails are available at each of these areas. Ungroomed trails take off from a variety of Sno-Parks (plowed parking areas) on the mountain.

 ### TIMBERLINE LODGE AND SKI RESORT (ages 5 and up)

Off Highway 26; (503) 622–7979; (503) 222–2211 (snow report); www.timberlinelodge.com. Call for snow levels, hours, and prices.

Timberline enjoys the longest ski season in North America, with more than a thousand acres of skiable terrain. A new Magic Carpet lift supports a wide range of children's learning programs. Foot passengers are also allowed on the **Magic Mile Super Express Chairlift** daily, weather and lift lines permitting. Ages 6 and younger Free of charge when accompanied by parents. If you're just visiting the mountain for the day, summer or winter, stop by the lodge to appreciate the impressive views and equally impressive 1930s construction in this National Historic Landmark. Built as a WPA project, the lodge has the classic rough-hewn, massive scale of the period. Have your kids try to find the various animals carved into wooden structures throughout the building.

93

The Dalles

The early French *voyageurs* gave the name *Le Dalle*, or "the trough," to the falls at a Native American fishery about 6 miles above the current site of town because of the frequency with which they were pulled under by the force of the water at the bottom of the falls. The falls have long since been covered with calm waters pooled behind The Dalles Dam.

  ### COLUMBIA GORGE DISCOVERY CENTER & WASCO COUNTY HISTORICAL MUSEUM (ages 5 and up)

 5000 Discovery Drive; (541) 296–8600; www.gorgediscovery.org. Summer hours, daily 10:00 A.M.–6:00 P.M.; January through mid-March Tuesday through Sunday, 10:00 A.M.–4:00 P.M. $6.50 adults; $3.50 ages 6–16; 5 and under **Free**.

You'll want to spend the whole day in this 50,000-square-foot facility, exploring two museums, talking with pioneers in the Oregon Trail Living History Park, walking the interpretive trail, or having lunch in the Basalt Rock Cafe on site. This is the official interpretive center for the Columbia River Gorge National Scenic Area, and its exhibits on geology, wildlife, and ancient cultures will add meaning to your travels in the Gorge.

FORT DALLES MUSEUM (ages 5 and up)

Fifteenth and Garrison Streets; (541) 296–4547. Open daily during summer. Call for hours, winter open days, and admission prices.

Housed in the last remaining building of Fort Dalles, the museum was built in the wake of the Whitman massacre across the river. Originally the surgeon's quarters, the building now aptly serves to tell the story of the early decades of the community. Outside, the grounds contain a wide range of horse-drawn vehicles, and across the street you can visit an old homestead, granary, and barn.

 ### DALLES DAM AND TOUR TRAIN (all ages)

A half-hour train ride starts from the visitor center, at the end of Cladfelter Way off exit 87 of Interstate 84; (541) 296–9778. Call for seasonal hours. **Free**.

A train ride tour of the dam provides a lot of history as well as fun. The pool of water behind the dam covers two Native American sites: a sacred burial ground and the ancient fishing grounds of **Celilo Falls.** Photographs in the **Seufert Visitor Center** show the fishing platforms built over basalt rocks so the Yakima Nation Indians could spear the salmon as they jumped the falls on their migration upriver. You'll also see petroglyphs that were recovered before the dam was built. You have the option to stop off at the powerhouse and fish ladders or a picnic area, and return on a later train. The center's collections and interpretive displays provide background on Lewis and Clark and other local history.

RIVERFRONT PARK (all ages)
Take Interstate 84 to exit 85; (541) 296–9533. Open dawn to dusk. **Free**.
Give your teenagers a relatively safe place to try out sailboarding. The offshore islands protect beginners from both the main river current and barge traffic. Equipment rentals and lessons are available through vendors operating at the park in the summer.

WONDER WORKS MUSEUM (ages toddler to 12)
419 East Second Street; (541) 296–2444. Open daily, 10:00 A.M.–4:00 P.M. $2.00 kids age 2 and over; adults and kids under 2 **Free**.
The kids will be entertained at this see-and-do museum that encourages kids to use their imaginations, learning through play and exploration. There are no "no-nos" here. Exhibits include a teepee, police car, and grocery store.

MEMALOOSE STATE PARK (all ages)
11 miles west of The Dalles; accessible only from the westbound freeway; (503) 478–3008 or (800) 551–6949; (800) 452–5687 (campground reservations); www.oregonstateparksorg. Campground open March through October; day-use area open year-round. Call for hours, fees.
You can see the lower and only remaining of two Memaloose Islands, which were sacred Native American burial grounds. Memaloose is the Chinook Indian word for "island of the dead." The park provides a cool summer oasis in the hottest part of the gorge.

un Facts
- The Dalles is one of the oldest inhabited locations in North America, serving as a center of the Native American trade for at least 10,000 years.
- The Dalles is one of the oldest incorporated cities in the United States.

DESCHUTES RIVER STATE RECREATION AREA (all ages)

Located east of The Dalles; on Highway 206; (800) 551–6949 or (503) 228–9561; (800) 452–5687 (campground reservations); www.oregonstateparks.org. Call for hours, fees.

This is where the Deschutes River flows into the Columbia. Recreation options include hiking, cycling, camping, boating, and—most popular—fishing. The Deschutes is one of Oregon's finest fishing rivers, popular among local Native Americans who dip-net fish from platforms along the river banks. An Oregon Trail exhibit provides information about the pioneers who turned south just beyond here to follow the Barlow Trail spur of the Oregon Trail rather than risk disaster on the Columbia River. You can even rent a covered wagon to camp in! For a shady walk, take the Atiyeh Deschutes River Trail through white alder and birch forest. Look for oriole nests that resemble hanging baskets.

MAYER STATE PARK (all ages)

Located ten miles west of The Dalles; (800) 551–6949 or (503) 228–9561; www.oregonstateparks.org. Day-use area. $3.00 day-use fee.

Call ahead to arrange for a **Free** naturalist-led tour. A swimming area in a small lake within the west side of the park is perfect for little ones. From the park, take the 9-mile scenic drive to Rowena Crest, a viewpoint high above the river that gives access to the Tom McCall Nature Preserve on the Rowena Plateau.

TOM MCCALL NATURE PRESERVE

Located on the Rowena Plateau, east of Hood River; (503) 230–1221; www.nature.org. Call for hours, fees.

This premier wildflower meadow, preserved by the Nature Conservancy, is best visited between early March and late May, when the blooms reach their peak. Hiking paths weave across the meadow and along the cliffs, but use caution because this is rattlesnake country.

Top Event in The Dalles

APRIL

Northwest Cherry Festival. A parade, live music, health fair, food court, and crafts are all a part of this week-long celebration of cherry blossoms. (800) 255–3385.

Where to Eat

IN HOOD RIVER

Carolyn's Restaurant. *1313 Oak Street; (541) 386–1127.* Check this place out for breakfast or lunch. If you need to head out of town early, they open at 6:00 A.M. daily here. $-$$

***Columbia Gorge* Sternwheeler.** *Located at the Port of Cascade Locks Marine Park, west of Hood River; (503) 223–3928 or (541) 374–8427.* Open June to October. Lunch, brunch, and dinner cruises, as well as special holiday trips, are available. Wednesday is Family Dinner Night. $$$

Pasquale's Ristorante. *Located in the Hood River Hotel, 102 Oak Avenue; (800) 386–1859 or (541) 386–1900.* Breakfast, lunch and dinner are served in this casually elegant place. Specialties are pasta and seafood. The sidewalk cafe offers a pleasant European ambiance. $$-$$$

IN MT. HOOD

Huckleberry Inn. *Government Loop Road; (503) 272–3325.* Open twenty-four hours a day, it's a great breakfast or lunch stop. $-$$$

Mt. Hood Brewing Company. *Government Camp Loop Road; (503) 622–0724; www.mthoodbrewing.com.* Families are more than welcome at this mountainside dining establishment. Parents can enjoy the local brew while kids partake of classic pub hamburgers and fries. $-$$$

Honey Bear Express. *Corner of Salmon River Road and Highway 26; (503) 622–5726.* Deli-style sandwiches, burgers, and take-out. Open daily. $-$$

IN PORTLAND

Alexis Restaurant. *215 West Burnside; (503) 224–8577.* This lively place is often crowded, so try to get there early for all your Greek favorites. If Greek food is new for the kids, try the extensive appetizer menu to give them a taste of some tantalizing possibilities. $$

Bread and Ink Cafe. *3610 Southeast Hawthorne; (503) 239–4756.* Open for breakfast, lunch, and dinner, this casual neighborhood cafe has been voted one of the best restaurants in Oregon. $$

Hamburger Mary's. *239 SW Broadway; (503) 223–0900.* If you've got a hankering for a good hamburger, you won't want to miss this place. It looks like a hole-in-the-wall, but it's really one of the best places in Portland to get a burger. $$

Tom's Pancake House. *12925 Southwest Canyon Road, Beaverton; (503) 646–2688.* Just as its name suggests, this place specializes in all flavors and types of pancakes, plus waffles and omelettes. Children's menu. $$

IN SANDY

Calamity Jane's Hamburger Parlor. *42015 Highway 26; (503) 668–7817.* You can choose from fifty different burgers, and the milkshakes are made with real ice cream. $$

THE DALLES

Cousin's Restaurant. *2116 West Sixth Street; (541) 298–5161; www.cousinsrestaurant.com.* Homestyle breakfast, lunch, and dinner spot well known for its cinnamon rolls, turkey sandwiches, and pot roast. $-$$

Where to Stay

IN HOOD RIVER

Best Western Hood River Inn. *1108 East Marina Way; (800) 828–7873 or (541) 386–2200; www.hoodriverinn.com.* Air-conditioned riverfront rooms, a restaurant, and a heated outdoor pool and spa are situated right in the heart of the Columbia River Gorge. Pets OK. $$–$$$$

Columbia Gorge Hotel. *4000 Westcliff Drive; (800) 345–1921 or (541) 386–5566; www.columbiagorgehotel.com; E-mail: cghotel@gorge.net.* This historic hotel, with its Spanish-style exterior, is all old-world luxury on the inside. The hotel was built in 1921 by lumber magnate Simon Benson on the site of an old Native American meeting ground. An inviting lobby and fireside coffee room don't seem geared to children, but little ones are welcome at this stately old hotel. They'll enjoy exploring the grounds outside, where an arched stone footbridge crosses a small stream that meanders through the property. Family suites are available. $$$$

Hood River Hotel. *Oak Street and First; (800) 386–1859 or (514) 386–1900; www.hoodriverhotel.com; E-mail: hrhotel@gorge.net.* This hotel, built in 1913, is on the National Historic Register and has been refurbished as an enjoyable hotel with reasonable rates and many rooms overlooking the river. In the comfortable lounge, a basketful of toys helps entertain the kids. $–$$$

MT. HOOD AREA

Huckleberry Inn. *Government Camp Business Loop Highway; (503) 272–3325.* Seventeen units. A restaurant, kitch-

enettes, and laundry facilities make this an especially handy place to stay during ski season. $–$$$

Timberline Lodge and Ski Resort. *Off U.S. 26 about 60 miles east of Portland; (800) 547–1406 or (503) 622–7979; www.timberlinelodge.com.* The oldest resort on the mountain is a convenient place to reserve for a winter ski vacation—or summer outdoor fun. Visitors appreciate the impressive views and the 1930s construction in this National Historic Landmark that was built as a WPA project. $$$–$$$$

Trillium Lake Basin Cabins. *P.O. Box 28, Government Camp 97028; (503) 297–5993.* Located at the base of Multorpor (Skibowl East), the cabins are close to the downhill ski centers along a lovely stream. From the cabin door you can walk to the ski area and ski right onto an extensive system of cross-country trails, or hike to Trillium Lake, where you can also camp in the summer. $$

IN PORTLAND

McMenamin's Edgefield Manor. *2126 Southwest Halsey Street; (503) 669–8610 or (800) 699–8610; www.mcmenamins.com/Edge/index2.html.* Once a farm home, this delightful refurbished bed-and-breakfast inn, pub, movie theater, and restaurant is a welcoming place for families to stop for lunch or overnight. $$–$$$

Mallory Hotel. *729 Southwest Fifteenth Avenue; (800) 228–8657 (reservations) or (503) 223–6311; www.malloryhotel.com.* One hundred forty-three rooms, thirteen suites. A spacious lobby with ornate wainscoting and an enormous chandelier create a warm welcome in this family-oriented facility located on the Max line. A reasonably priced restaurant, laundry service, and 2:00 P.M. checkout make this place a hidden gem in downtown Portland. $$$-$$$$

Days Inn. *1414 Southwest Sixth Avenue; (503) 221–1611; (800) 329–7466; www.daysinn-gowest.com.* One hundred eighty rooms. Right in the heart of downtown Portland, this is an excellent choice for families. Each bright and cheery room has a small library of hardbound books. You'll also find laundry service, an outdoor swimming pool and complimentary newspaper. $$-$$$

DoubleTree Lloyd Center. *1000 Northeast Multnomah Street; (503) 281–6111, (800) 996–0510; www.double treelloydcenter.citysearch.com.* Four hundred seventy-six rooms. Glass elevators give you a bird's-eye view of the modern, spacious lobby and the Portland environs. There are two more formal restaurants plus a friendly family-style coffee shop. Just across the street is the Lloyd Center mall, with an ice-skating rink, dozens of eateries and enough shops to provide hours of entertainment for everyone. $$-$$$$

Radisson Hotel, *1441 Northeast Second Avenue; (877) 777–2704 or (503) 233–2401.* Two hundred thirty-six rooms. Complimentary newspapers, coffeemakers, continental breakfasts, in-room movies, laundry services, and a heated outdoor pool offer something for every family member. $$$-$$$$

IN SANDY

Best Western Sandy Inn. *37465 Highway 26, Sandy; (800) 528-1234 or (503) 668–7100.* A spa, indoor pool, suites, continental breakfast, and exercise room await you in this establishment next to Mt. Hood. $-$$$

IN THE DALLES

Quality Inn. *2114 West Sixth Street; (541) 298–5161; www.qualityinn-the dalles.com.* Eighty-five units. Kids love the Old West exterior and you'll love the outdoor swimming pool, indoor spa, in-room coffee maker, and access to fitness center. $$

For More Information

Beaverton Area Chamber of Commerce. *4800 South West Griffith Drive, #100, Beaverton, OR 97005; (503) 644–0123; www.beaverton.org; E-mail: info@beaverton.org.*

Canby Area Chamber of Commerce. *P.O. Box 35/266 North West First, #C, Canby, OR 97013; (503) 266–4600; www.canby.com/chamber; E-mail: chamber@canby.com.*

Port of Cascade Locks Visitor Center. *P.O. Box 307/Marine Park Drive, Cascade Locks, OR 97014; (503) 374–8619; www.gorge.net/cgeda/cgeda/meportl.htm.*

Columbia River Gorge Visitors Association. *404 West Second Street, The Dalles, OR 97058; (800) 984–6743; www.gorge.net/crgva; E-mail: crgva@gorge.net.*

Molalla Area Chamber of Commerce. *P.O. Box 578, 103 South Molalla Avenue, Molalla, OR 97038; (503) 829–6941; www.molallachamber.com; E-mail: macc@molalla.net.*

Mount Hood Information Center. *P.O. Box 819, 65000 East Highway 26, Welches, OR 97067; (503) 622–4822.*

Portland Metropolitan Chamber of Commerce. *221 NW Second, Portland, OR 97209; (503) 228–9411; www.pdx-chamber.org; E-mail: chamber@pdxchamber. org.*

Portland/Oregon Visitors Association. *26 Southwest Salmon Street; Portland,OR 97204; (800) 962–3700 or (503) 222–2223; www.pova.com; E-mail: info@pova.com.*

Hood River Chamber of Commerce. *405 Portway Avenue, Hood River, OR 97431; (541) 386–2477; www.hoodriver. org; E-mail: hrccc@gorge.net.*

The Dalles Area Chamber of Commerce. *404 West Second Street, The Dalles, OR 97058; (800) 255–3385 or (503) 296–2231; www.thedalleschamber. com; E-mail: tdacc@gorge.net.*

Troutdale Area Chamber of Commerce. *P.O. Box 245, 338 East Historic Columbia River Highway, Troutdale, OR 97060; (503) 669–7473; www. troutdalechamber.org.*

Washington County Visitors Association. *5075 South West Griffith Drive, #120, Beaverton, OR 97005; (800) 537–3149 or (503) 644–5555; www.wcva.org; E-mail: wcva@pinc.com.*

Woodburn Area Chamber of Commerce. *P.O. Box 194, 2233 Country Club Road, Woodburn, OR 97071; (503) 982–8221.*

Other Important Resources

- **Portland Parks and Recreation.** *1120 Southwest Fifth Avenue, Suite 1302; (503) 823–2223; www.parks.ci.portland.or.us; E-mail: pkweb@ci.portland.or.us*

- **State Campground Guide.** *(800) 547–7842*

- **State Park Campsite and Reservations.** *(800) 452–5687; www. oregonstateparks.org*

- **www.el.com/to/portland**

The Willamette Valley

Oregon's Willamette Valley represented the dream, the inspiration that brought 300,000 people from the middle west of the young nation on a 2,000-mile trek laden with untold hardship. It was the promise of land so rich you could sow corn in the morning and harvest it in the afternoon, of rivers teeming with fish, and of forests running thick with deer and elk. Today, the Willamette Valley is still the agricultural heartland of the state. In summer you're never very far from a roadside fruit and vegetable stand, where you can buy produce that was washed on the vine with the morning's dew. U-pick fields abound, too, starting with strawberries in late May or early June, moving through peaches and cherries in July, and raspberries and blueberries in August. In fall, apples, pears, walnuts, and filberts are ready for gathering.

Newberg and McMinnville

 CHAMPOEG STATE PARK (ages 5 and up)
Located seven miles east of Newberg; take Highway 278 west from Interstate 5. (800) 551–6949 for information; (800) 452–5687 for reservations; www. oregonstateparks.org. Park open dawn to dusk. $3.00 park admission fee.

Once a small townsite and the seat of the first provisional government body on the West Coast, Champoeg (sham-poo-ee) is now a quiet riverside retreat not far from the bustle of the big city. Before it was used by settlers, the site was a Kalapuya Indian village. Much of this area's history is described in the exhibits

Fun Facts It was at Champoeg State Park that the first Oregon settlers voted in 1843 for the formation of a provisional government.

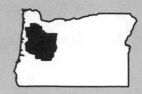

THE WILLAMETTE VALLEY

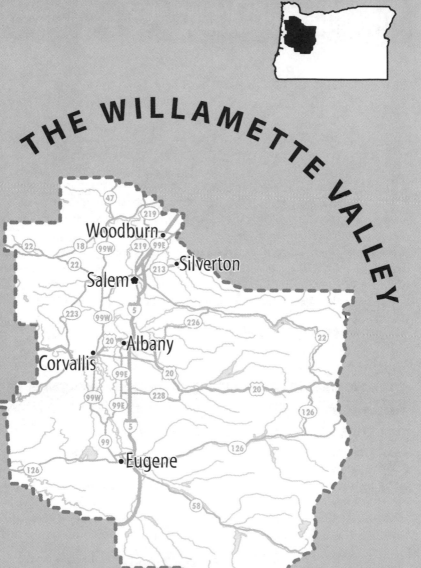

47

219

Woodburn

18   219 99E

22   99W

22   •Silverton

213

Salem•

223   99W

5

226

20 •Albany   22

Corvallis

99E

20

99W   228   20

99E

126

5

99

126

126

•Eugene

58

at the Visitor Center, near the park entrance. Ten miles of walking and cycling trails are good ways to explore, and a map is available at the Visitor Center which shows both the paths and the original location of town buildings swept away by an 1860 flood. Tour **Newell House,** the **Pioneer Mothers Log Cabin Museum,** and, in summer, take a guided walk to tour historic **Manson Farmstead** and old Champoeg townsite.

FLYING M RANCH (ages 5 and up)

23029 Northwest Flying M Road, Yamhill, 10 miles west of McMinnville; (541) 662–3222; www.flying-m-ranch.com; E-mail: flyingm@bigplanet.com. Open year-round; call for hours. Cabins sleep two to ten, $60–$200; rustic camping $12; hourly horseback rides $15 weekdays, $17 weekends; day-long rides $65; kiddie rides $4.25 for 15 minutes. Call for times and reservations.

Set in the foothills of the Coast Range along the North Yamhill River, the ranch offers a rustic country experience within easy reach of the city. In addition to horseback rides, you can enjoy fishing, swimming, volleyball, and other sports and walking the many trails through forest and meadow. The lodge dining room serves breakfast, lunch, and dinner.

Top Events Around Newberg

SUMMER

Champoeg Historical Pageant. The history of Oregon, from Native American legends of Mt. Hood's fight with Mt. Adams over the Squaw Mountain (now known as Mt. St. Helens) to rowdy celebrations of the Hudson's Bay trappers and the arrival of Oregon Trail pioneers, is played out in this educational summer event 7 miles south of Newberg off Highway 219. (503) 678–1251.

SEPTEMBER

Champoeg Fall Harvest Festival. Old-time crafts, entertainment, covered-wagon rides, and a mountain-man encampment. (503) 678–1251.

Oktoberfest. Visit this Bavarian celebration in Mt. Angel on a weekday to avoid the crowds. Although the Biergarten is for adults only, much of the entertainment, such as pony rides, miniature carnival rides, puppet shows, and magicians, is geared to families with young children. (541) 845–9440 or www.oktoberfest.org; info@oktoberfest.org.

EVERGREEN AVIATION MUSEUM (ages 5 and up)

3850 Southwest Three Mile Lane, 4 miles southeast of McMinnville off Highway 18; (503) 434–4180; www.sprucegoose.org. Open daily 9:00 A.M.–5:00 P.M. $9.00 adults; $5.00 students; 5 and under Free.

Get "up close and personal" with historic, world-famous aircraft—the most famous of which is the Hughes Flying Boat, affectionately called the Spruce Goose. Designed as a cargo vessel to transport men and materials over long distances, it was the biggest airplane ever built. Its history is one of personal sacrifice, determination, and technological development. The museum houses a number of other aircraft and offers hands-on activities for visitors of all ages.

Aurora

Aurora, a small community northeast of Woodburn, began as a German-American communal society. The followers of religious visionary Wilhelm Keil established the first West Coast religious commune in 1855, and its appearance has changed little since then. In fact, the center of town has been designated a National Historic District. You can reach Aurora by traveling east about 2½ miles from exit 278 on Interstate 5, or by driving north on State Highway 99E from Woodburn for about 8 miles.

OLD AURORA COLONY MUSEUM (ages 5 and up)

212 Second Street; (503) 678–5754. Call for hours, fees.

A guide takes you through the old ox barn and a rough log cabin as well as other original buildings used by commune members. Your kids will appreciate the frontier life demonstrations that emphasize the amount of work necessary to survive day-to-day. Pick up a self-guided walking-tour brochure at the Historical Society's **William Keil & Co. Store.**

Top Aurora Events

JUNE

Strawberry Social. Hosted by the museum, the shortcake and ice cream social helps raise funds for the museum. (503) 678-5754.

AUGUST

Aurora Colony Days. Historic town celebration of its pioneer past. (503) 678-2288.

Salem

Just 20 years ago, Salem was a sleepy town that housed Oregon's Capitol. But in recent years, the city has metamorphosed into a bustling center of commerce and culture. Renovated historic buildings, coffee houses, and department stores all add to the fabric of Salem's spirited city blocks.

STATE CAPITOL (ages 8 and up)

900 Court Street Northeast; (503) 986–1388; www.oregonlink.com/ capitol_tour. Self-guided tours available throughout the year; during summer months building tours available every half hour. **Free**.

Salem's most visible and most visited landmark, the Capitol building is white marble topped with a 23-foot-high sculpture of the golden Oregon Pioneer. Inside, large murals depict elements of Oregon's history on a grand scale. Give your kids a taste of both history and contemporary state government with a stop at the Capitol building.

A.C. GILBERT'S DISCOVERY VILLAGE (all ages)

116 Marion Street Northeast, under the Marion Street Bridge that crosses the Willamette; (503) 371–3631; www.acgilbert.org. Open Monday through Saturday, 10:00 A.M.–5:00 P.M.; Sunday, noon–5:00 P.M. Admission $4.00, children 2 and under **Free**.

This place is a must on your Salem itinerary. A.C. Gilbert is the man who gave children of the 1940s and 1950s the original Erector Sets, chemistry sets, and other fun and educational toys. The two historic houses have become a hands-on exploratorium for children, with innovative exhibits and activities in the sciences, arts, and humanities. Plan to spend several hours here because the kids will want to try everything at least twice.

Kid-friendly Books *Best Hikes with Children in Western and Central Oregon.* Bonnie Henderson, 1992; paperback.

MISSION MILL MUSEUM VILLAGE (ages 5 and up)

1314 Mill Street, off Twelfth Street SE; (503) 585–7012; www.oregonlink.com/ mission_mill. Open Monday through Saturday, 10:00 A.M.–5:00 P.M. $6.00 adults; $4.00 ages 6–18, under 6 **Free**.

Hour-long guided tours of the mill and three historic houses that date from the 1840s begin at the ticket booth on the grounds. There's also a charming gift shop with old-fashioned ambience.

MARION COUNTY HISTORICAL SOCIETY MUSEUM (ages 5 and up)

260 Twelfth Street, on the northwest corner of Mission Mill Village; (800) 874–7012; (503) 364–2128; E-mail: mchs@open.org. Open Tuesday through Saturday, 9:30 A.M.–4:30 P.M. $2.00 adults; $1.00 children.

The exhibits begin with the Kalapuya Indians and cover pioneer life and the development of Salem as the seat of state governance. The prize possession of the museum is a 125-year-old dugout canoe, which especially impresses kids.

ENCHANTED FOREST (all ages)

8462 Enchanted Way Southeast; located between exits 244 and 248 just off Interstate 5 seven miles south of Salem; (503) 371–4242 or (503) 363–3060; www.enchantedforest.com. Open daily from March 15 through March 31 and May through Labor Day, 9:30 A.M.–6:00 P.M. Closed October 1 to March 15. $6.95 adults; $6.25 ages 3–12, 2 and under Free*. Extra fees for large rides.*

Some little ones may not be ready for the Haunted House or the Ice Mountain or Timber Log rides, and it may take a while to convince them that walking into the witch's mouth won't mean they will be eaten, but everything else is appropriate for any age. Bring your own picnic basket, or dine at the cafeteria that serves hot dogs and burgers.

THRILLVILLE U.S.A. (ages 5 and up)

(503) 363–4095. Call for hours of operation, which vary by season. $1.00 per ticket, $18.00 for twenty-two tickets.

Attractions for the intrepid include bungee jumping; "The Ripper," a giant rollercoaster; and the "Sky Coaster," which hoists riders 150 feet, then free-falls for 50 feet to swoop through the sky at 50 miles per hour. There are kiddie rides, bumper boats, mini-golf, go–carts, games of skill, and giant waterslides.

WESTERN ANTIQUE POWERLAND MUSEUM (ages 5 and up)

3995 Brooklake Road Northeast, Brooks; (503) 393–2424; www.antiquepower land.com. Open daily, 10:00 A.M.–6:00 P.M., April through September; 10:00 A.M.–4:00 P.M. in winter. Call for admission fees and special programs.

This vast collection of antique farm equipment, from steam engines to kerosene tractors as well as horse-drawn plows and sowers, is massive enough to grab the attention of kids of all ages.

 BUSH PASTURE PARK (all ages)
Located off Mission Street between High and Twelfth Streets; (503) 363–4714 or (503) 588–6261; www.oregonlink.com/bush_house/index.html. Call for hours. Park and art center **Free***; Bush House Museum open Tuesday–Sunday, 2:00–5:00 P.M. October through April, noon–5:00 P.M. May through September. $3.00 adults; $2.50 students; $1.50 ages 6–12; under 6* **Free***.*

The beautiful **Bush House Museum** and its surrounding gardens, plus the 1882 Conservatory and **Bush Barn Art Center,** all provide an agreeable setting for an afternoon family outing. In July, the three-day Salem Art Show draws artists and craftspeople from all over the country who sell their high quality wares in the park's shady grove.

Top Salem Events

JULY

Salem Art Fair & Festival. A plethora of local artists and craftspeople fill the park and sell their wares at booths. Performers and children's activities complete the schedule of events. (503) 581-2228; www.scva.org.

JULY–AUGUST

Great Oregon Steam-Up. During this event at the **Western Antique Powerland Museum,** kids have a chance to ride on some of their huge examples of antique farm equipment, and there are demonstrations of old-style threshing, flour milling, and blacksmithing. (503) 393-2424; www.antiquepowerland.com.

AUGUST–SEPTEMBER

Oregon State Fair. Walk through the animal exhibition areas, laugh at the crowing roosters and odd-looking ducks, try to guess which bunny should get the blue ribbon, and watch the 4-H kids trying to keep their pigs clean before the show. Dozens of food booths offer everything from hot corn on the cob, slathered with butter, to Thai noodles. (503) 947-3247; www.fair.state.or.us.

SILVER FALLS STATE PARK (all ages)

Located in the Cascade foothills, 26 miles east of Salem by way of State Highway 22 and State Highway 214; (800) 551–6949 or (503) 873–8681, ext. 31 (information); (800) 452–5687 (campground reservations); www.oregonstate parks.org. Call for hours. Camping and $3.00 day-use fees are charged in summer. Campground closes for winter months.

The park includes over twenty-five miles of trails for hiking, biking, and horseback riding. The park also has ten waterfalls, half of which cascade more than 100 feet down basalt bluffs. Horse rentals are available from H.O.R.S.E.S. For the Physically Challenged (503–873–3890); $25 per hour; 10:00 A.M.–5:00 P.M. daily, May through September, weather permitting.

 OREGON GARDEN (all ages)

In Silverton, 15 miles northeast of Salem off Interstate 5; (541) 874–8100; www.oregongarden.org. Open daily in summer, 9:00 A.M.–6:00 P.M.; call for off-season hours. $1.00.

Determined to become a rival to the famous Butchart Gardens in British Columbia, the Oregon Garden is growing to become a world-class botanical garden of 240 acres. Currently 60 acres are open to the public and include the Children's Garden, natural meadows and wetlands, an ancient oak grove, and a lovely loop trail through a variety of plant specimens. It will be fun to return every year to watch the garden grow!

 MINTO-BROWN ISLAND PARK AND WILDLIFE REFUGE (all ages)

Head south on Commercial Street about one and a half miles until you reach River Road, looking carefully for the rustic brown sign; (800) 874–7012 or (503) 581–4325. Open dawn to dusk.

More than 20 miles of walking trails, jogging paths, and cycling routes are found in this 900-acre park, plus lots of opportunities for birdwatching, especially blue heron.

 WILLAMETTE QUEEN STERNWHEELER

City Dock at Riverfront Park in Salem; (503) 371–1103; www.willamettequeen. com. Call for prices, schedules, and reservations.

The graceful sternwheeler was once an important mode of transportation on the Willamette River, taking people and products to their destinations. Now passengers enjoy leisurely dinner cruises and riverbank sites on the deck.

Family Favorites in the Willamette Valley

1. **Champoeg State Park,** Newberg
2. **Bush Pasture Park,** Salem
3. **Silver Creek Falls,** near Salem
4. **Mary's Peak,** near Corvallis
5. **Alsea Falls,** near Corvallis
6. **The Oregon Gardens,** Silverton
7. **Gilbert House Children's Museum,** Salem
8. **Lane County Historical Museum,** Eugene
9. **Eugene Saturday Market**
10. **Lively Park Swim Center,** Springfield

Independence

Independence marked the end of an arduous covered-wagon trek from Independence, Missouri. The town is now loaded with antiques stores, which probably won't thrill the kids, but you can lure them on with promises of treats at **Taylor's Fountain,** 296 South Main Street, (503) 838–1124, one of the few old-fashioned drugstore soda fountains remaining in the state.

 HERITAGE MUSEUM (ages 5 and up)
112 South Third Street; (503) 838–4989; E-mail: herimusm@open.org. Open Wednesday and Saturday, 1:00 P.M.–5:00 P.M.; Thursday through Friday, 1:00 P.M.–4:00 P.M. **Free.**
You'll find all sorts of pioneer paraphernalia. It's fun trying to figure out what some of the kitchen gadgets were used for!

Monmouth

Oregon's only "dry" town is located about 15 miles southwest of Salem. It's also home to Western Oregon University, Oregon's distinguished four-year college for students seeking credentials in special education.

PAUL JENSEN ARCTIC MUSEUM (ages 5 and up)

Located at Western Oregon University, 590 West Church Street; (503) 838–8468. Open Wednesday through Saturday, 10:00 A.M.–4:00 P.M. Admission is by donation.

Your kids will enjoy seeing the more than 3,000 artifacts gathered by Jensen, who was once president of the college and who traveled to the Arctic on several expeditions. Children shiver at the diorama of wolves snarling at a massive caribou. Special attractions are a sod house and a 27-foot walrus-skin boat, which were given to Dr. Jensen by inhabitants of St. Lawrence Island.

Albany

Historians credit Albany with having the most varied historic buildings in the state. Many, built between 1875 and 1915, are in three districts, all of which are on the National Register of Historic Places. On Sundays in the summer, you can take a horse-drawn carriage tour led by costumed guides who describe the houses and their history.

MONTEITH HOUSE MUSEUM (ages 5 and up)

518 Second Avenue Southwest; (800) 526–2256 or (541) 928–0911. Open Wednesday through Sunday, noon–4:00 P.M., mid-June through September; other times by appointment. **Free***, but donations appreciated.*

Visit this home for a closer look at one of the most authentic restored buildings in Oregon and the first frame structure constructed in Albany in 1849.

WAVERY LAKE PARK (ages 3 and up)

On Pacific Boulevard and Salem Avenue; (541) 917–7777. Park open daily year-round; boat rentals daily, noon–6:30 P.M. June through Labor Day, weather permitting. Paddleboat rentals $4.00 per half hour.

Once a log-holding pond, this little lake has become a roadside gem. Feed the resident ducks, have a picnic, walk around the lake, or rent a paddleboat for fun.

ALBANY FIRE MUSEUM (ages 6 and up)

120 Thirty-fourth Street SE; (541) 967–4389. Open by appointment only. **Free***.*

This small museum presents the history of fire suppression.

ALBANY REGIONAL MUSEUM (all ages)

136 Lyon Street; (541) 967–7122; www.albanyrm.org. Open Monday through Saturday, noon–4:00 P.M.; other times by appointment. Free.

Old Albany memorabilia, photos, and artifacts fill this regional museum. Peer into a turn-of-the-century doctor's office and sit in a chair from a shoeshine stand that was popular in Albany for decades.

 ## BRYANT AND MONTIETH PARKS (all ages)

Located along the Willamette River, near Northwest Water Street; (541) 917–7777 or (800) 526–2256. Open daily, dawn to dusk. Free.

The Willamette River is one of the few rivers in the U.S. that flows north. Boating and water skiing are popular along the river. Bluegill, crappie, smallmouth bass, and catfish can be caught where the Willamette and the Calapooia rivers join at Bryant Park in town. You can also fish for trout, steelhead, and salmon in season. Fishing licenses are not required for children under 14; licenses are available at most sporting goods stores.

  ## FOSTER LAKE (all ages)

Located 29 miles east of Albany off Highway 20; (541) 367–5127. Open April through October. Free for day use.

Sunnyside Park on Foster Lake offers a boat ramp, moorage, swimming, water skiing, fishing, picnic areas, volleyball courts, and access to Foster Lake for a full day of recreation for your family. The park has 162 tent/trailer sites, 104 with water and electric hook-up, and restrooms, showers, and a group camping site.

 ## LINN COUNTY HISTORICAL MUSEUM (ages 5 and up)

101 Park Avenue, Brownsville, sixteen miles south of Albany; (541) 466–3390. Open Monday through Saturday, 11:00 A.M.–4:00 P.M.; Sunday, 1:00 P.M.–5:00 P.M. Free admission but donations appreciated.

Relics of pioneer life are displayed in settings much as they would have appeared during Oregon's early days. Seven old railroad cars have been incorporated into the museum, as well as a covered wagon that arrived in 1865 by way of the Oregon Trail, and a collection of miniature sleighs and horse-

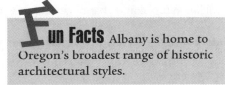

Fun Facts Albany is home to Oregon's broadest range of historic architectural styles.

111

drawn vehicles. An exhibit on the Calapooia (or Kalapuya) Indians documents some of the history of this culture, which was decimated by smallpox brought by white missionaries.

Top Albany Area Events

SUMMER

River Rhythms Summer Music Series. Located in Albany's beautiful Montieth Park, the Thursday night program brings nationally known entertainers. Arrive early to stake out seating with blankets or lawn chairs. Bring your picnic basket or select from a variety of food vendors.

Mondays at Montieth. Local musicians and groups take the stage for free concerts every Monday night in summer.

FOURTH OF JULY WEEKEND

Albany World Championship Timber Carnival. Located at the Timber Linn Memorial Park on Knox Butte Road, this annual event features buckers and cutters, loggers, and ax throwers who compete in the half-century-old carnival. (541) 928-2391; www.timbercarnival.com.

JULY

Linn County Pioneer Picnic. Held every year since 1887, this is the oldest annual celebration in Oregon. Participate in horseshoe tournaments, watch the Kiddie parade, and enjoy the logger's jamboree and a flower show. Held in Brownsville's Pioneer Park. (541) 466-3380.

For information on these Albany events, call (800) 526-2256 or (541) 928-0911; www.albanyvisitors.com.

Corvallis

Corvallis, home to Oregon's oldest state university, is the quintessential college town. It's also a good central location from which to explore the coast, wildlife refuges, and charming rural communities.

OREGON STATE UNIVERSITY (ages 5 and up)

LaSells Stewart Center (conference and performing arts center) *Twenty-fifth Street across from Parker Stadium; (541) 737–2402; oregonstate.edu. Call for hours, schedules.* Free.

Take a walk along the many campus walkways and enjoy the abundant landscaping, public artwork, and varied architecture. The conference center, situated on campus as well, sponsors a wide variety of events throughout the year and brings performances designed for family entertainment.

CORVALLIS BIKE PATHS (ages 5 and up)

(800) 334–8118 or (541) 757–1544. Always open. **Free**.

In all, there are more than 25 miles of bike paths and bike lanes in Corvallis. The city is fringed with several sections of bike paths set off from the roadways to offer safe cycling for families with children. A favorite route is the wide former roadway that connects Oregon State University with the **Benton County Fairgrounds** at Fifty-third. The mile-long section runs through fields where cows, horses, and llamas graze, and past the **Irish Bend Covered Bridge.**

Another favorite cycling spot is along the Willamette in **Riverfront Park.** From the parking area near the boat ramp at the end of Tyler Avenue and First Street, you can cycle south to a small loop where the Mary's River flows into the Willamette. You can also continue out to **Avery Park,** along the Mary's River and on to the Bruce Starker Arts Park, where you can feed ducks on the ponds or let the kids explore the play structure. In summer concerts are often held in the grassy amphitheater. Rent bikes for adults and kids at least 5 feet tall at **Peak Sports,** 129 Northwest Second, (541) 754-6444. Call for prices, hours.

MAJESTIC THEATRE (all ages)

115 Southwest Second Avenue; (541) 757–6977; www.majestic.org; E-mail: mail@majestic.org. Call for hours, prices, and schedules.

This completely renovated 1913 vaudeville house features a wide range of concerts, plays, and productions for families year-round. Local singer-songwriter Jory Aronson—Corvallis's female equivalent to Raffi— often brings her show to the stage, and you're likely to find puppet shows, storytellers, and plays such as Roald Dahl's *Charlie and the Chocolate Factory* on the playbill.

MARY'S PEAK (ages 5 and up)

From Corvallis take State Highway 34 west about 18 miles to Mary's Peak Road (Forest Road 30); (541) 750–7000. Open dawn to dusk. **Free**.

The most recognizable landmark to the west of Corvallis, Mary's Peak offers prime family recreation. In spring and summer, the wildflowers blaze on the hillsides near the peak of the 4,097-foot mountain, and in wintertime the hillsides ring with children's shrieks as they hurtle down snowy slopes on inner tubes and sleds. Two trails serve both hikers and cross-country skiers, depending on the season, and the 360-degree view from the summit is something you won't want to miss. Camping is available between late May and October at six sites near the summit.

ALSEA FALLS (ages 5 and up)

  Farther west on State Highway 34, turn south at the small town of Alsea toward Monroe; you can also reach the falls from State Highway 99W south of Corvallis, off the Benton County Scenic Loop Drive through Alpine; (800) 334–8118 or (541) 757–1544. Call for hours. **Free** *for day use; call (541) 375–5646 for campground information.*

Just driving to Alsea Falls is a wonderful adventure. From Highway 99W you pass through the quaint little hamlets of Alsea and Alpine that are tucked away in Oregon's forested coastal range. From Highway 34 you'll travel several miles of gravel road winding through dense forest. A small campground, a well-maintained picnic area, and an easy 1.9 mile-loop await you at Alsea Falls. Take the easy hiking path at the trail sign, and enjoy a walk among second-growth hemlock and Douglas fir.

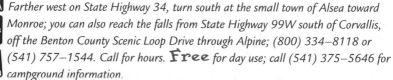

An Adventure to Remember There's nothing more exhilarating than a drive in Northwestern forest on a fall afternoon. When you travel south from Corvallis and drive west on winding State Highway 34, you will come upon **Alsea Falls,** one of the most scenic waterfalls west of the Cascade Mountains. The falls, which are an easy walk from the parking lot for people of all ages, slither over monstrous black basalt boulders and continue meandering to a shallow stream. Picnic tables line this fragrant forest and invite you to tarry near the water's gentle sounds.

SHEEP BARNS, OREGON STATE UNIVERSITY (all ages)

7565 NW Oak Creek Drive; (541) 737–2903. Open 8:00 A.M.–6:00 P.M. daily. **Free**.

If you're lucky, you'll witness the birth of a baby lamb or watch a mother tenderly washing her newborn. Lambing starts in mid-January and continues through March.

AVERY PARK (ages 5 and up)

Located along the Mary's River south of U.S. 20 at the foot of Southwest Fifteenth Street; (541) 754–1701. Open dawn to dusk. **Free**.

The park delights children with its unusual playground equipment. "Dinosaur bones" and a full-size retired train engine get the kids' vote for the park's favorites. They're located to the left of the park entrance, beyond the small community rose garden. To the right of the entrance, there's another play structure and access to the Mary's River for wading.

 MCDONALD FOREST (ages 5 and up)

Trail begins at the Forestry Club Cabin in Peavy Arboretum, about 5 miles north of Corvallis off State Highway 99W; (541) 737–4452. Open dawn to dusk. **Free**.

Oregon State University owns this research forest, which offers several walking, mountain biking, and horse trails. A trail map and brochure are usually available at the trailhead that points out fifteen stops that demonstrate forest management practices.

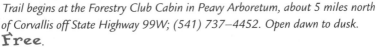 **FINLEY WILDLIFE REFUGE (ages 5 and up)**

26208 Finley Refuge Road, off U.S. Highway 99W, 10 miles south of Corvallis; (541) 757–7236; www.rl.fws.gov/visitor/oregon.html. Open dawn to dusk; office hours 7:00 A.M.–4:30 P.M. Monday through Thursday, until 3:30 P.M. Friday. **Free**.

Hundreds of thousands of migrating waterfowl winter along the Willamette Valley and find a safe haven at the 5,325-acre refuge, where you and your children can enjoy walks throughout the year. Even very young children can manage the **Woodpecker Loop Trail,** which winds over 1¼ miles of gentle terrain through forest, meadow, and wetland environments. Have your kids approach the pond slowly and watch and listen for the squeak of the frogs as they leap into the water. A brochure, usually available at the trailhead (at a small parking lot about 3.6 miles west of Highway 99W on Refuge Road) identifies the woodpeckers you might see as well as plant and other animal species along the trail.

 BENTON COUNTY HISTORICAL MUSEUM (ages 5 and up)

1101 Main Street, located in Philomath, 7 miles west of Corvallis; (541) 929–6230. Open Tuesday through Saturday, 10:30 A.M.–4:30 P.M. **Free**.

The museum is housed in what was the first college in the territory. Its interpretive exhibits provide insights into the region's pioneer and early industrial life. A rotating art exhibit and a portion of the Horner Collection—a collection of natural history and archaeological artifacts—are other interesting dimensions of the museum.

 OSBORN AQUATIC CENTER (all ages)
1940 New Highland Drive; (541) 766–7946. Call for hours. $3.50 adults; $3.00 ages 6–17; $2.50 ages 5 and under.

The recent addition of "Otter Beach"—an outdoor pool with water cannons, floor geysers, a play structure, pools and falls, and a 22-foot slide—make this a place for year-round water fun for everyone in the family.

Top Corvallis Events

JULY

Da Vinci Days. Named after that famous Renaissance artist, scientist, and inventor Leonardo da Vinci, this event attracts thousands for three days of arts, science, and fun. The Campo di Kids helps youngsters with activities that change annually, such as fish printing—taking scaly flounder or rockfish, dipping it in ink, and rolling it on paper to create an indelible impression—to a long 4-foot-high wooden easel that snakes about 40 feet through the park with buckets of chalk provided. Music on three stages sets the background sound. (541) 757–6363; www.davinci-days.org.

SEPTEMBER

Fall Festival. Arts and crafts booths, food booths, live music, and entertainment focus on creativity. Kids get a chance for some hands-on creativity of their own. (541) 752–9655; www.proaxis.com/~corfallfest; E-mail: corfallfest@proaxis.com.

Oregon Folklife Festival. Music, crafts, and food are the centerpieces of this old-fashioned celebration. (541) 754–3601; E-mail: info@oregonfolk life.com.

Eugene

Eugene, Oregon's second-largest city, is located at the confluence of the Willamette and McKenzie rivers in the midst of farmland and forests that stretch to the foothills of the Cascade Mountains to the east and the Oregon Coast Range to the west. The University of Oregon is housed here on a beautiful campus crisscrossed with walking paths. Several lush Eugene parks invite outdoor enthusiasts to jog, cycle, and walk.

HENDRICKS PARK (all ages)

Located at the foot of Summit Avenue (off Agate Street); (541) 682–5333; www.ci.eugene.or.us/PW/PARKS/Hendricks. Always open. **Free**.

A blur of glorious color peaks in the springtime with more than 6,000 rhododendrons—both native and hybrid. May is the best month for a visit to this twelve-acre garden, but at any time of year you can enjoy a walk through this lush wooded park. **Free** guided tours are offered each spring.

WILLAMETTE SCIENCE AND TECHNOLOGY CENTER (all ages)

2300 Leo Harris Parkway off Centennial; (541) 682–7888; www.efn.org/~ wistec; E-mail: wistec@efn.org. Open Friday, noon–5:00 P.M.; Saturday and Sunday, 11:00 A.M.–5:00 P.M. $4.00 adults; $3.00 ages 4–17; 3 and under **Free**.

WISTEC is a hands-on, user-friendly environment in which kids can explore natural wonders, all the while learning about physics and science concepts. They can shout into an echo tube, experiment with the force of pendulums, or watch what happens when they electrify a bubble.

LANE ESD PLANETARIUM (ages 5 and up)

2300 Leo Harris Parkway, on the same site at WISTEC; (541) 687–7827 or (541) 461–8227; www.laneplanetarium.org. Call for program hours. Admission $4.50 adults; $4.00 students; $3.50 ages 11 and under.

The planetarium is one of the largest facilities of its kind between San Francisco and Vancouver, British Columbia. It offers year-round weekend programs on touring the solar system, exploring the night sky across the seasons, or learning about cosmic phenomena.

UNIVERSITY OF OREGON'S MUSEUM OF NATURAL HISTORY (ages 5 and up)

1680 East Fifteenth Avenue; (541) 346–3024. Open Tuesday through Sunday, noon–5:00 P.M. 𝔉𝔯𝔢𝔢 *admission but donations appreciated.*

Kids get a strong sense of Oregon's very early history through the museum's displays of Native American artifacts, including a pair of 9,000-year-old sagebrush sandals. Changing exhibits explore other cultures throughout the world.

 UNIVERSITY OF OREGON MUSEUM OF ART (ages 5 and up)

Located on campus at 1430 Johnson Lane; (541) 346–3027. Open Wednesday, noon–8:00 P.M., Thursday through Sunday, noon–5:00 P.M. Closed major holidays. $3.00 suggested donation; children 13 and younger 𝔉𝔯𝔢𝔢.

Visiting exhibits bring a variety of subjects to the campus, from photography to wall-size contemporary oils. The permanent displays include first-rate collections of Asian art, Northwest and American contemporary art, and photography.

 # *R*afting the McKenzie River (ages 10 and up)

Explore the river aboard rubber rafts with a variety of whitewater guide services:

- **River Runner Supply.** *78G Centennial Loop; (541) 343–6883. Call for hours, fees. Kayak and raft rentals and guided tours.*

- **Oregon Whitewater Adventures.** *39620 Deerhorn Road, Springfield; (541) 746–5422; www.oregonwhitewater.com. Guided raft trips $75–$95 per day, $50 per half day, 15–20 percent discount for children 12 and under.*

Other river rafting services include:

- **Oregon River Sports.** *1640 West Seventh Avenue; (541) 334–0696 or (888) 790–7235, www.oregonriversports.com. Raft rentals $55–$125 per day. Guided trips $49–$95; prices include lunch. Also canoe and kayak rentals for use on the canal in Alton Baker Park, $6–$8 per hour.*

LANE COUNTY HISTORICAL MUSEUM (ages 5 and up)

740 West Thirteenth Avenue; (541) 682–4242 or (541) 682–4239; www.lcog.org/admin/museum.html. Open Wednesday through Friday, 10:00 A.M.–4:00 P.M.; Saturday, noon–4:00 P.M. $2.00 adults; 75 cents ages 3–17, under 3 Free.

With collections dating from the 1840s, your kids will imagine themselves along the Oregon Trail or getting dressed up for a flapper's party in the 1920s, or riding an early child's bicycle with odd-sized wheels. Inquire about the numerous educational programs the museum offers. You can request a guided tour from one of the museum's docents.

 OREGON AIR AND SPACE MUSEUM (ages 5 and up)

90377 Boeing Drive, off Airport Road; (541) 461–1101. Open Monday through Saturday, noon–4:00 P.M. $5.00 adults; $3.00 ages 13–18; $2.00 ages 6–12; 5 and under Free.

A growing exhibit that now includes an F-4 Phantom jet, a forty-year-old Cessna L-19 that flew in the Korean War, and the oddly shaped Bullet, a home-built plane that never made it off the ground as a commercial venture. Exhibits trace the development of the space industry, and a gift shop sells model planes, T-shirts, and books.

 PAUL'S BICYCLE WAY OF LIFE (ages 5 and up)

152 West Fifth Avenue; (541) 344–4105; www.bicycleway.com. Open weekdays 9:00 A.M.–7:00 P.M., weekends 10:00 A.M.–5:00 P.M. Rentals $12–$15 per day.

Eugene is a town that reveres cycling. You can tell because of the extensive bike paths and lanes throughout the town, and the investment in sophisticated cycling bridges that cross the Willamette and McKenzie rivers.

 FIFTH STREET PUBLIC MARKET (all ages)

Located at 296 East Fifth Street; (541) 484–0383; www.5thstmarket.com. Open daily 10:00 A.M.– 6:00 P.M.

Seventy-five shops and numerous restaurants and ethnic-flavored cafes capture Eugene's eclectic essence. French and Middle Eastern cafes nestle with a Thai restaurant and fabulous bakeries. Artisan booths with wood-framed photographs stand near boutiques with hand-blown glass objects and earthen pottery. There's a new Nike store next door and the kids will enjoy the mini-museum depicting the lives of renowned track and field heroes.

EUGENE SATURDAY MARKET (all ages)

Eighth and Oak Streets downtown; (541) 686–8885; www.eugenesaturday market.com. April through November; Holiday Market held in Lane County Fairgrounds Exhibit Hall, Thirteenth and Jefferson (call for dates and hours). Open Saturday, 10:00 A.M.–5:00 P.M.

Here's another venue that's uniquely Eugene but with even more unusual entrepreneurial enterprises—from farmers selling fresh-cut flowers and garden-grown fruits and vegetables, to artisans with quilts, tie-dyed kids' clothing, jewelry, and wonderful wooden handcrafted toys. It's billed as Oregon's oldest weekly open-air crafts festival. The international food court lets you experience tastes of the world.

LANE ICE CENTER

796 West Thirteenth; (541) 682–4292. Call for regular hours; $5.00 adults; $4.00 children. Family Night, Tuesday and Thursday, $4.25; 7:00 P.M.–8:30 P.M.

The ice arena is home to the Eugene Blues hockey team, with games held throughout the winter months. When the team isn't on the ice, it's your family's turn.

 LIVELY PARK SWIM CENTER (all ages)

6100 Thurston Road, Springfield; (541) 747–9283 or (541) 736–4244. Wave pool hours: Monday, Wednesday, 6:30–8:30 P.M.; Friday 3:30–5:00 P.M. and 6:30–9:00 P.M.; Saturday, noon–5:00 P.M. and 6:30–9:00 P.M.; Sunday, noon–5:00 P.M. Admission $5.00; $2.50 under 3; groups of six or more $4.00; family unit $6.00 plus $1.75 each.

The first indoor wave pool on the West Coast opened its doors in Springfield in 1989 and has been drawing hordes of families ever since. The huge pool contains not only the wave pool but a larger-than-usual children's wading pool (complete with floating rubber duckies), a Jacuzzi, a lap pool, and a 136-foot water slide. You can bring your cooler and eat at one of the many tables. Family changing rooms are equipped with private showers, potties, and sinks, so your little ones don't have to go into the larger dressing room alone. The noise level seems overwhelming sometimes, but that helps contribute to the "lively" atmosphere.

 SPRINGFIELD MUSEUM (ages 5 and up)

590 Main Street; (541) 726–3677 or (541) 726–2300; www.springfield museum.com. Open Tuesday through Friday 10:00 A.M.–5:00 P.M.; Saturday, noon–4:00 P.M. $1 per person.

A variety of changing exhibits and a permanent collection of objects ranging from pioneer toys to men's ties invites even locals to visit more than once.

FERN RIDGE LAKE (ages 5 and up)

Located just 12 miles from downtown Eugene by way of Clear Lake Road off State Highway 99W; (541) 937–2131. Open dawn to dusk. Minimal parking and day-use fee.

Here's another spot that's popular with the locals for camping, picnicking, swimming, waterskiing, sailing, and sailboarding. **Perkins Peninsula Park** offers a swim area, playing field, boardwalk, and interpretive nature trail.

FALL CREEK STATE RECREATION AREA (ages 5 and up)

Located off State Highway 58 about 15 miles southeast of Eugene; (541) 937–1173 or (800) 551–6949; (800) 452–5687 for campground reservations; www.oregonstateparks.org. Always open. $3.00 day-use fee.

When the summer heat starts to get to you, take the family to one of the many nearby swimming holes. Fall Creek has four campgrounds and a picnic area borders the stream that flows into the reservoir. A few swimming holes beyond the Puma Creek Campground offer a little more privacy.

FALL CREEK NATIONAL RECREATION TRAIL (ages 5 and up)

Located about 15 miles west of Eugene on State Highway 58; take the turnoff at Jasper-Lowell through the town of Lowell, turn right at North Shore Road and continue for about 11 miles. The 14-mile trail begins opposite the Dolly Varden Campground on the creek's south bank. For maps and information, visit the Willamette National Forest office at 211 East Seventh Avenue in Eugene (541) 465–6521.

An old-growth forest and paths lush with maiden and sword ferns give hikers a true sense of getting away from it all without a long or tedious drive.

AUFDERHEIDE NATIONAL SCENIC BYWAY
WILLAMETTE NATIONAL FOREST (ages 5 and up)

Located east of Eugene; follow State Highway 58 to State Highway 126; turn at Forest Road 19. The drive follows the South Fork of the McKenzie River and the North Fork of the Middle Fork of the Willamette River from Oakridge (30 miles southeast of Eugene) to the small community of McKenzie Bridge. (541) 782–

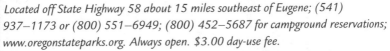
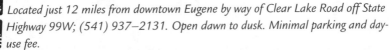

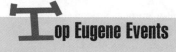

op Eugene Events

MAY

Fiesta Latina. Annual Latin-American cultural celebration featuring food, local art, music, and dancing. (541) 344–5070.

JUNE

Oregon Bach Festival. The critically acclaimed festival features a series of children's performances as well as Free noon concerts. Most performances are located at the **Hult Center for the Performing Arts.** (800) 457–1486 or (541) 682–5000; www.oregonbachfestival.com.

JULY

Oregon Country Fair. Every summer, it's as if the clock has stopped somewhere in the late '60s. The Oregon Country Fair draws an amazing crowd of old hippies and new yuppies and their families for what one coordinator called "a walking Whole Earth catalog." The event offers an amazing variety of food booths to satisfy carnivores, vegetarians, and vegans alike. Entertainment ranges from vaudeville and mime to folk and rock 'n' roll. The "Energy Park" demonstrates alternative energy sources and the "Community Village" offers exhibits on political, social, cultural, spiritual, and environmental concerns. (541) 343 4298; www. oregoncountryfair.org.

Children's Celebration. This annual event celebrates being a child—no matter what age you are! Island Park in Springfield is transformed into a child's world. (541) 736–4544; www.willamalane.org.

AUGUST

Oregon Festival of American Music. Performances by renowned musicians ranging from gospel to jazz and blues are the heart of this program, which is located at the Hult Center for the Performing Arts and the outdoor Cuthbert Amphitheater. (541) 687–6526 or (800) 248–1615; www.ofam.org; E-mail: info@ofam.net.

SEPTEMBER

Eugene Celebration. The annual downtown Eugene Celebration held in mid-September has activities such as face painting and miniature golf in the Kid Zone, dozens of food booths, and continuous live entertainment. Don't miss the largest three-day street party in the state. (541) 681–4108; www.eugenecelebration.com.

2283 or (541) 822–3381. Open dawn to dusk. $5.00 day-use fee at some parking areas (NW Forest Pass).

Willamette National Forest is a beautiful drive, along which there are many places to stop so the kids can run and explore in old-growth forests and woodland streams and waterfalls. Of particular interest to kids is the **Delta Nature Trail,** a half-mile loop through towering old-growth trees, some of which are up to 500 years old.

 ### SALT CREEK FALLS (ages 5 and up)

Located just an hour southwest of Eugene; turnoff located off Willamette Highway 58; look for Salt Creek Falls sign. (541) 465–6521; www.fs.fed.us/r6/willamette. Northwest Forest Pass day-use fee, $5.00.

Oregon's second-highest waterfall, which tumbles over tall basalt cliffs, presents a blend of history and natural beauty as well as outdoor recreation. Interpretive panels tell of the ladies and gentlemen who rode the train to this spot for a day's picnic outing in the 1920s, and of the 7,000-year-old evidence of Molalla and Kalapuya Indian activity in these canyons. Walking trails lead to shaded picnic spots and an observation platform that gives you a bird's-eye view of the 286-foot falls. A 2.5-mile loop hike to Diamond Creek Falls takes about two hours.

 ### WALDO LAKE (ages 5 and up)

Located in the high Oregon Cascades southeast of Eugene; (541) 937–2129; www.fs.fed.us/r6/centraloregon.

Waldo Lake is one of the purest, clearest lakes in the world, according to water specialists. At an elevation of 5,414 feet, Waldo Lake's summer recreation period is fairly short. Three Forest Service campgrounds provide a few amenities (like flush toilets) that make camping less rustic. Hiking trails connect to other lakes, such as tiny Betty Lake, which is shallow enough to warm for swimming in the summer. Mountain bikers frequently use the 22-mile **Waldo Lake Trail,** which circles the lake. Trail information is available from the Oakridge Ranger Station on State Highway 58 near Oakridge.

 ### ODELL LAKE AND CRESCENT LAKE (all ages)

Located on West Odell Road off State Highway 58, approximately 70 miles east of Eugene; (541) 433–3200; www.fs.fed.us/r6/centraloregon. Always open. **Free.**

Boat rentals, swimming beaches, hiking trails, picnic areas, and campgrounds make these lakes easy to enjoy with the family. In winter-

123

time the lodges are open for cross-country skiers or for downhill enthusiasts skiing at nearby Willamette Pass. Three resorts offer cabins and
lodge rooms, boat rental, restaurants, and ski rentals. All are open year-
round; call for hours and rates.

- **Odell Lake Lodge.** *East end of Odell Lake; (541) 433–2540; www.
odelllakeresort.uswestdex.com; E-mail: odelllake@bendnet.com.*

- **Shelter Cove Resort.** *On west end of Odell Lake; (541) 433–2548.*

- **Crescent Lake Lodge.** *(541) 433–2505.*

WILLIAMETTE PASS (ages 5 and up)

*Southwest of Eugene on Highway 58; (541) 345–7669; www.willamettepass.com.
Generally open by mid-November, 9:00 A.M.–4:00 P.M.; twilight skiing 12:30–
9:00 P.M. Friday and Saturday. Adults $31; ages 6–10 $20; 5 and under*
Free *with adult.*

You'll find daytime and night skiing on six runs and one of the best
ski instruction programs for children anywhere. Skiing begins when the
snow covers the slopes, usually in December. There are also several miles
of groomed cross-country trails. The Cascade Summit Lodge has a
restaurant for skiers who need to warm up with a cup of steaming
cocoa and a bite to eat. Both downhill and cross-country ski rentals are
available, and child care is offered.

DORRIS RANCH (ages 5 and up)

*At the intersection of South Second and Dorris Streets; (541) 736–4544. Open
daily at 6:00 A.M. to dusk.* **Free***.*

Experience Oregon's history with a visit to Dorris Ranch. Now a living history farm, it welcomes families to walk among the seventy-five
acres of lush orchards, seventy-five acres of riverfront forest, and forty
acres of pasture and wetlands. A one-and-a-half-hour self-guided walk-

ing tour takes you
through each of
these environments
along a level, 2-
mile trail. The edu-
cational programs
offered March

Fun Facts Dorris Ranch in Springfield
was the first commercial filbert orchard in
the United States, beginning in 1892.

through December are well worth joining.

MT. PISGAH (ages 8 and up)

33735 Seavy Loop Road; to reach the trailhead, take Interstate 5 south of Eugene to exit 188, then follow signs to Mt. Pisgah Arboretum along Seavy Loop Road. Cross the bridge over the Coast Fork of the Willamette River, then turn right and take the trailhead from the parking lot at the end of the road; (541) 747–3817 or (541) 741–4110; www.efn.org/~mtpisgah; E-mail: mtpisgah@efn.org. Free.

It's fairly steep in places, and you can get quite muddy if it has been raining, but the views from the top make the climb worth it. The sighting pedestal on the mountain top will tantalize your kids. Local outdoor author Bonnie Henderson suggests bringing lots of paper and crayons so kids can create rubbings of the bas-relief fish, birds, leaves, and shells that decorate the 40-inch-tall bronze pedestal. The relief map on top identifies visible landmarks. Watch for poison oak along the trail and "cow pies" underfoot. There are now 7 miles of all-weather trails criss-crossing the 208-acre park.

Where to Eat

IN NEWBERG

Pasquale's Italian Cuisine. *111 West First Street; (503) 538–0918.* Fine dining at family-oriented prices. $$-$$$

IN SALEM

Karma's Cafe. *1313 Mill Street; (503) 370–8855.* You can eat soup and sandwiches on the deck outdoors, which is right in the middle of Mission Mill Village. $

Alessandro's. *120 Commercial Street NE; (503) 370–9951.* Locals say this restaurant, snuggled near a lovely little park, offers the best Italian food in town. Good service and a family friendly atmosphere make lunch or dinner stops memorable. $$-$$$

IN ALBANY

Wine Depot & Deli. *Two Rivers Market, 300 Second Avenue; (541) 967–9499.* This is a good spot to pick up sandwiches for a picnic lunch. $

Novak's Hungarian Restaurant. *2835 Santiam Highway Southeast; (541) 967–9488.* A legend in Albany, Novak's warm and inviting ambience is obvious right when you walk in the door. Delicious homemade breads and noodle dishes will appeal to the kids while mom and dad experiment with some of the more exotic dishes. $-$$

IN CORVALLIS

Nearly Normal's. *109 Northwest Fifteenth Street; (541) 753–0791.* A casual eatery in an old house near Oregon State campus, it offers a nice variety of vegetarian and international cuisine. Ingredients are as fresh as can be. Kid friendly. $

New Morning Bakery. *219 Southwest Second (541–754–0181) and 1870 Southwest Third (541–757–1821).* Open for desserts, breakfast, lunch, and dinner. Incredibly decadent pastries are available at both locations. Affordable monster-size cookies and delicious salads and soups give everybody something to savor. A children's play area is equipped with toys, books, and child-size tables and chairs. $

IN EUGENE

Glenwood Restaurants. *2588 Willamette (541–687–8201) or 1340 Alder (541–687–0355).* Casual food and atmosphere; voted best family dining by *Eugene Weekly* four years in a row. $–$$

Mazzi's Italian Food. *Fifth and Willamette; (541) 485–4444.* This is the splurge restaurant—meals are good but pricey and kids will adore eating in an old train boxcar or the 1912 train depot. $$$$

Oregon Electric Station. *1545 Willamette Street; (541) 344–2371.* It's an easy location to miss, but don't pass up the opportunity to have truly fresh and delicious fish and chips. Outdoor counter service and seating. $

Taco Loco. *900 West Seventh Avenue; (541) 683–9171.* A lively and visually stimulating eating establishment that serves Mexican and Salvadorean food, it was voted People's Choice Best Mexican in a local restaurant survey. $–$$

Where to Stay

IN WOODBURN AND SILVERTON

Champoeg State Park. *(800) 452–5687, for reservations.* The campground and park are northwest of Woodburn, due west of Wilsonville; take exit 278 from Interstate 5 and follow signs to the park. $

IN SALEM

Best Western Mill Creek Inn. *3125 Ryan Drive Southeast; (800) 346–9659 or (503) 585–3332.* One hundred nine units. Mini-suites and large two-room suites. Fitness room, pool. Restaurant next door. In-room fridge, microwave. Free shuttle to Salem Airport. $$$–$$$$

Rodeway Inn. *3195 Portland Road Northeast, (503) 585–2900.* Forty units. Free in-room coffee. Outdoor heated pool. Refrigerators and microwaves. $$–$$$

IN ALBANY

Brier Rose Inn. *206 Seventh Avenue Southwest; (541) 926–0345.* Bed-and-breakfast in an enchanting historic house. $$$

Hawthorn Inn & Suites. *251 Airport Road Southeast; (800) 527–1133 or (541) 928–0921; www.hawthorn.com.* Fifty units. Cable TV. Pets welcome. Pool and spa available. $–$$$

Motel Orleans. *1212 Price Road Southeast; (800) 626–1900 or (541) 926–0170.* Seventy-eight units. Cable TV. Pets welcome. Pool available. $$

IN CORVALLIS

Super 8 Motel. *407 Northwest Second Street; (800) 800–8000 or (541) 758–8088.* One hundred one rooms. Located on the banks of the Willamette River, this budget motel is close to downtown. Indoor pool and spa. Small pets welcome. $–$$

IN EUGENE

Best Western Green Tree Inn. *1759 Franklin Boulevard; (541) 485–2727.* Sixty-five units. Spa, pool, and workout room. Pets welcome. Central location

near the University of Oregon campus. $$–$$$

Best Western New Oregon Motel. *1655 Franklin Boulevard; (541) 683–3669.* One hundred twenty-eight units. Reasonably priced rooms also have refrigerators. Families will also appreciate the indoor pool, whirlpool tub, sauna, and exercise room after a day of traveling. $$–$$$

Phoenix Inn Hotel. *850 Franklin Boulevard; (800) 344–0131 or (541) 344–0001; www.phoenixinn.com. E-mail: phoenixinn@uswest.net.* Ninety-seven units. At this centrally located hotel, you'll receive a complimentary breakfast and have access to a pool, jacuzzi, and fitness center. $$–$$$

For More Information

Albany Visitors Association. *250 Broadalbin Street SW, Suite 110, Albany, OR 97321; (800) 526–2256 or (541) 928–0911; www.albanyvisitors.com; E-mail: albanyinfo@albanyvisitors.com.*

Aurora Chamber of Commerce. *21558 Highway 99E, Aurora, OR 97002; (503) 678–2228; www.cdds.com/chamber. html.*

Corvallis Convention and Visitors Bureau. *420 Northwest Second Street, Corvallis, OR 97330; (800) 334–8118 or (541) 757–1544; www.visitcorvallis.com/ ccvb/; E-mail: info@visitcorvallis.com.*

Eugene Area Chamber of Commerce. *1401 Willamette Street, Eugene, OR 97440; (541) 484–1314; www. eugenechamber.com; E-mail: info@ eugenechamber.com.*

Eugene Convention & Visitors Association of Lane County. *P.O. Box 10286, 115 West Eighth, Suite 190, Eugene, OR 97440; (800) 547–5445 or (541) 484–5307; www.cvalco.org; E-mail: tourism@cvalco.org.*

McKenzie River Chamber of Commerce. *P.O. Box 1117, 44643 McKenzie Highway, Leaburg, OR 97489; (541) 896–3330; www.el.com/to/ mckenzierivervalley; E-mail: mcrvco@ aol.com.*

Monmouth-Independence Chamber of Commerce. *148 Monmouth Street, Independence, OR 97351; (503) 838–4268; www.open.org/mice; e-mail: mice@ open.org.*

Newberg Chamber of Commerce. *115 North Washington, Newberg, OR 97132; (503) 538–2014; www.newberg. org.*

Salem Convention & Visitors Association. *1313 Mill Street, Southeast, Salem, OR 97301; (800) 874–7012 or (503) 581–4325; www.svca.org or www. salemvisitorcenter.com.*

Woodburn Area Chamber of Commerce. *P.O. Box 194, 2233 Country Club Road, Woodburn, OR 97071; (503) 982–8221.*

Central Oregon and the Cascades

In many ways Central Oregon is the state's playground. It's here that we can find virtually any kind of outdoor recreation that teases our ambitions—mountain climbing, rock climbing, whitewater rafting, skiing, swimming, hiking, bicycling, fishing, and horseback riding. The area's climate is ideal for the outdoor-bound. In summer, less rain falls here than in many other areas of the state. Winter brings snow to the mountains, but a well-equipped highway department keeps roads passable.

Posh family resorts at Sunriver, Black Butte, Seventh Mountain, and Eagle Crest, among others, draw visitors every season of the year. The forests, rivers, and lakes of the region create a lush backdrop for camping and outdoor recreation. And there is a wealth of educational opportunities for outings to lava fields, museums, and historic sites. You'll want to take your time here and then return to see what new experiences each season has to offer.

Bend

DRAKE PARK'S MIRROR POND (all ages)
Take Bond Street and turn on Franklin Street heading west; (541) 389–7275; www.bendparksandrec.org. Always open. **Free**.

A wide variety of waterfowl plays a predominant role in this aptly named section of the Deschutes River, which flows through the town of Bend. There are even a pair of swans from Queen Elizabeth's royal swannery here. A broad, green parkland hugs the shore and a children's playground sits just across the bridge at Harmon Park.

CENTRAL OREGON AND THE CASCADES

Warm
Springs
Madras
Sisters
Prineville
Redmond
Bend
LaPine

SAWYER PARK (all ages)

Located just a half-mile northwest of the Bend River Mall; (541) 389–7275; www.bendparksandrec.org. Day use. **Free**.

This 61½-acre park has both developed and natural settings, with picnic tables, drinking water, and toilets.

DESCHUTES RIVER (all ages)

(541) 389–7275; www.bendparksandrec.org. Day use. **Free**.

Equally enticing for fishing and hiking, the 3-mile-long **Deschutes River Run Trail** follows the Deschutes River from Sawyer Park to Northwest First Street in Bend. You'll see lots of joggers, mountain bikers, and walkers on this popular trail.

THE FUNNY FARM (all ages)

64990 Deschutes Market Road, halfway between Bend and Redmond; (541) 389–6391. Open 11:00 A.M.–5:00 P.M. daily; extended hours in summer. Admission by donation.

This family amusement park features a bowling-ball garden, an electric kaleidoscope, a life-size outdoor chess board, and four acres of other silly, zany, and fun activities.

*F*amily Favorites in Central Oregon

1. High Desert Museum
2. Lava Lands Visitor Center
3. Lava River Cave
4. Lava Cast Forest
5. Mount Bachelor Ski Resort (winter and summer)
6. Pine Mountain Observatory
7. Osprey Observation Point
8. Reindeer Ranch at Operation Santa Claus
9. Three Creeks Lake
10. Museum at Warm Springs

..OT BUTTE STATE SCENIC VIEWPOINT (all ages)

 Take Northeast Greenwood, which winds to the top of the butte; (800) 551–6949; www.oregonstateparks.org. Always open. **Free**.

To get a great view of the Cascades and the surrounding area without going far from town, take a short trek to this volcanic cinder cone within the city's limits. It provides a perfect 360-degree view of the various peaks—Mt. Hood, Jefferson, Washington, Three-Fingered Jack, Broken Top, Bachelor, Newberry Crater, and the Three Sisters—as well as the Deschutes River as it wends its way north.

DESCHUTES COUNTY HISTORICAL SOCIETY (all ages)

 129 Northwest Idaho; (541) 389–1813. Open Tuesday through Saturday, 10:00 A.M.–4:30 P.M. $2.50 adults; $1.00 ages 6–15; under 6 **Free**.

Exhibits of artifacts of the county's colorful history give insight into the lives of Native Americans and pioneers. The timber industry's early days are also explored in displays.

HIGH DESERT MUSEUM (all ages)

 59800 South Highway 97, located just off U.S. 97, 3 miles south of Bend; (541) 382–4754; www.highdesert.org. Open daily, 9:00 A.M.–5:00 P.M. except major holidays. $8.50 adults; $7.50 ages 13–18; $4.00 ages 5–12, children under 4 **Free**.

Besides the spectacular array of exquisite dioramas, there's a Desertarium with live animals scurrying about in their natural habitats, a homestead exhibiting the details of harsh pioneer life in the central desert, and a forestry exhibit with a working sawmill. The museum also sponsors special programs and live animal presentations at regular intervals throughout the day (May through September).

LAVA LANDS VISITOR CENTER (ages 5 and up)

 Located eleven miles south of Bend on U.S. 97; (541) 593–2421; www.fs.fed.us/rb/centraloregon. Visitor center is open daily in summer, rest of year Wednesday through Sunday, 9:00 A.M.–5:00 P.M. $5.00 car entrance fee (NW Forest Pass).

You'll feel as though you're in another world entirely, as if you've somehow landed on the moon on this volcanic cinder cone, where the 360-degree view is stunning. Imagine, as you look at the remains of a giant lava flow, what it must have looked like as a molten river. An interpretive trail snakes over the lava fields and through an adjoining pine forest. Regular programs include guided walks, demonstrations, and talks on the human and volcanic history of the region.

An Adventure to Remember

You'll have a deeper knowledge of the hardships early pioneers faced after visiting Central Oregon's **High Desert Museum,** a veritable treasure chest of natural history, anthropology, and wildlife displays. A rustic cabin, tiny as today's fabricated tool shed, reflects the pioneer settler's keen ability to make use of every nook and cranny. The spare multipurpose room holds cast iron pots and pans, a wooden washboard, a pine-framed bed, and an open pantry, demonstrating among other things how dramatically complex our society has become since the turn of the century. During the live raptor program, kids can view injured or orphaned birds of prey. Afterwards, wildlife educators give them a chance to feel a hawk's wing and examine a kestrel's skull. Also on the museum grounds are a tiny stream and pond where large rainbow trout swim, and rocky beds where otters frolic and porcupines lounge. An old sawmill, a Basque sheepherder's wagon, and exhibits on Native American and pioneer history all reflect the museum's painstaking attention to detail. If you go nowhere else during your stay in Central Oregon, be sure to visit this extraordinary museum.

LAVA RIVER CAVE (ages 10 and up)

Located about 12 miles south of Bend; (541) 383–5300 or (541) 593–2421. Open May to mid-October, call for seasonal hours. $3.00 adults; $2.50 ages 13–17; 12 and under Free; *$2.00 for lantern rental.*

How would you like to take your kids out for a bit of spelunking? One of the more fascinating discoveries around Central Oregon happened when a trapper stumbled across a huge cave while hunting in 1889. In 1923 geologists studying the cave realized that it continued underground far deeper than any cave previously discovered. This cave is the longest uncollapsed lava tube in Oregon, extending nearly 5,200 feet from end to end. Bring flashlights and extra batteries or rent propane lanterns at the entrance. Wear sweaters and long pants because the cave is always about 42°F. Get ready for an experience that will have your kids shivering, not from the cold but because it's a bit spooky to be underground in a long cavern lighted only by your flashlights. Their imaginations will run riot. Stairs take you down into the cavern, where ice stalactites and stalagmites form in winter. Children love the echo chamber, where you can hear voices from farther ahead return as strange sounds.

un Facts

■ The **Lava River Cave** is the longest continuous river tube in Oregon.

■ The big obsidian flow at the **Newberry Volcano** was created 1,300 years ago and now covers 700 acres.

LAVA CAST FOREST (ages 5 and up)

Located 14 miles south of Bend; take U.S. 97 south, then turn east directly across from the Sunriver turnoff for 9 miles to the trailhead; (541) 383–5300 or (541) 593–2421. Open daily, May through October, dawn to dusk. $5.00 vehicle permit (NW Forest Pass).

Somewhat deceptively named, this isn't really a forest of trees embedded in lava. Rather, you'll find the hollow impressions left by trees caught in the path of a lava flow, casting molds in the hardening lava. Explore the area on a paved, self-guided mile-long nature trail.

MT. BACHELOR (ages 5 and up)

Located 22 miles west of Bend on Cascade Lakes Highway; (800) 829–2442 or (541) 382–2442. Open daily; call for hours. Lift tickets $42 adults, $35 teens (13–18), $24 children 6–12, children 5 and under Free. *Surcharge on holidays.*

Families can find both summer and winter recreation here. Ski rentals are available, including a complete selection of children's alpine and Nordic skis. A day lodge lets you warm up with a cup of hot chocolate or a piping hot lunch. The cafe remains open in the summer, too, and the rental shop switches from skis to mountain bikes. The summer excursion chair takes you on a scenic trip to Pine Marten Lodge at the 7,200-foot level, where you can enjoy lunch or dinner with incredible views. Several designated hiking trails at the top allow you to explore the full panorama of Central Oregon.

BACHELOR DOWNHILL BIKE TRAILS (ages 12 and up)

Located just 22 miles west of Bend on Cascade Lakes Highway; (800) 829–2442 or (541) 382–2442. Open daily, 10:00 A.M.–4:00 P.M. Call for bike rental prices.

Visitors also like exploring Mt. Bachelor's terrain in the summer. Trails looping the base of the mountain eventually wind through high desert landscape and over to Sparks and Todd lakes. Bikes can be rented at Mt. Bachelor.

RAFTING (ages 8 and up)

A number of outfitters in the area offer whitewater rafting trips on the Deschutes, one of Oregon's most challenging whitewater rivers. Most day trips average about $75 per person. In addition to those operating from area resorts, other outfitters include:

- **All Star Rafting.** *(800) 909–7238.*

- **Rapid River Rafters.** *(800) 962–3327 or (541) 382–1514.*

- **Deschutes Whitewater Services.** *(541) 395–2232.*

    Whitewater trips on this stretch of the Deschutes are geared for families with teenage children because of the hazards inherent in rafting in turbulent rapids.

PINE MOUNTAIN OBSERVATORY

Located 35 miles east of Bend. Take U.S. 20 to Millican, then turn 9 miles south from the marked road; (541) 382–8331 (after 3:00 P.M.). Open to the public Memorial Day through Labor Day, Friday and Saturday evenings, or by special appointment. Call first. Suggested donation of $3.00.

    University of Oregon's astronomical research facility features 15-, 24-, and 32-inch telescopes. Scientific discoveries that have been made here have been published worldwide. This is the only major observatory in the northwestern United States.

SUNRIVER (ages 3 and up)

Located about 15 miles southwest of Bend; (800) 547–3922 or (541) 593–1000; www.sunriver-resort.com. Resort always open.

    Sunriver, one of the first resorts to combine a lodge with private home development, is now a premier family resort. From horseback riding to ice skating, mountain biking to whitewater rafting, the resort offers an array of recreational opportunities with something to please everyone. **Goody's Soda Fountain** (541–593–2155), with the aroma of fragrant homemade waffle cones wafting through the air, is the refreshment stop of choice for families. All these activities cost extra, of course, but the advantage is a well-planned "one-stop-shopping" approach located in the heart of Oregon's lovely high desert region.

SUNRIVER NATURE CENTER & OBSERVATORY (ages 5 and up)

Located 18 miles south of Bend in Sunriver Resort; turn right on Abbott Drive, then follow signs to the marina and stable; (541) 593–4394; www.sunrivernature center.org. Open daily 9:00 A.M.–5:00 P.M. in summer, Tuesday–Saturday 10:00 A.M.–4:00 P.M. rest of year. $2.00 adults; $1.00 12 and under. The observatory is open Tuesday–Sunday, 9:00–11:00 P.M. in summer; call for hours rest of year. $6.00 adults, $4.00 children 12 and under.

Families can learn more about astronomy at the observatory, wildlife, and natural and cultural history through living history programs and other exhibits.

BLACK BUTTE STABLES (ages 8 and up)

The company's stables are at three locations, depending on the season. (541) 595–2061 or (541) 549–6765. Call for prices, hours.

The stables offer guided trail rides, full pack trips, and wagon rides.

SHEVLIN PARK (all ages)

Located five miles west of Bend on Shevlin Park Road; (541) 389–7275. Open all year, dawn to dusk. **Free.**

Over 500 acres of forested land that rim Tumalo Creek await you. In summer take one of several trails that wander up Tumalo Creek, where kids enjoy exploring in the water. Several new facilities offer pleasant picnic spots.

Top Bend Events

JULY

Cascade Cycling Classic. Racers from around the globe compete in challenging cycling events. Spectators especially favor the evening criterium races. (541) 385–8655.

AUGUST

Sunriver Music Festival. Classical and pops music plus a children's concert make this a sure bet for your resort stay. (541) 593–1084.

Cascade Festival of Music. Classical and world music are satisfying offerings at this annual event in Drake Park; children's musical parade is a sure hit. (541) 382–8381.

Cascade Lakes Scenic Highway

CASCADE LAKES SCENIC HIGHWAY (all ages)

To reach the highway from Bend, take Franklin Avenue west past Drake Park, then follow the signs; (800) 949–6086. The road beyond Mt. Bachelor is closed in winter and often doesn't open until June. **Free**.

Also called "Century Drive" because it's almost 100 miles of beautiful scenery, this road circles a chain of impressive mountain lakes. Take a week or two to explore the area, if you can, stopping at a different lake every night, or getting to know one or two very well.

TODD LAKE (ages 5 and up)

(541) 383–4000; www.fs.fed.us/r6/centraloregon. Call about hours and winter closures. $5.00 day-use fee (NW Forest Pass).

You'll have to carry your camping gear in from the parking area about 200 yards, but the reward is a beautiful wedge of clear, mountain water in an alpine meadow, with a view of **Broken Top** in the background. A path circles the lake and provides a perfect opportunity for exploring. In August the lakeshore comes alive with frogs, which guarantee the kids extra fun. Picnic tables on the west shore provide shady spots for having lunch, but you can also take your picnic basket and blanket and dine in a sunny meadow on the north shore.

BOATING

You can rent canoes in Bend at two locations:

- **Alder Creek Kayak & Canoes.** *345 SW Century Drive, (541) 389–0890.* Kayaks and canoes available for rent. Lessons and classes also available.

- **Bend Outdoor Center.** *55 Northwest Wall, Building "C"; (541) 389–7191 or (541) 388–0361. Call for hours, prices.* Kayaks and rafts are available for rent here.

ELK LAKE (ages 5 and up)

Located 29 miles southwest of Bend; (541) 383–4000; www.fs.fed.us/r6/centraloregon. Call about hours, winter closures. $5.00 trail permit, $10.00 vehicle permit for camping.

Three Forest Service campgrounds and two picnic areas provide a base of operation if you're camping, or the lodge is the place to stay if you want a bit more comfort. This lake is popular with small sailboats and sailboarders as well. For information on the lodge, ask the operator for mobile phone number YP7–3954 or write to P.O. Box 789, Bend, OR 97709. In winter the lodge will bring you in from the Mt. Bachelor Sno-Park by Sno-Cat for cross-country ski holidays.

OSPREY OBSERVATION POINT (all ages)

Located on the west shore of Crane Prairie Reservoir 45 miles southwest of Bend; (541) 383–4000; www.fs.fed.us/r6/centraloregon. Always open. $5.00 day-use fee (NW Forest Pass).

Watch osprey circling over the lake and listen to their piercing cries calling to one another as they seek their dinner from the lake below. Osprey were once an endangered species, but with the ban on DDT and with protected habitats such as these, osprey are now a more common sight on Oregon lakes and rivers. This area remains one of a handful of designated osprey nesting sites in the United States. Take the ¼-mile nature trail from the parking lot and help your kids spot the nests atop tall poles. It's quite a vision to observe an osprey make a successful dive, then return to the nest with a wriggling trout clutched in its talons.

Fun Facts The Osprey Observation Point, established in 1969, is one of the few osprey nesting areas in the United States.

LaPine

The **Cascade Lakes Scenic Highway** turns east again on State Highway 42, toward LaPine. Along the way, take State Highway 43 to Pringle Falls along the Deschutes River.

NEWBERRY NATIONAL VOLCANIC MONUMENT (all ages)

Located 24 miles south of Bend on U.S. 97; (541) 383–5300; www.fs.fed.us/r6/centraloregon. Call about hours, winter closures. $5.00 car entrance fee (NW Forest Pass).

Newberry National Volcanic Monument stands starkly on the horizon. The newest national monument in the West, Newberry was designated in 1990 for its unique scenic, recreational, and scientific value. The giant caldera within Newberry Crater holds two crystal-clear alpine lakes, Paulina and East, as well as the Big Obsidian Flow, deposited by an eruption more than 1,500 years ago. Native Americans used the sharp black obsidian to make tools and spear- and arrowheads. If you come across a historical or cultural artifact along the trail, such as an Indian arrowhead, feel free to pick it up and hold a piece of history in your hands for a moment, but then replace it so those who follow you might also appreciate its significance. To remove any such artifact is against federal law.

Walk with your kids along the 1-mile interpretive trail through the center of the flow, but caution them about the cutting edges of this dense volcanic glass. In August this area is alive with frogs migrating up the flow from Lost Lake—your kids will go wild!

Throughout the summer, park naturalists at Newberry National Volcanic Monument offer **Free** educational and interpretive programs, usually at a small outdoor amphitheater near the Big Obsidian Flow.

Sisters

When first driving into this small western town, you could be forgiven for thinking the calendar has dropped about a hundred years. If it weren't for the cars, the town's clapboard, false-front buildings and wooden boardwalks would make you believe you were back in the Old West. Many of the shops are geared for tourists, but your kids will appreciate the ice cream parlor on Main Street.

METOLIUS RIVER (all ages)

Just 8 miles west of Sisters; (541) 595–6711; www.metoliusriver.com. **Free**.

The headwaters of the Metolius River rush full force out of the ground, a sight that will amaze your kids and rekindle your own appreciation of the wonders of nature. This is one of the premier fly-fishing rivers in the state, completely set aside for catch-and-release fishing. Good places to get a look at some lunkers are on the small viewing platform near the bridge where the river flows in front of the **Camp Sherman Store,** about 5 miles north of U.S. 20, and at the state hatchery about 5 miles beyond. The store also has one of the best selections of hand-tied flies I've come across.

SKIING

Folks in Sisters have two downhill and three cross-country ski areas to choose from, all within 45 miles of town. **Mt. Bachelor** is certainly the largest of these, but one other also deserves consideration.

HOODOO SKI BOWL (ages 5 and up)

Located 22 miles northwest of Sisters; (541) 822–3799 or (541) 822–3337; www.hoodoo.com. Closed Wednesdays except during school vacation; call for hours. $30 adults ($28 weekday); $23 children ($20 weekday); under 5 Free.

The "bowl," which offers excellent downhill skiing with a variety of slopes, is the second oldest ski area in Oregon. The groomed cross-country trails at the resort can be enjoyed for a fee, but equally fun trails take off from the Sno-Park below the mountain. Sometimes you'll see mushers racing their sled dog teams on broad stretches of forest service roads in the summer.

THREE CREEKS LAKE (ages 5 and up)

Located about 17 miles south of Sisters; (541) 549–7700; www.fs.fed.us/r6/ deschutes. Call for hours, winter closures. $5.00 day-use fee (NW Forest Pass).

You'll find this lake is a beautiful spot to spend a weekend, a week, or just an afternoon. The shore of the lake has a shallow, gradual shelf that is perfect for wading, and the small marina on the lake rents rowboats by the day or the hour. The water in this lake is so clear that you can see to the bottom at its deepest point, some 30 feet below the surface. A small stream runs into the lake from **Little Three Creeks Lake** above. Walk along the stream in search of brook trout, crawdads, or other critters. The lush, green meadow

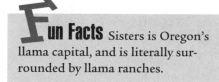

Fun Facts Sisters is Oregon's llama capital, and is literally surrounded by llama ranches.

surrounding Little Three Creeks comes alive during August when tiny frogs make their way from the lake to the forest.

OREGON LLAMAS (ages 8 and up)

61702 Teal Road in Bend; (888) PAC–LAMA or (541) 382–5028; tom@pack llama.com. $150 per person per day, 15 percent discount for children under 12.

If you'd like a different kind of adventure, try a llama trek. Central Oregon has become a popular place to raise these gentle Andean animals, and local hikers have taken advantage of their docility as pack animals. They take pack trips into the local Mt. Jefferson and Three Sisters Wilderness areas. The Bend Chamber of Commerce (541-382-3221) can provide a list of other outfitters for back-country trips, both with llamas and on horseback.

WIZARD FALLS (ages 5 and up)
Located about five miles north of Camp Sherman on U.S. 20, just east of Black Butte, turn north at sign for Metolius River and drive to Road 1419; (541) 549–7700. Open as weather permits. Free.

The Metolius River passes through a narrow channel of deep rock and forms these grand falls. The spot is as hazardous as it is beautiful, so keep your kids on the bridge when you stop to admire it.

WIZARD FALLS FISH HATCHERY (all ages)
Located just across the bridge at Wizard Falls; (541) 549–7700. Open as weather permits. Free.

The kids can feed the enormous brook trout, including some unusual specimens like albino trout, with food available from a coin-operated dispenser. Interpretive displays describe the life of a trout and how the hatchery helps enhance the native populations in the river.

Top Events in Sisters

JUNE

Sisters Rodeo. A parade, pancake breakfast, and four rodeo performances draw people from all over the state. (541) 549-0121; www.sistersrodeo.com.

JULY

Sisters Quilt Show. All the buildings in town are festooned with quilts. (541) 549-0251; www.stitchinpost.com.

Redmond

 ## CROOKED RIVER RAILROAD COMPANY TRAIN (ages 6 and up)

Three miles north of Redmond off Highway 97 and O'Neil Road; (541) 548–8630; www.crookedriverrailroad.com. Office hours 9:00 A.M.–5:00 P.M. weekdays; 10:00 A.M.–4:00 P.M. Saturday; train runs for Friday and Saturday dinner and Sunday brunch and supper; prices vary; $59–$71 adults; $38 ages 4–12; $20 ages 3 and under.

This 1800s-era dinner train rides 19 miles through the Crooked River Valley, past rim-rock canyons and high desert. Entertainment features Wild West characters who take you back in time to the era of train robberies and adventure. Special holiday and murder-mystery trains.

 ## SMITH ROCK STATE PARK (all ages)

9241 Northeast Crooked River Drive, located 25 miles north of Bend; from U.S. 97 north of Redmond, follow signs to the park; (800) 551–6949 or (541) 548–7501. Open year-round, dawn to dusk. $3.00 day-use fee.

This is a mecca for rock climbers and photographers. Your kids are probably too young to climb, but you can watch climbers scale the rock faces in the park, then rappel down on brightly colored ropes. The 641-acre park is filled with dramatic rock spires rising above the Crooked River Canyon. Walk along 2 miles of developed trails to the river or ridge (keep to the trail to reduce erosion) and watch for wildlife such as deer and nesting geese, hawks, falcons, eagles, and osprey. On your way, stop at the **Juniper Junction** store, 9297 Northeast Crooked River Drive, (541-548-4786) for a huckleberry ice cream cone.

 ## PETERSEN ROCK GARDEN AND MUSEUM (all ages)

Located off U.S. 97 at Sixty-first Street and follow signs; (541) 382–5574. Open 9:00 A.M. daily, closing time varies by season. $3.00 adults; $1.50 teens; 50 cents ages 6–11; under 6 Free.

The late Mr. Petersen spent seventeen years creating this 4-acre park of miniature bridges, lily ponds, buildings, towers, and gardens, using varicolored rocks to create the designs.

op Redmond Events

JULY

4th of July Parade. If you're here during Fourth of July weekend, help this friendly community celebrate Independence Day by cheering participants in an old-fashioned parade. (541) 923–5191.

NOVEMBER–DECEMBER

Starfest Light Tour. This holiday light show features dozens of displays that can be enjoyed from the family car or in a horse-drawn carriage. Santa's there too! (541) 923–2453.

SANTA IN REDMOND

 OPERATION SANTA CLAUS (all ages)

4355 West Highway 126, Redmond; located 2 miles west of Redmond; (541) 548–8910. Open daily, call for hours.

Christmas in July? Make that Christmas all year at Operation Santa Claus reindeer ranch. More than 100 reindeer live at this ranch, where the owners believe in keeping the spirit of the holiday going all year. Take a self-guided tour or wander through the gift shop. Come see the newborns in May and June.

Madras

 LAKE BILLY CHINOOK (all ages)

2 miles southwest of Madras (U.S. 26 to Culver Highway, then follow signs to lake); (800) 551–6959; www.oregonstateparks.org. Call for hours, winter closures. $3.00 vehicle permit.

Three rivers feed into the waters of Lake Billy Chinook, named for an Indian guide who helped Captain John Frémont in his mapping expeditions to Oregon. The lake is now a haven for summer water fun in the midst of Oregon's high desert country.

143

COVE PALISADES STATE PARK (all ages)

7300 S.W. Jordan Road; (800) 551–6949; (800) 452–5687 for reservations; www.oregonstateparks.org. Open daily, $3.00 day-use fee.

The park straddles the Deschutes and Crooked River arms of the lake and is the center of much recreation activity. Boat ramps, swimming beaches, campgrounds, and picnic tables are provided. The two campgrounds, one on the Deschutes River and another overlooking the Crooked River from above on the cliffs, are closed in winter. There are three public day-use areas and a private restaurant that's open May through September.

Cove Palisades Marina (541-546-3412), on the Crooked River arm of the lake, rents fishing and waterskiing boats, patio boats, and jet skis. In summer, park rangers offer interpretive programs, and just up from the Deschutes Campground to the northeast, you'll find a large boulder of basalt with Indian petroglyphs. You can walk to the beach along a trail across from the entrance station at Deschutes River Campground, but keep the eyes and ears open for rattlesnakes.

ROUND BUTTE OVERLOOK PARK (all ages)

Located 15 miles southwest of Madras near the town of Culver off U.S. 97; (503) 464–8515 or (800) 542–8818. Open daily, May 25–September 30, 8:00 A.M. to dusk. Free.

The park includes a picnic area and interpretive center overlooking Round Butte Dam and Lake Billy Chinook.

RICHARDSON'S ROCK RANCH (all ages)

Located 11 miles north of Madras (pronounced Mad Russ) near milepost 81; (541) 475–2680. Open daily, 7:00 A.M.–5:00 P.M. weather permitting.

Kids of all ages can enjoy an afternoon of rockhounding here, digging for thunder eggs—those drab, round rocks that, when split in two, reveal formations like miniature worlds in crystal, opal, agate, or cinnabar. The thunder egg is the Oregon state rock, and its name comes from an Indian legend about a battle between the thunder spirits residing in Mt. Jefferson and Mt. Hood.

Top Madras Event

MAY

Collage of Culture. Country music, Latin salsa, traditional Indian dances, and ethnic food—what more could you want in this event that celebrates cultural diversity? (541) 475-2350.

When they became angry with one another, the spirits hurled the agate-filled balls at one another, sounding their thunder with each toss. The result of their ire is resting in rock beds, about 4,000 acres of which are within the Richardson family ranch. Digging is available daily, weather permitting, and rock picks are provided. Thunder egg splitting services are also available at the shop, and finished rock products are sold. Rocks are just 50 cents but you can also pay by the pound for what you take out.

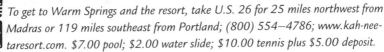

Warm Springs Indian Reservation

KAH-NEE-TAH RESORT (all ages)
To get to Warm Springs and the resort, take U.S. 26 for 25 miles northwest from Madras or 119 miles southeast from Portland; (800) 554–4786; www.kah-nee-taresort.com. $7.00 pool; $2.00 water slide; $10.00 tennis plus $5.00 deposit.

Everyone will enjoy the traditional aspects of a stay at this tribal-owned and -operated resort that retains the rugged natural beauty of its surroundings. Kids love swimming in the pools, one fed by hot springs, and the other with a fountain depicting bears holding salmon spouting water. Activities include salmon bakes, fry bread, dancing and drumming, and storytelling and singing. You can rent cabins, lodge rooms, tepees, or campsites for RVs. Recreation also includes fishing and kayaking on the Deschutes, hiking along trails, horseback riding, working out at the fitness center, or playing tennis or golf.

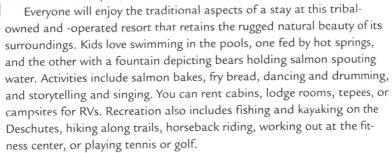

MUSEUM AT WARM SPRINGS (ages 5 and up)
2189 U.S. 26; (541) 553–3331. Open daily, 9:00 A.M.–5:00 P.M. $6.00 adults; $3.00 ages 5–12; 4 and under **Free**.

The homeland for more than 3,400 members of Warm Springs, Wasco, and Northern Paiute tribes, Warm Springs Reservation has developed a thriving tourist industry as well as a center that seeks to enlighten visitors about the rich traditions of Northwest Native American culture. The stunningly beautiful museum is one place you won't want to miss. Completed in 1993, it was created to provide a legacy to the generations that follow: "Preservation of the past, the birthright of your heritage, and the inheritance of our hopes and dreams for the future." The history of the Confederated Tribes unfolds in a state-of-the-art permanent exhibit of audiovisual presentations and displays, which include prized heirlooms from tribal families, historic photographs, and murals. Traditional

145

dwellings—a tule mat lodge, wickiup, and plankhouse—show how people lived in ancient villages. Beadwork, basketry, clothing, and other artifacts are also displayed. A multimedia exhibit draws you into the traditional singing, drumming, and dancing of the tribes, which is a marvelous experience to appreciate with your family. Walking trails along Shitike Creek lead to picnic areas and an amphitheater where performances and demonstrations are staged in the summer.

OLALLIE LAKE NATIONAL SCENIC AREA (ages 5 and up)
(541) 822–3381; www.fs.fed.us/r6/mthood or www.olallielake.com. Call for hours, seasonal closures. $5.00 vehicle fee (NW Forest Pass).
This area covers nearly 11,000 acres in both the **Mt. Hood National Forest** and the **Warm Springs Reservation.** The many lakes that dot the region of pine and fir forests reflect the grandeur of Mt. Hood to the north and Mt. Jefferson to the west. A resort on Olallie Lake offers small cabins for rent, as well as a store with fishing and camping supplies and boat rentals. No motors or swimming are allowed on the lake because it provides drinking water for local residents. You can swim in Head Lake and First Lake, both just off the road to the north of Olallie Lake.

OLALLIE TRAIL (ages 5 and up)
(541) 822–3381.
The trail circles Olallie Lake and spur trails lead to several other lakes. You can pick up a map of area trails from the ranger station near the entrance to the Scenic Area, or at the resort store on Olallie Lake. Access to Olallie Lake is not suitable for trailers and requires a car in good condition.

Where to Eat

IN BEND
Westside Bakery and Cafe. *1005 Northwest Galveston; (514) 382–3426.* On the way out of town, heading toward the Cascade Lakes Scenic Highway, you'll come across this dining establishment with unusual and eclectic decor which includes a red-nosed moose head, old movie posters, and Native American paraphernalia. The menu offers a wide variety of options for both parents and children. You can even grab goodies to go from the bakery. $

Legends Publick House. *125 Northwest Oregon Avenue; (541) 382–5654.* Upscale dining in a casual setting makes this a popular place for locals and visitors. $$

Mexicali Rose. *301 Northeast Franklin Avenue; (541) 389–0149.* This festive place has been voted Best Mexican Restaurant in several restaurant surveys. $$–$$$

IN SISTERS

Bronco Billy's Ranch & Saloon. *190 East Cascade Street; (541) 549–7427.* At this favorite watering hole, you also can find lunch and dinner with a western flair. Barbecued ribs, links and chicken are renowned rib-sticking entrees. $–$$$

Kokanee Cafe. *Located 15 miles west of Sisters in Camp Sherman; (541) 595–6420.* Many would agree this hidden gem offers the best of Northwest cuisine. Fresh local ingredients are always featured in the small but carefully chosen list of featured dinner entrees. Closed November through March. Call first. $$$–$$$$

Papandrea's Pizza. *442 East Hood; (541) 549–6081.* This cozy pizza parlor has a very local, friendly feel.

Where to Stay

IN BEND

Bend Riverside Motel. *1565 Northwest Hill Street; (800) 284–2363 or (541) 389–2363.* One hundred ninety-four rooms. The large piece of property that houses this facility is right next to the Deschutes River and Pioneer Park. Less expensive rooms are cramped, but for slightly more, you get room to stretch out and views of the river. An indoor pool, sauna, and a tennis court are available. $$–$$$

Best Western Entrada Lodge. *19221 Century Drive; (800) 528–1234 or (541) 382–4080.* Seventy-nine rooms. Situated a few miles west of Bend among tall pine trees, this peaceful place is close to Mt. Bachelor and doesn't offer all the fanfare that other establishments do. But it includes a continental breakfast, an outdoor pool, and a whirlpool. $$–$$$

Black Butte Ranch. *P.O. Box 8000, Black Butte Ranch, 97759; (800) 452–7455; www.blackbutteranch.com.* Up to 120 homes and condos. Black Butte is a volcanic cinder cone that rises to a 6,436-foot elevation. The year-round resort offers both lodge rooms and condominiums, as well as private homes rented by the day or week. Cycling on miles of paved trails, plus tennis, swimming, and golf, round out many a family vacation. $$$–$$$$

Sunriver Lodge and Resort. *P.O. Box 3609; (800) 801–8765 or (541) 593–1221; www.sunriver-resort.com.* Private homes and condos are for rent on a nightly and weekly basis. Horseback riding, ice skating, mountain biking, and whitewater rafting make this a perfect "one-stop" resort site. $$$–$$$$

IN LAPINE

Best Western Newberry Station. *16515 Reed Road and U.S. 97; (800) 210–8616 or (541) 536–5130.* Forty units. Continental breakfast, an indoor swimming pool and a spa give families a pleasant respite. $

Paulina Lake Resort. *P.O. Box 7, LaPine; (541) 536–2240; www. paulinalakeresort.evisionsite.com.* The resort is open mid-June through October and mid-December through mid-March. Camping is available along the lakes and Paulina Creek. Paulina Lake Resort and **East Lake Resort** (541-536-2230) both offer cabins. They also provide boat rentals and restaurants serving breakfast, lunch, and dinner (Paulina only). Paulina's resort is also open for winter recreation. $$–$$$$

West View Motel. *51371 U.S. 97 South; (541) 536–2115.* Nine units. Pets are allowed. Some kitchenettes are available. $

IN SISTERS

Best Western Ponderosa Lodge. *505 U.S. 20 West; (541) 549–1234; www.bestwestern.com.* Forty-eight units. Continental breakfast, a swimming pool, and spa pool are offered to guests, who will also appreciate the proximity to downhill skiing, golf, and fishing. $$–$$$

Comfort Inn at Sisters. *540 U.S. 20; (541) 549–7829.* Fifty units. Continental breakfast is available here and pets are allowed with prior approval. You'll also find an indoor swimming pool and laundry facilities. $$–$$$$

Sisters Motor Lodge. *511 West Cascade; (541) 549–2551.* Eleven units. Full breakfast is provided and you'll be close to golf, skiing, tennis, and fishing. Kitchenettes are available also. Pet friendly. Nonsmoking. $$–$$$$

IN REDMOND

Eagle Crest Resort. *1522 Cline Falls Road; (800) 682–4786 or (541) 923–2453; www.eagle-crest.com.* One hundred thrity units. Exercise rooms, indoor and outdoor pools, kitchenettes, and a restaurant give families plenty of options. $$$–$$$$

Redmond Super 8 Motel. *3629 Twenty-first Place; (800) 800–8000 or (541) 548–8881; www.super8.com.* Eighty-five units. Continental breakfast, indoor pool and spa, and laundry facilities are provided. Pets are allowed. $$–$$$

IN MADRAS

Best Western Rama Inn. *12 Southwest Fourth Street; (888) RAMA-INN or (541) 475–6141.* Forty-seven units. Continental breakfast, a sauna, and an exercise room are offered here. $–$$

Sonny's Motel. *1539 Southwest U.S. 97; (800) 624–6137 or (541) 475–7217.* Forty-four units. Kitchenettes and laundry facilities are available. Pets allowed. $$–$$$

IN WARM SPRINGS

Kah-Nee-Tah Resort. *P.O. Box K, Warm Springs, 97761; (800) 554–4786 or (541) 553–1112; www.kah-nee-taresort. com.* One hundred sixty-nine rooms, twenty teepees, and fifty RV sites.

Kayaking and whitewater-rafting opportunities are available on the Deschutes, along with hiking, horseback riding, working out at the fitness center, and playing tennis or golf. Two restaurants serve American and Northwest cuisine. The resort museum is outstanding. $$–$$$

For More Information

Bend Chamber of Commerce. *777 NW Wall Street, Bend, OR 97701; (541) 382–3221; www.bendchamber.org.*

Bend Visitor & Convention Bureau. *63085 N. Highway 97, Bend, OR 97701; (541) 382–8048.*

Central Oregon Visitors Association. *572 SW Bluff Drive, Suite C, Bend, OR 97702; (800) 800–8334; www.visitcentraloregon.com.*

LaPine Chamber of Commerce. *P.O. Box 616, LaPine, OR 97739; (541) 536–9771; www.lapine.org; E-mail: info@lapine.org.*

Redmond Chamber of Commerce. *446 Southwest Seventh Street, Redmond, OR 97756; (541) 923–5191; www.redmondcofc.com/.*

Sisters Area Chamber of Commerce. *352 West Hood Avenue; P.O. Box 430; Sisters, OR 97759; (541) 549–0251; www.sisterschamber.com; E-mail: info@sisterschamber.com.*

Southern Oregon

The southern region of Oregon encompasses the diversity of the whole state: coast, mountains, valleys, high desert. Your choices for family fun are equally diverse—from birdwatching on Oregon's largest lake to exploring its only national park, from riding a wild river to watching Shakespeare performed in one of the world's preeminent Shakespearean theaters. In winter, southern Oregon is transformed into a frosty playground. In summer the warm, dry weather provides an open invitation to outdoor recreation.

Ashland

Ashland's population of 19,000 swells to more than 50,000 when the renowned Shakespearean festival season is at its peak. While we wouldn't recommend introducing your children to Shakespeare with a play like *King Lear*, the theater inevitably offers one of the Bard's twelve comedies on its playbill each year. Experiencing a play in the open-air Elizabethan Theatre is wonderful, but spend a little extra to rent a cushion and lap robe—it will make all the difference if the night becomes chilly. Another enjoyable pastime in Ashland is dining, and for a town this size there are a number of remarkably good restaurants.

 OREGON SHAKESPEARE FESTIVAL (ages 8 and up)
15 South Pioneer Street, P.O. Box 158, Ashland, 97520; (541) 482–2111; www.orshakes.org. Plays run from February to October. Call for prices, schedules. Tickets range from $25 to $34.

Three theaters, the **Elizabethan Theatre,** the **Angus Bowmer Theatre,** and a new theater, scheduled to open in March 2002, which will replace the Black Swan Theater, all offer top-notch productions. The

SOUTHERN OREGON

Crater Lake National Park

Lakeview

Klamath Falls

Medford
Ashland

Roseburg

Grants Pass

Cave Junction

140
395
140
395
140
31
97
97
39
97
58
138
232
97
62
66
62
230
140
62
138
5
227
234
5
199
99
238
5
38
138
42
199
46
199

Bowmer offers both Shakespeare and contemporary plays while the Elizabethan is strictly dedicated to the Bard.

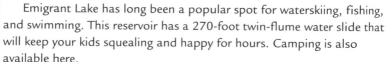

un Facts Ashland is home to the internationally acclaimed **Oregon Shakespeare Festival,** held every year from February until October.

 ### OREGON SHAKESPEARE FESTIVAL BACKSTAGE TOURS (ages 5 and up)

15 South Pioneer Street; (541) 482–4331. Reservations required; tours start at 10:00 A.M. to 11:45 A.M. daily except Monday. Prices range from $5.00 to $10.00, depending on the season.

With an actor as a guide, you get a behind-the-scenes look at how a theatrical production is put together. Your kids will especially enjoy the costumes and props, which they're allowed to touch.

 ### OLD ASHLAND WALKING TOURS (ages 8 and up)

Meet at the Plaza Information Booth at 10:00 A.M. daily except Sunday, July through mid-September; (541) 552–9159; E-mail: jpetersn@mind.net. Adults $5.00, children $2.00, families $12.00.

 ### EMIGRANT LAKE (all ages)

Located six miles southeast of Ashland on State Highway 66; (541) 774–8183 or (541) 776–7001. Open dawn to dusk. $3.00 vehicle pass.

Emigrant Lake has long been a popular spot for waterskiing, fishing, and swimming. This reservoir has a 270-foot twin-flume water slide that will keep your kids squealing and happy for hours. Camping is also available here.

 ### HYATT LAKE (all ages)

Located farther along State Highway 66; (541) 482–2031. Open dawn to dusk. Call for day-use entrance fees.

You'll find more water recreation as well as winter fun at Hyatt Lake, a high Cascade lake that will reward you with a view of Mt. McLoughlin.

 ### MT. ASHLAND (ages 5 and up)

1745 State Highway 66, located 18 miles from the city center heading south; (541) 482–2897; www.mtashland.com. Usually opens Thanksgiving weekend; call for hours. Lift tickets range from $11 to $27.

With four chairlifts and more than twenty ski runs on a 1,150-foot vertical slope, Mt. Ashland should be on the to-do list for any family that enjoys downhill skiing. A ski school and rental shop cater to those interested in giving the slopes a try for the first time, and the day lodge offers meals and great views. Summer hiking is terrific here too. The Pacific Crest Trail crosses Mt. Ashland Inn's parking area and several spur trails lead to scenic viewpoints and picturesque streams.

WILD AND SCENIC ROGUE RIVER RAFTING (ages 8 and up)

Many local outdoor operators run trips out of Ashland, including:

■ **Noah's River Adventures**
53 North Main Street, P.O. Box 11, Ashland 97520; (800) 858–2811 or (541) 488–2811; www.noahsrafting.com. Call for schedules. Half-day Rogue River trip $69; one-day Rogue River or Upper Klamath trip, $119–$149. Family discount plans available.

Noah's offers half-, full-, and multi-day floats and family scenic "sunsoaker" trips without the whitewater.

■ **Adventure Center**
40 North Main Street; (800) 444–2819 or (541) 488–2819; www. raftingtours.com. Call for schedule; runs early spring to early fall. $69 half-day; $119–129 all day. Discounts available for families.

This company runs eight different rivers, including the Rogue and Wild Upper Klamath, and supplies transportation, gear, and food. They also offer a simple float trip for families with pre-school age children.

■ **Raft the Rogue**
21171 State Highway 62, Shady Cove; (800) 797–7238 or (541) 878–3623; www.rafttherogue.com; E-mail: rafttherogue@gartech.com. Call for schedule; runs early spring to early fall. Raft for a family of four, $45; family of 6, $55; larger rafts $65 and up.

This company rents the rafts and delivers you to the river; you do the rest!

 LITHIA PARK (all ages)
Located off just Siskiyou Boulevard; (541) 488–5340. Open dawn to dusk.
Free.

A green and lovely place with Ashland Creek creating a musical backdrop, Lithia Park is at the heart of this romantically small town. Designed by John McLaren, the architect who gave San Francisco Golden Gate Park, Lithia Park is now a recognized National Historic Site. Near the entrance to the park is a small fountain, bubbling forth water from Lithia Springs, a mineral springs that has been said to have curative powers.

Top Ashland Events

JUNE

Feast of Will. This celebration dinner in Lithia Park, complete with period music and dancing, marks the opening of the Elizabethan Theatre each season. (541) 482-4331.

DECEMBER

Holiday Festival of Lights. Be sure to attend the community's yuletide festival if you're in the area during the holidays. It lasts the whole month. (541) 482-3486.

YEAR-ROUND

Southern Oregon University Theatre Arts. The university presents a variety of classics, musicals, and contemporary plays each academic year. (541) 552-6348.

Medford

Medford's prosperity turned from gold in the 1800s to agricultural activity— it's still a major world center for pears—and a strong timber industry. That great American pastime—baseball—can be appreciated on a professional level in Medford, home of the Southern Oregon A's.

 BUTTE CREEK MILL (ages 5 and up)
402 Royal Avenue North, Eagle Point; (541) 826–3531. Open Monday through Saturday, 9:00 A.M.–5:00 P.M.
Free.

Oregon's only original water-powered gristmill has been operating continuously since 1872, when two 1,400-pound French buhr millstones were brought around Cape

Fun Facts Medford is home to Oregon's only original water-powered gristmill. Located in Eagle Point, **Butte Creek Mill** is listed on the National Register of Historic Places.

Horn by ship, then transported over the mountains by a wagon. The building itself, open for self-guided tours, is a living museum. Your kids will be intrigued by the way the waterwheel turns the stones to grind the grains into flour. To continue the old-fashioned family entertainment, bring a picnic to enjoy in the park across the stream, and walk across the Antelope Creek Covered Bridge, also nearby. You can also buy Butte Creek Mill products at the Country Store located on the property.

 ### HARRY AND DAVID
1314 Center Drive #A; (877) 322–8000; (541) 864–2278; www.harryand david.com. On weekdays, tours leave every half-hour, 9:30 A.M. until 1:45 P.M. By reservation only. $5.00 per person, under 12 Free.

If your kids love fruit, take them on a tour of one of the largest mail order companies in the world. The tour takes you through the plant that packages gift baskets of delectable fruits, from Oregon-grown ruby silk pears to ruby cream bananas; to the candy kitchen where an assortment of chocolate truffles are created before your eyes; and on to the bakery, where baklava, loaf cakes, and fruit pastry confections will get your mouths watering—just in time to return to the retail store. You can also visit the store on your own, without the benefit of a guided tour.

MEDFORD RAILROAD PARK
Located near the Rogue Valley Mall on Berrydale Avenue off Table Rock Road; http://sorcnrhs.railfan.net/medfordpark.htm; E-mail: sorcnrhs@railfan.net. Open second and fourth Sundays from April through October, 11:00 A.M.–3:00 P.M. Free *but donations appreciated.*

Train buffs have put together miniature steam, diesel, and electric trains that run along a mile of track. Parents and kids are welcome to take rides. Bring lunch to eat in the picnic pavilion.

   ### JOSEPH P. STEWART STATE RECREATION AREA (all ages)
Located 35 miles northeast of Medford on Highway 62; (800) 551–6949 or (541) 560–3334. Always open. Free.

The park has a marina with a cafe and store and a swimming beach for cooling off during the summer. It also features 5½ miles of hiking trails and a 6-mile bike trail. Camp sites are available too.

SOUTHERN OREGON HISTORY CENTER
106 North Central Avenue; (541) 773–6536; www.sohs.org. Open Monday through Friday, 9:00 A.M.–5:00 P.M. Free.

Exhibits include the traditional collections of pioneer artifacts, as well as informative displays on early farming and mining in the region.

op Medford Events

APRIL

Pear Blossom Festival. Among the activities are the 10-mile Pear Blossom Run, bicycle races, arts and crafts, and a parade. (541) 734-7327.

SUMMER

Medford's Bear Creek Park. Concerts are held in the park on Sunday evenings. (541) 774-2400.

OCTOBER

Medford Jazz Jubilee. More than a hundred performances give families plenty of options for a weekend of great music entertainment. (800) 599-0039 or (541) 770-6972.

JACKSONVILLE

Located just west of Medford, Jacksonville was at the heart of southern Oregon's Gold Rush that began in 1852, and the entire town has since been put on the National Register of Historic Places. If you'd like to explore the town and learn more about its history, take a narrated carriage or trolley ride through town.

 JACKSONVILLE MUSEUM OF SOUTHERN OREGON HISTORY (ages 5 and up)

206 North Fifth Street; (541) 773–6536; www.sohs.org. Open Wednesday through Saturday, 10:00 A.M.–5:00 P.M.; Sunday, noon–5:00 P.M. $3.00 adults; $2.00 ages 6–12; under 6 Free (covers Children's Museum also).
Exhibits feature Native American artifacts and pioneer pottery.

 JACKSONVILLE HISTORY STORE (ages 5 and up)

California and Third Streets; (541) 773–6536. Open Wednesday through Sunday, 10:00 A.M.–5:00 P.M.
Offerings include wonderful replicas of children's toys from long ago as well as a good selection of folk art.

CHILDREN'S MUSEUM (all ages)

206 North Fifth Street; (541) 773–6536. Same hours as Jacksonville Museum of Southern Oregon History.

This child-oriented attraction is located in the adjoining County Jail. Kids appreciate the pioneer exhibit area, where the usual museum refrain, "Look but don't touch," doesn't apply. The collection of antique toys is also a favorite.

GIN LIN MINING TRAIL (ages 5 and up)

Located 15 miles south of Jacksonville in the Rogue River National Forest; (541) 899–1812; www.fs.fed.us/r6/rogue. Always open. Free.

The trail tells the story of a Chinese miner whose claim on this stretch of the Siskiyous yielded more than a million dollars in gold dust. An interpretive brochure, available at the trailhead, describes numbered stops along the way. The easy ¾-mile walk takes off from the Flumet Flat Campground in the Rogue River National Forest.

APPLEGATE LAKE (all ages)

Located in Rogue River National Forest, 23 miles southwest of Medford; (541) 899–1812. Always open; water levels may restrict recreation activity. Some Free sites; others require a $5.00 fee.

The lake is a great place to spend the day swimming, boating, fishing, or hiking on one of several trails around the lake. Hartish Park, on the west shore, is a charming spot for picnicking.

Top Jacksonville Events

JUNE TO LABOR DAY

Britt Festivals. Renowned musicians converge here to wow audiences in a peaceful outdoor setting. (800) 882–7488.

JULY

Children's Festival. Held on the Britt grounds, this event is especially fun for children ages two to twelve. The whole family can enjoy arts and crafts, food, and live entertainment. (541) 776–7286.

DECEMBER

Victorian Christmas. Strolling carolers and horse-drawn carriage rides add a festive holiday atmosphere in this famous Gold Rush town. (541) 899–8118.

Grants Pass

The Rogue River is one of the most popular destinations in Oregon, and it runs through Grants Pass. Immortalized by writer Zane Grey, this mighty 215-mile river is famous worldwide for its stunning beauty, from the headwaters in Crater Lake National Park to the Pacific Ocean. The wild and scenic section of the river brings thousands to challenge its whitewater canyons in rafts and kayaks.

HELLGATE JETBOAT EXCURSIONS (ages 8 and up)

966 Southeast Sixth Street; (800) 648–4874 or (541) 476–2628; www. hellgate.com. Operates May to September; call for schedules. Hellgate Quick and Scenic Trip: $26 adults; $16 children. This is a two-hour, 36-mile trip.

The original jet boat tour company on this part of the river, Hellgate trips leave from the Riverside Motel, off Seventh Street, to either Hellgate Canyon (made famous by John Wayne's *Rooster Cogburn*) or Grave Creek. The brunch and dinner trips include a meal at the OK Corral.

Grants Pass Parks
Take both your picnic and a Frisbee to any of four parks in and near town where your family can play Disc Golf. You toss your whirling disc at the "holes," which are actually wire baskets mounted atop poles.

- **Riverside Park (all ages).** *Located downtown on the Rogue River; (541) 471–6435. Open dawn to dusk.* Riverside Park has a nine-hole course that is perfect for beginners.

- **Tom Pearce Park (all ages).** *Located off Foothill Boulevard about 5 miles from Grants Pass's town center; (541) 474–5285. Open dawn to dusk.* This park has a "pro" eighteen-hole course that's used in competitions.

- **Indian Mary Park (all ages).** *Located on the Merlin-Galice Road about 10 miles from Exit 61 off Interstate 5; (541) 474–5285. Open dawn to dusk.* There's a nine-hole course as well as camping and picnicking facilities.

- **Wolf Creek Park (all ages).** *Located in the small town of Wolf Creek about 18 miles north of Grants Pass off Exit 76; (541) 474–5285. Open dawn to dusk.* Here you'll also find a nine-hole course as well as camping and picnicking facilities.

op Grants Pass Events

MAY

Boatnik Festival. Adventurous whitewater buffs compete over a 50-mile course on the Rogue River. A parade, art show and carnival are also a part of this lively weekend event. (800) 547–5927 or (541) 476–7717.

AUGUST

Josephine County Fair. This old-fashioned event with carnival rides and pig races is certain to entertain your brood. A favorite event is the four-wheel-drive log pull. (541) 476–3215; www.jocofair.com.

AUGUST–SEPTEMBER

Jedediah Smith Mountain Man Rendezvous. The rendezvous takes you back to another era, one filled with brawny mountain adventurers and pioneer women who forged a new life in this vast, wild land. It includes demonstrations of the firearms, lifestyle, clothing, and crafts of that period. (541) 476–2040.

 GRANTS PASS HISTORICAL WALKING TOUR (ages 5 and up)

 (800) 547–5927 or (541) 476–5510 or (541) 479–7827; www.grantspass chamber.org. Always open. 𝐅𝐫𝐞𝐞.

Take a self-guided walking tour of the town's historical neighborhoods, where you will see some of the most impressive early twentieth-century architectural styles in Southern Oregon. Downtown Grants Pass is now a National Historic District, and many of these buildings also house irresistible antique shops and restaurants.

 VALLEY OF THE ROGUE STATE PARK (all ages)

Located about 10 miles east of Grants Pass, just off Interstate 5 near the town of Rogue River; (800) 452–5687 (for reservations); (800) 551–6949 or (541) 582–1118 (for information); www.oregonstateparks.org. Open year-round for camping, dawn to dusk for day use. 𝐅𝐫𝐞𝐞 *for day use. $10–$18 for camping, depending on season and type of accommodation.*

Perhaps one of the most popular campgrounds in the state as a result of its proximity to Interstate 5, Valley of the Rogue also offers a picnic area along the river, which lets you watch boaters launch rafts and kayaks into this placid body of water. Across the river is the site of a fort, and the land around the park itself was once used briefly as a reservation for Takilma Indians.

 HOUSE OF MYSTERY AT THE OREGON VORTEX (all ages)
4303 Sardine Creek Road, Gold Hill; past Valley of the Rogue State Park about 3 miles on Interstate 5; (541) 855–1543. Open daily, March to May and September to October, 9:00 A.M.–5:00 P.M. (last tour at 4:15 P.M.); June to August, 9:00 A.M.–6:00 P.M. (last tour at 5:15 P.M.) $7.50 adults; $5.50 ages 5–11; under 5 **Free**.

This is the spot of "The Oregon Vortex," which proprietors claim is the area of unusual phenomena that Native Americans called "The Forbidden Ground." Kids love the strange sensations produced by trying to stand up straight when the walls and floors around all seem slanted. The visual phenomena are fun to experience, and, who knows, maybe it's not just an optical illusion.

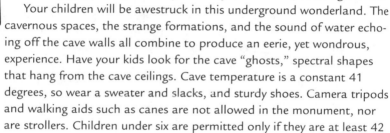

Cave Junction

Cave Junction, Oregon's third-oldest town, sits in what is called the Illinois Valley, where the east and west forks of the Illinois River join on the journey down the Siskiyou mountainsides toward the Rogue River and the sea. More than a dozen creeks find their way into the Illinois in Cave Junction, making rushing waters a common sound just about anywhere in town. **Illinois River State Park** lies less than a mile south of Cave Junction along the West Fork Illinois River. On hot days your kids will appreciate the cooling water and will enjoy splashing among the rocks. There are picnic tables for a leisurely riverside lunch.

 OREGON CAVES NATIONAL MONUMENT (ages 5 and up)
19000 Caves Highway, located 19 miles from Cave Junction on State Highway 46; (541) 592–2100; www.nps.gov/orca. Cave tours closed winter; trails open year-round. Call for tour times, which vary seasonally. $7.50 adults, $5.00 ages 6–11.

Your children will be awestruck in this underground wonderland. The cavernous spaces, the strange formations, and the sound of water echoing off the cave walls all combine to produce an eerie, yet wondrous, experience. Have your kids look for the cave "ghosts," spectral shapes that hang from the cave ceilings. Cave temperature is a constant 41 degrees, so wear a sweater and slacks, and sturdy shoes. Camera tripods and walking aids such as canes are not allowed in the monument, nor are strollers. Children under six are permitted only if they are at least 42 inches tall and can handle the sometimes steep stairways on their own. There's a special **Free** 20-minute tour for those under 42 inches in height.

While you wait for the tour to start, explore aboveground, where a nature trail leads you on a cliff-top loop about ¹⁄₁₀ mile long. Trailside signs identify the plant life, and you're likely to encounter a little wildlife along the way as well. **No Name Trail,** about 1¹⁄₁₀ miles round-trip, takes you past gurgling mountain streams and mossy cliff sides, through dense forest with wildflowers in the undergrowth. Another trail follows **Cave Creek** 1⁸⁄₁₀ miles to Cave Creek Campground. Allow three hours for your visit.

OUT 'N' ABOUT TREESORT (ages 5 and up)

300 Page Creek Road, Takilma; (800) 200–5484 or (541) 592–2208; www. treehouses.com. Tours $2.50; rentals $80–$150; horseback riding $20 per hour; tree climbing/rappelling $20 per lesson.

One of the most unusual places to stay is a bed and breakfast that rents a standard ground-level cabin (very cozy, sleeps five) and, thanks to revised permits, the proprietor can allow people to spend the night in the lofty perch of a white oak tree. The family tree house has two cabins linked by a swinging bridge. Kids think this is the next thing to heaven— or Disneyland. The freshwater swimming pool is fed by river water. Horseback riding is available, with guided trail rides (for ages eight and older). Tours are offered daily in summer and off-season weekends from noon–5:00 P.M. You can tour unoccupied treehouses and experience the Mountain View Treeway—a high-rise walkway that includes 90-foot and 45-foot suspension bridges.

OREGON CAVES CHATEAU (all ages)

*20000 Caves Highway; (541) 592–3400. Call for hours. Closed end of December to February. **Free** for day visitors.*

This 1934 chateau is a treasure trove of the past and a designated National Historic Landmark. The six-story lodge is nestled among waterfalls in the rugged Siskiyou Mountains. Most of the furnishings have been making people comfortable for more than sixty years. Park rangers hold slide talks here, and you can treat your kids to an ice cream cone at the beautiful old wooden soda fountain. Lodging is available from mid-March through December.

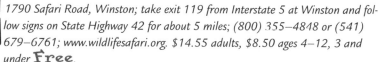

Roseburg

DOUGLAS COUNTY MUSEUM OF HISTORY AND NATURAL HISTORY

123 Museum Drive, located next to the County Fairgrounds, follow signs from Interstate 5 at exit 123; (541) 957–7007; www.co.douglas.or/museum. Open weekdays, 9:00 A.M.–5:00 P.M., Saturday 10:00 A.M.–5:00 P.M., noon–5:00 P.M. Sunday and holidays. $3.50 adults; $1.00 ages 4–17; 3 and under Free.

This is a surprisingly large museum with a nationally acclaimed collection in four separate wings. Exhibits range from the prized million-year-old saber-toothed tiger to an 1890 steam donkey used in local logging camps. Native American artifacts that predate Crater Lake, a "mud wagon" that traveled the roads of nineteenth-century Southern Oregon, and a large collection of historic photographs will have your kids enthralled. They'll love the hands-on Discovery Room too.

WILDLIFE SAFARI

1790 Safari Road, Winston; take exit 119 from Interstate 5 at Winston and follow signs on State Highway 42 for about 5 miles; (800) 355–4848 or (541) 679–6761; www.wildlifesafari.org. $14.55 adults, $8.50 ages 4–12, 3 and under Free.

You'll find an open zoo where emus peck at your car windows and baby pygmy goats in the petting area beg for food in ice cream cone cups. African elephants provide entertainment twice daily, and your child can ride one of these giant creatures, pretending to be a Raja on a tiger hunt in the jungles of India. Trains run, weather permitting, within the central Safari Village, and you can grab a bite to eat in the White Rhino restaurant. Check out the botanical gardens, too.

DIAMOND LAKE CORRALS (ages 8 and up)
DIAMOND LAKE BICYCLING (ages 5 and up)

Located near Diamond Lake Lodge, 76 miles east of Roseburg along the North Umpqua Highway; (800) 733–7593; www.diamondlake.net. Open year-round.

Trail rides from a few hours long to overnight can be arranged through the resort.

You can also rent mountain bikes to ride along the paved 12-mile bike path that circles the lake, and is transformed into a cross-country ski trail in winter. Cross-country skis, inner tubes, and snowmobiles also can be rented from **Diamond Lake Lodge.**

An Adventure to Remember

An Adventure to Remember Snuggled tightly in the rolling hills of western Douglas County, **Wildlife Safari** has come a long way since its beginnings in the 1970s as a for-profit open-zoo enterprise. Today, the 600-acre savanna successfully provides a natural habitat that closely resembles the native homes of elephants, bears, gazelles, rhinos, zebras, and ostriches, among others. And it's now a member of the Safari Game Search Foundation, a non-profit organization dedicated to the conservation, education, research, and rehabilitation of animals.

The grounds provide a marvelous opportunity for you and your family to observe animal interaction in an unrestrained, bucolic setting. If you're near Roseburg, include this destination in your travels.

BICYCLING AND RAFTING

A number of outfitters offer guided fishing and whitewater trips on the North Umpqua River. Two local outdoor specialists are:

- **North Umpqua Outfitters.** *222 Oakview Drive; (541) 673–4599 or (888) 789–7152; www.nuorafting.com. Call for schedules, prices.*

- **Oregon Ridge and River Excursions.** *P.O. Box 495, Glide 97443; (541) 496–3333 or (888) 454–9696; www.rafting.rosenet.net. Call for schedules, prices.*

The Oregon Ridge part of the latter's name refers to mountain bike excursions, which they also offer. This North Umpqua River outfitter offers daily excursions.

STEWART PARK (all ages)

Located on Stewart Parkway on the west side of town, off Garden Valley Road; (541) 672–7701. Open dawn to dusk. **Free**.

Kids love climbing on the old steam locomotive in the large playground. The 230-acre park also has horseshoe pits and tennis courts, wide green fields, and a nature trail leading from the wildlife pond through an old orchard and along the North Umpqua River. On summer Tuesday evenings, take your kids to an outdoor concert at the band shell.

SUSAN CREEK FALLS TRAIL (ages 5 and up)

Starts in the day-use area of the Susan Creek Campground, off State Highway 138 about 28 miles east of Roseburg; (541) 440–4930; www.or.blm.gov. Always open. $11.00 per campsite per night.

This 2-mile trail leads to a group of fascinating Indian mounds. You'll walk through a young forest of mixed conifers and madrones with a thick undergrowth of salal, fern, and huckleberry. At ¾ mile, the falls cascade nearly 70 feet down a cliff side into a boulder-bordered pool. Beyond the falls, follow the footbridge up a fairly steep hill for another ½ mile to the Indian mounds—ceremonial rock piles prepared by young men in spiritual quest. These are cultural treasures that should not be disturbed. The location also houses 31 campsites that are open May through October.

⊥op Roseburg Events

JUNE

Umpqua Valley Roundup and Parade. This event features the only summertime Professional Rodeo Cowboy's Association rodeo, plus arts and crafts, and dancing. (541) 672–2648.

JUNE–AUGUST

Music on the Half Shell. Located in lovely Stewart Park, this *Free* summer series features a variety of music programs ranging from zydeco and Cajun to African. Pack a picnic dinner and relax! (800) 444–9584, ext. 10; www.halfshell.org.

JULY

Graffiti Week. 1950s car owners from the West Coast gather for car shows, a fun run, concerts, and '50s-style fun. (800) 444–9584.

Crater Lake National Park

CRATER LAKE NATIONAL PARK (all ages)
P.O. Box 7, Crater Lake 97604; (541) 594–2211, Ext. 402; (541) 830–8700 for lodging and boat-tour information; www.crater-lake.com. Park is open year-round; camping available when snow clears in early summer; lodging available mid-May through mid-October. $10 for a seven-day vehicle pass.
North entrance is located off State Highway 138, from Roseburg; two visitor centers, Steel Information Center, at the junction of the south entrance road and Rim Drive, and the Rim Village Visitor Center near the east end of the parking area, provide a wealth of informational materials. The park entrance at the south

gate is off State Highway 62, which runs between Medford and Klamath Falls. In winter, access to the park is by way of State Highway 62 only. Rim Drive is closed in winter, but intrepid Nordic skiers can take the 33-mile unplowed road circling the rim of the lake on skis. Watch for ice, and check with park rangers for avalanche warnings before you begin.

It's difficult not to describe Crater Lake in superlatives: The bluest water, the most dramatic contrasts, and the clearest air all leave visitors invigorated for days. Away from the lake itself, the forests are rich with surprises—deep river canyons, sparkling waterfalls, bright and delicate wildflowers. You'll want to take your time exploring here. The geology and history of the area are equally fascinating. In the last 750,000 years, explosive eruptions created a series of volcanic peaks along what we now call the Cascade Range. Mt. Mazama, which holds Crater Lake in its peak, was one of these, and for 500,000 years it erupted regularly. About 8,000 years ago, the most violent eruption of all took place in a series of massive explosions forty-two times more powerful than Mt. St. Helens's 1980 blast. The winds scattered as much as 6 inches of ash over 5,000 square miles, covering eight states and three Canadian provinces. In the **Pumice Desert,** north of the rim, the ash is 50 feet deep. The eruptions emptied the mountain of magma, removing the support for the mountain peak. The peak collapsed, forming the bowl-shaped caldera that, at first, was too hot to hold water. As volcanic activity slowed, the caldera filled with water. The volcano has been silent for 4,000 years.

> # Fun Fact
> Crater Lake is the deepest lake in North America, the second deepest in the Western Hemisphere, and the seventh deepest in the world.

Many children prefer the Klamath Indian version of events that created the mountain lake. A battle began between the god of the world above, Skell, who lived on Mt. Shasta to the south, and the evil god of the world below, Llao. Skell won the battle, beheading the mountain of Llao and forever ridding the world of his evil influence, leaving in his place a beautiful mirrored lake that reflects the sky. Look for **Llao Rock,** which dominates the northwest portion of the lake and faces **Skell Head,** across the lake on the east side. From the parking lot at the rim, walk the paved path down to the **Sinnott Memorial Overlook,** where a rock shelter hewn from the side of the caldera provides a breathtaking view. A topographical relief map of Mt. Mazama shows the lake, **Wizard Island,** and the surrounding area. Along the park's south entrance road on State Highway 62, stop at one of several pullouts or picnic areas to view a breathtaking canyon through which Annie Creek runs more than 250 feet below.

To explore the environs of Crater Lake more deeply, take the **Annie Creek Trail,** which leaves between Loops D and E in the Mazama Campground and follows a 1⁷⁄₁₀-mile loop descending 200 feet to the valley floor and along the stream before ascending the rim to complete the circuit. Other trails to explore are the **Castle Crest Wildflower Trail,** a ⁴⁄₁₀-mile loop that begins across from the Steel Information Center just beyond the junction of East and West Rim drives, and the **Godfrey Glen Nature Trail,** about 1 mile beyond Mazama Village on the road to the rim. Rangers sometimes lead walks, or you can purchase inexpensive leaflets at the trailhead. The only safe—and legal—access to the lake is the 1-mile **Cleetwood Cove Trail,** on the West Rim Road about 13 miles from Rim Village. You must be in good physical condition to attempt this steep hike down the walls of the caldera. Once there, you can dip your feet in the water or try your hand at catching some of the kokanee salmon or rainbow trout that remain in the lake, which was stocked with these species between 1888 and the 1940s, when park rangers decided to allow the lake to return to its natural state. During summer, boat tours of the lake are offered from this point. The **Volcano Cruise Boat Tour** is the only company allowed to have a boat on the lake and offers up-close views from inside the caldera. You can also stop and spend some time on Wizard Island, returning on a later tour. The two-hour narrated tour takes you past the **Phantom Ship,** remnants of an older volcano and dike that were exposed after the great eruption. The boat tours operate daily late June through mid-September, weather permitting. You can rent skis at the **Rim Village store** from Thanksgiving to April. The **Llao Rock Cafe and Gift Shop** are open daily. There are no camping or lodging facilities available in the park from mid-October through late May.

Free Things to Do in Crater Lake

- **Mazama Campground Amphitheater.** Your family will enjoy the public programs offered in the amphitheater in summer, including guided nature walks and evening talks.

- **Steel Information Center.** The center shows the "Crater Lake Movie" every half hour in summer.

Klamath Falls

Klamath Falls sits on the southern tip of Upper Klamath Lake, the largest lake in the state at 58,992 acres, with Mt. McLoughlin casting its reflection in the waters. In summer months you can hop aboard a restored 1906 trolley through the downtown area to get a sense of the area and its history.

 BALDWIN HOTEL MUSEUM (ages 5 and up)

31 Main Street; located in the old Baldwin Hotel; (541) 883–4207. Open June through September, Tuesday through Saturday, 10:00 A.M.–6:00 P.M. Admission based on number of floors toured. Two floors $3.00, four floors $4.00. Family rates available.

Guided tours take you back to the early 1900s, with the original furnishings and many photographs by the builder's talented daughter.

 FAVELL MUSEUM OF WESTERN ART AND INDIAN ARTIFACTS (ages 5 and up)

125 West Main Street; (541) 882–9996; www.favellmuseum.com. Open June through September, Monday through Saturday, 9:30 A.M.–5:30 A.M.; Wednesday through Saturday the rest of the year. $4.00 adults; $2.00 ages 6–16.

Arrowheads, ceremonial knives, stone- and beadwork, basketry, and pottery captivate the kids. See the silver treasure from an abandoned wagon train and tour the walk-in vault display of miniature working firearms, including a Gatling gun.

 KLAMATH COUNTY MUSEUM (ages 5 and up)

1451 Main Street; (541) 883–4208. Open Tuesday through Saturday, 9:00 A.M.–5:00 P.M. $2.00 adults, $1.00 students.

Natural history, Indian and pioneer history, and agricultural development are all on display in the museum. Your kids will see up close some of the birds and animals they might encounter in the natural areas around Klamath Falls, and they'll learn about the geothermal energy resources that have been used in the area for centuries.

 UPPER KLAMATH LAKE (all ages)

Located north of Klamath Falls on U.S. 97; (800) 445–6728 or (541) 884–0666; www.klamathnwr.org. Always open. Free.

On the northwest shore are two marked **canoe trails** that wind through the tule marshes. Redwing blackbirds perch like sentinels on the cattails, and white pelicans soar on the high winds above. Pick up a checklist of the 250 bird species to be seen in the refuge and have your kids see how many they can check off during your stay.

UPPER KLAMATH CANOE TRAIL (all ages)

Begins at Malone Springs launch 4 miles from the junction of State Highway 140 and West Side Road (take Rocky Point turnoff), northwest of Klamath Falls; (530) 667–2331; www.klamathnwr.org/ukcanoe.html. Open dawn to dusk.

The canoe trails meander through marsh land on the edge of Upper Klamath Lake. You can rent canoes at **Rocky Point Resort** on Rocky Point Road (541-356-2287; www.rockypointoregon.com).

OVER THE HILL LIVE STEAM CLUB (all ages)

Located 27 miles north of Klamath Falls; (541) 783–3030; www.sscom.org/oth.html. Open Sunday, 10:00 A.M.–3:00 P.M. Memorial Day through Labor Day. Call about prices.

The club operates a one-eighth-scale train park that is open to the public from the weekend before Father's Day to Labor Day weekend. Bring a picnic to enjoy at tables set up for guests. The trains, a mixture of diesel and live steam engines, pull cars with comfortable seats, roomy enough for adults, along thousands of feet of track.

SUN PASS RANCH (all ages)

52125 Highway 62; P.O. Box 499; Fort Klamath 97626; (888) 777–9005 or (541) 381–2259; www.virtualcities.com/ons/or/c/orc4701.htm; E-mail: sunpass@aol.com. Open year-round. Bed-and-breakfast $75; guided horseback tours $25 per person for the first hour.

Located in a pristine rural setting, the ranch offers horseback riding and river float trips, pony rides, mountain bike rentals, cross-country skiing, fly-fishing, and a ranch-style bed and breakfast.

Fun Facts

- The area boasts the largest wintering population of American **bald eagles** in the forty-eight contiguous states.

- **Upper Klamath Lake**, at 58,992 acres, is the largest lake in Oregon.

COLLIER MEMORIAL STATE PARK (all ages)

Located 30 miles north of Klamath Falls; (800) 551–6949 or (541) 783–2471; www.oregonstateparks.org. Open dawn to dusk; call for museum hours. **Free**.

The museum side of the park is open year-round and houses rotating exhibits; camping is closed in winter. Straddling the highway, the park has a beautiful picnic area in a shaded ponderosa pine forest alongside the Williamson River and an open-air logging museum across the highway that some claim has the largest collection of logging equipment in the nation. Children appreciate the sense of scale and the absence of "do not touch" signs. There's also an authentic pioneer village with buildings relocated from their original sites.

 ### FORT KLAMATH MUSEUM (all ages)

Located on Highway 62, 2 miles south of Crater Lake; (800) 445–6728 or (541) 883–4208. Open Thursday through Monday, 10:00 A.M.–6:00 P.M. June through August. **Free** *but donations appreciated.*

The museum is now a military post that was established in 1863. The displays depict the Modoc Indian War of 1872–73. In the park are the graves of the fearless Modoc chief Captain Jack and three braves who fought against the U.S. Army in the most extensive Indian war in the West.

Top Klamath Events

AUGUST

Klamath County Fair & Jefferson Stampede Rodeo. You'll receive a two-for-one series of events that fill your entire weekend. (541) 883-3796.

DECEMBER

Snowflake Festival. A holiday bazaar, a parade, a toy show, a holiday play, and a tree lighting help usher in the holiday season. (541) 883-5368.

Lakeview

First settled in the 1870s by sheep and cattle ranchers, Lakeview calls itself the "tallest town in Oregon" because it has the highest elevation above sea level of any incorporated town in the state.

SCHMINCK MEMORIAL MUSEUM (ages 5 and up)

128 South "E" Street; (541) 947–3134. Open Tuesday through Saturday, 1:00–5:00 P.M.; closed December to January. $2.00 adults; children under 13 Free.

Kids love the doll and toy collection in the basement, and the old vacuum cleaners behind the kitchen area will bring on a few giggles. Baseball fans will covet the silk baseball cards of such early players as Ty Cobb and Rebel Oakes.

 WARNER CANYON SKI AREA (ages 8 and up)

Located 10 miles northeast of Lakeview off State Highway 140 in the Fremont National Forest; (541) 947–6040; www.fs.fed.us/r6/freemont/rogs/warncan. htm or www.lakecountychamber.org/warner_canyon_ski_area.org (lists current schedule and prices). Call for hours, lift prices.

With fourteen downhill runs and several miles of Nordic trails, as well as great sledding opportunities, this county-run ski area is a great place for families with a hankering for some outdoor winter fun.

 FORT ROCK STATE NATURAL AREA (all ages)

Located north of Silver Lake, 7 miles off State Highway 31; (800) 551–6949; www.oregonstateparks.org. Always open. Free.

This area rises nearly 400 feet from the desert shelf. Archaeologists discovered a pair of 9,200-year-old woven sandals here and one is now housed in the Lake County Museum.

 FORT ROCK STATE MONUMENT (all ages)

Located 1 mile north of the rock, within Fort Rock State Park; (541) 938–6055 or (800) 551–6949; www.oregonstateparks.org. Open dawn to dusk. Free.

A half-mile trail takes you inside an ancient volcanic maar that rose within a 40-mile-wide lake, which Native Americans lived by more than 10,000 years ago.

 LAKE COUNTY MUSEUM (ages 5 and up)

118 South G Street; (541) 947–2220. Open May through October, Monday through Saturday, 9:00 A.M.–4:30 P.M.; February through April, Wednesday through Friday, 10:00 A.M.–4:00 P.M. Closed November through January. $2.00 adults; children Free.

Historical displays portray with artifacts the Native American culture indigenous to the area.

op Lakeview Events

JUNE

Junior Rodeo. For a chance to see young people compete on horseback, come to this event held early in the summer. (541) 947–6040.

SEPTEMBER

Lake County Round-Up. The event is held during the Lake County Fair. A wild-cow milking contest is guaranteed to have your kids roaring with laughter. (541) 947–6040.

FREMONT NATIONAL FOREST

Located 8 miles west of Lakeview on State Highway 140; (541) 947–2151; www.fs.fed.us/r6/fremont. Always open.

Fremont National Forest has an abundance of lakes and streams for you to explore with your kids. **Drews Reservoir** is a popular spot for waterskiing as well as fishing and swimming. **Cottonwood Meadow Lake,** north of State Highway 140, is surrounded by aspen and pine forests, with a trail that circles the lake and connects two camping areas. South of the highway, **Lofton Reservoir, Heart Lake,** and **Holbrook Reservoir** are accessible from various U.S. Forest Service roads, and all are well maintained even though some are gravel.

amily Favorites in Southern Oregon

1. Oregon Shakespeare Festival, Ashland

2. Rogue River, near Ashland

3. Oregon Caves National Monument

4. Crater Lake National Park

5. The House of Mystery, near Grants Pass

6. Favell Museum of Western Art and Indian Artifacts, Klamath Falls

7. Fremont National Forest, near Lakeview

8. Susan Creek Falls Trail, near Roseburg

9. Wildlife Safari, Winston

10. Douglas County Museum of History and Natural History, Roseburg

Where to Eat

IN ASHLAND

Alex's Plaza Restaurant. 35 North Main Street; (541) 482–8818. Sitting alongside Ashland Creek, Alex's has a diverse menu sure to please everyone. $–$$$

Ashland Creek Bar and Grill. 92½ East Main; (541) 482–4131. Also nestled along the creek, this place serves burgers, sandwiches, and salads. $$

Ashland Bakery and Café. 38 East Main Street; (541) 482–2117. Enjoy morning pastries and cappuccino at breakfast, or a lunch of delicious home-style soup and bread; dinner also served. $$

Señor Sam's. 1634 Ashland Street; (541) 488–1262. The specialty is healthy Mexican food. The restaurant received the "Best Burritos" in Ashland vote. $

IN MEDFORD

Hometown Buffet. 1299 Center Drive; (541) 770–6779; www.buffet.com. Nothing fancy, just plenty of choices and the largest salad bar in town. It's a very affordable place to feed the whole family. $$

IN JACKSONVILLE

Bella Union Restaurant. 170 West California; (541) 899–1770; www.bellau. com. It may be housed in the building where the Bella Union Saloon was one of seven local saloons in 1868, but you won't find typical saloon fare in this upscale spot. Instead your choices will include pasta, pizza, steak, and seafood. $$

IN GRANTS PASS

The Laughing Clam. 121 Southwest G Street; (541) 479–1110. The menu at this casual family restaurant is varied enough to make everyone happy. $

Yankee Pot Roast. 720 Northside Sixth Street; (541) 476–0551. Fine family dining in comfortable surroundings. $$–$$$

Wild River Brewing & Pizza Co. 595 Northeast E Street; (541) 471–7487. Here's a pizza place that serves its specialty with a flair. Parents appreciate the local microbrew. $–$$

IN ROSEBURG

La Hacienda. 940 Northwest Garden Valley Boulevard; (541) 672–5330. Good Mexican food. $–$$

Brutke's Wagon Wheel. 227 Northwest Garden Valley Boulevard; (541) 672–7555. This pasta and prime rib eatery is a local family favorite. $$$–$$$

Cafe Espresso. 368 Southeast Jackson; (541) 672–1859. This is a good place to stop for a snack of cookies or pastries and good java. $

IN CRATER LAKE NATIONAL PARK

Llao Rock Cafe. P.O. Box 7, Crater Lake 97604; (541) 594–2211, Ext. 402; www. crater-lake.com. The cafeteria menu features simple fare: hamburgers, soups, chili, and a salad bar. $

IN KLAMATH FALLS

Mia and Pia's Pizzeria and Brewhouse. *3545 Summers Lane; (541) 884–7777.* $$

IN LAKEVIEW

Indian Village Restaurant. *508 North First Street; (541) 947–2833.* A gift shop and arrow collection displayed on the walls of the restaurant and lounge will interest the kids. The standard steak-and-burgers menu is a safe bet. $–$$

Where to Stay

IN ASHLAND

Mt. Ashland Inn. *550 Mt. Ashland Ski Road; (800) 830 8707 or (541) 482–8707; www.mtashlandinn.com.* Five guest rooms. Located in a large log chalet; all rooms have private baths. The inn's owners will shuttle guests to the ski lodge, only 3 miles up the road. $$–$$$

Hyatt Lake Resort. *7979 Hyatt Prairie Road; (541) 482–3331.* RV and tent sites are available plus all kinds of activities to enjoy with your kids, including horseback riding, boating, mountain biking, and fishing in summer and cross-country skiing and general snow play in winter. $

Stratford Inn. *555 Siskiyou; (800) 547–4741 or (541) 488–2151.* Just 5 blocks from the Shakespeare festival, this inn provides continental breakfast and has laundry facilities, a pool, and a spa. $$$

Windmill Inn of Ashland. *2525 Ashland Street; (800) 547–4747 or (541) 482–8310.* The inn offers kitchenettes and refrigerators plus continental breakfasts. Pets are welcome. $$$–$$$$

Bed-and-breakfast referrals are available through two different agencies in Ashland: **Ashland B&B Clearinghouse,** *(800) 588–0338; www.opendoor.com/clearinghouse;* **Ashland's B&B Network,** *(800) 944–0329; www.ABBNet.com.*

IN MEDFORD

Cedar Lodge Motor Inn. *518 North Riverside; (800) 282–3419 or (541) 773–7361; www.oregonfishing.com/cedarlodge.* Eighty units. A restaurant and continental breakfast are both conveniences available to inn guests. Pets are welcome too. $–$$$

Best Western Pony Soldier Inn. *2340 Crater Lake Highway; (800) 634–7669 or (541) 779–2011; www.bestwestern.com.* Seventy-three units. There's a restaurant on the complex and continental breakfast is available. It also has an outdoor pool and a spa pool. $$–$$$

Windmill Inn of Medford. *1950 Biddle Road; (800) 547–4747 or (541) 779–0050.* One hundred twenty-three units. A playground nearby makes parents and kids happy. Laundry facilities and kitchenettes are available too. $$–$$$

IN JACKSONVILLE

The Stage Lodge. *830 North Fifth Street; (800) 253–8254 or (541)*

899–3953. Twenty-seven rooms, two suites. Resembling a nineteenth-century stage stop, this two-story lodge has attractive decor that matches the rest of the town's ambience. They serve a continental breakfast too. $$–$$$$

Wolf Creek Inn. *100 Front; (541) 866–2474; www.wolfcreekinn.com.* Eight rooms. One of the state's oldest hostelries, the inn originally opened for business in 1880 as a stop along the Oregon-to-California stagecoach line. The rooms have been restored to reflect the authentic pre-1900 style. Includes continental breakfast. $$

IN GRANTS PASS

Riverside Inn Resort & Conference Center. *971 Southeast Sixth Street; (800) 334–4567 or (541) 476–6873; www. riverside-inn.com.* One hundred sevety-four units. This full-service inn stands next to the Rogue River, where the Hellgate jetboats take off. It has an outdoor pool, a spa pool, and a restaurant. $$$$

Travelodge. *1950 Northwest Vine Street; (888) 515–6375 or (541) 479–6611; www.travelodge.com.* Sixty-two units. A restaurant, continental breakfast, and laundry facilities make this a convenient place for families. $$$

IN CAVE JUNCTION

Oregon Caves Lodge. *20000 Caves Highway, P.O. Box 128; Cave Junction 97523; (541) 592–2100; call for open season.* Twenty-two units, four suites. This rustic six-story lodge was built in 1934. Nestled deep in the Siskiyou National Forest, there are plenty of opportunities for outdoor activities including nearby hiking and cave exploration. $$$–$$$$

IN ROSEBURG

Howard Johnson Express Inn. *978 Northeast Stephens Street; (800) 446–4656.* Thirty units. The full-service inn offers continental breakfasts, kitchenettes, an indoor swimming pool, and laundry facilities. $$

Windmill Inn of Roseburg. *1450 Northwest Mulholland; (800) 547–4747; www.windmillinns.com.* It has a swimming pool, whirlpool and sauna, guest bicycles, and a complimentary continental breakfast. Family packages available. $$

Big K Guest Ranch. *20029 State Highway 138 West near Elkton, about 40 miles northwest of Roseburg; (800) 390–2445 or (541) 584–2295; www.gib-k.com.* The Kesterson family welcomes guests in twenty modern, log-sided cabins on their ranch, which rests along 10 miles of the Umpqua River. They offer horseback riding, fishing, horseshoes, and lots of exploring possibilities. $$$–$$$$

East Lemolo Campground. *North off Highway 138, located 75 miles east of Roseburg on Road 2610; (541) 498–2531; www.fs.fed.us/r6/umpqua.* Fifteen pretty sites are located on Lemolo Lake. The campground has vault toilets, picnic tables, and fire rings, and the lake offers fishing and water skiing opportunities. $

Diamond Lake Campground. *West off Highway 138 about 80 miles east of Roseburg on Road 4795; (877) 444–6777; reserveusa.com.* Fireplaces, running water, flush toilets, and showers provide a little extra luxury to this camping experience. $

Diamond Lake Resort. *76 miles east of Roseburg along the North Umpqua Highway; (800) 733–7593; www.diamondlake.net.* A resort offers the sparkling solitude of a Cascade mountain lake but with amenities to enhance your family's fun. Hiking, biking, and horseback riding are all available in the vicinity. Motel rooms $$-$$$; cabins $$$$.

IN CRATER LAKE NATIONAL PARK

Crater Lake Lodge. *P.O. Box 2704, White City 97503; (541) 830–8700; www.crater-lake.com.* Seventy-one rooms. Located in Rim Village, extensive reconstruction work that began in 1989 is now complete. The lodge is open mid-May through mid-October. $$$$

Mazama Village Motor Inn. *(541) 830–8700; www.crater-lake.com.* Forty units. The inn is located in Mazama Village complex. Open June to September. $$$-$$$$

Mazama Campground and **Lost Creek Campground** (tents only). First-come, first-served. Campground spaces cannot be reserved and usually fill up by early afternoon in summer. $

IN KLAMATH FALLS

Best Western Klamath Inn. *4061 South Sixth Street; (877) 882–1200 or (541) 882–1200.* Fifty-two rooms. Continental breakfast and indoor pool. $$-$$$

Maverick Motel. *1220 Main Street; (800) 404–6690 or (541) 882–6688.*

Forty-nine units. You can cool off in the summer in the outdoor pool. They serve a continental breakfast and welcome pets too. $

Quality Inn & Suites. *100 Main Street; (800) 732–2025 or (541) 882–4666.* Eighty-one units. The facility offers a wide range of accommodations, some of which have kitchenettes. Continental breakfast is served and there's a restaurant on the premises. $$-$$$

Rocky Point Resort. *Located on upper Klamath Lake off Highway 14, 25 miles from Klamath Falls; (541) 356–2287.* Boat rentals, tent sites, and RV hookups as well as dining rooms, showers, and laundry facilities are offered. $

IN LAKEVIEW

Aspen Ridge Resort. *Located off Forest Road 3790 about 16 miles south of State Highway 140; (800) 393–3323 or (541) 884–8685; www.aspenrr.com.* Lodge rooms and self-catering cabins overlook a meadow where the ranch's cattle and buffalo roam. Horseback riding trips take you into the surrounding forest. In winter you can strap on cross-country skis or hop on a snowmobile. $$$-$$$$

Lakeview Lodge Motel. *301 North "G" Street; (541) 947–2181.* Forty units. The motel has a spa pool and an exercise room. Pets are welcome. $$-$$$

For More Information

Ashland Visitor Information Center. *110 East Main Street, Ashland, OR 97520; (541) 482–3486; www.ashlandchamber. com.*

Southern Oregon Visitors Association. *548 Business Park Drive, Medford, OR 97501; (800) 448–4856 or (541) 779–4691; www.sova.org; E-mail: sova@jeffnet.org.*

Grants Pass–Josephine County Chamber of Commerce/Grants Pass Visitors and Convention Bureau. *1995 Northwest Vine Street, Grants Pass, OR 97526; (800) 547–5927 or (541) 476–7717; www.visitgrantspass. org or www.grantspasschamber.org; E-mail: gpcoc@grantspass.com or vcb@visitgrants pass. org.*

Illinois Valley Chamber of Commerce. *201 Caves Highway, P.O. Box 312, Cave Junction, OR 97526; (541) 592–2631 or (541) 592–3326.*

Jacksonville Chamber of Commerce. *185 North Oregon Street, P.O. Box 33, Jacksonville, OR 97530; (541) 899–8118; www.jacksonvilleoregon.org; E-mail: jvillechamber@wave.net.*

Klamath County Department of Tourism. *507 Main Street, Klamath, OR 97601; (800) 445–6728 or (541) 884–0666; www.klamathcounty.net; E-mail: tourism@co.klamath.or.us.*

Klamath County Chamber of Commerce. *507 Main Street, Klamath, OR 97601; (541) 884–5193; www.klamath. org; E-mail: inquiry@klamath.org.*

Lake County Chamber of Commerce. *126 North East Street, Lakeview, OR 97630; (541) 947–6040; www.lakecountychamber.org.*

Medford Visitors & Convention Bureau. *101 East Eighth Street, Medford, OR 97501; (800) 469–6307 or (541) 772–6293 or (541) 779–4847; www.visit medford.org; E-mail: medjacc@magick.net.*

Roseburg Visitors and Convention Bureau. *410 Southeast Spruce Street, Roseburg, OR 97470; (800) 444–9584 or (541) 672–9731; www.visitroseburg.com.*

Eastern Oregon

The rolling wheatlands of the Columbia River Valley give way to the high Blue Mountains and Wallowa Mountains before dropping sharply into Hells Canyon of the Snake River. Grande Ronde River's colorful, carved canyons, the sage-scented high desert, and the painted hills around the John Day Fossil Beds testify to vast changes wrought over fifty million years of geological evolution. The landscape recalls the days of cowboys and bronco-busting, pioneers and wagon trains, sometimes so vividly that one feels transported back in time. One of the least-populated areas of the state, much of northeastern Oregon remains untouched, the terrain preserved as early pioneers would have encountered it. Walking in the actual path of the wagon trains and reading the words of the pioneer women and men who trod these paths imparts a sense of the past your kids won't find in any history books.

Baker City

This Old West gold mining town has recaptured its history by resurrecting its original name: Baker City. For years, the name had been shortened to Baker, but with the approach of the Oregon Trail Sesquicentennial celebrations, the town mined its roots for a wealth of historic interest. For a while in the 1960s, Baker was known as the site of "No Name City," the fictional location created for filming *Paint Your Wagon*, with Clint Eastwood and Lee Marvin. A complete frontier town was constructed for the filming, and a replica is displayed at the Oregon Trail Regional Museum.

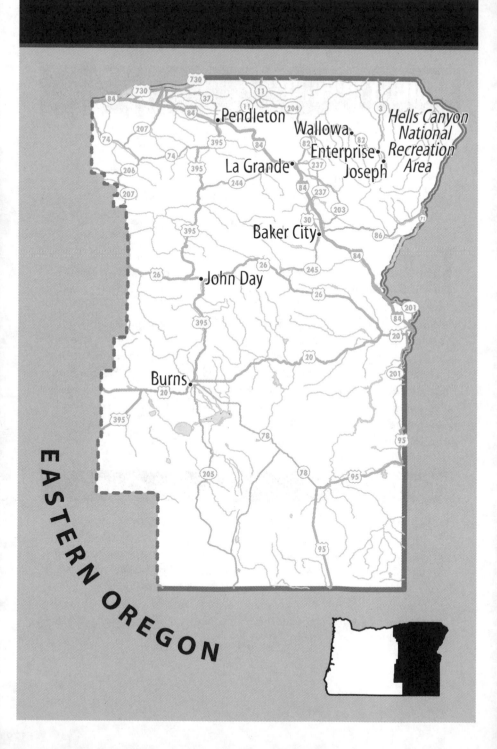

EASTERN OREGON

NATIONAL HISTORIC OREGON TRAIL INTERPRETIVE CENTER (all ages)

Located at Flagstaff Hill, about 5 miles from Baker City on State Highway 86; (541) 523–1843; www.or.blm.gov/NHOTIC; E-mail: Nhotic_Mail@or.blm.gov. Open daily, April 1 through October 31, 9:00 A.M.–6:00 P.M.; November 1 through March 31; 9:00 A.M.–4:00 P.M. $5.00 adults; $3.50 children.

Plan to spend all day here. At the heart of the center are exhibits of life-size figures speaking out as if you're overhearing their conversations along the trail. The historical accuracy and details are absorbing for both parents and children. In three minitheaters, well-made films integrated into a scenic backdrop provide insight into the experience of Oregon's early pioneers. Your kids can try to pack a miniature wagon with all the supplies needed to make the journey, having to make some tough choices about what to leave behind—a puzzle that can keep determined youngsters occupied for hours! Walking trails take you down the hill to several spots where wagon ruts are visible among the sagebrush. Some of the 4²⁄₁₀ miles of trails are quite steep, so you'll want to be in good shape. Ticks, rattlesnakes, and scorpions are local pests to be aware of on your walk. Take water, too, especially if you're walking in the heat of the day. A pioneer encampment and an old mine site are additional attractions.

 OREGON TRAIL REGIONAL MUSEUM (ages 5 and up)

2480 Grove Street; (541) 523–9308. Open daily, 9:00 A.M.–5:00 P.M., May 1 through October 30 (or by appointment). $3.50 adults; 75 cents children; $8.00 family rate.

Often confused with the National Historic Oregon Trail Interpretive Center, this museum, too, is worth a visit. A schoolroom replica includes some old schoolbooks your children will have fun looking through. An impressive rock and mineral collection, a fire wagon, and old carriages are other favorites. The replica of the complete frontier town built for the filming of *Paint Your Wagon* is on display.

 ALDER HOUSE MUSEUM (ages 5 and up)

2305 Main Street; (541) 523–9308. $4.00 adults; $1.00 children; $10.00 family. Call for hours.

You can take a guided tour of this restored historic house, which once belonged to Leo Alder, Baker City's greatest benefactor.

OREGON TRAIL MINIATURE GOLF (all ages)

42576 Old Trail Road; off Cedar Street at Interstate 84, exit 302; (541) 523–9348. Open daily, 10:00 A.M.–dusk, May 1 to October (weekends only in October). $4.00 for 36 holes; 6 and under **Free** *with an adult.*

Interestingly, this place combines trail lore with a bit of family recreation. Two outdoor miniature courses, eighteen holes each, are built around pioneer and mining themes. Old buildings, covered bridges, a mine shaft with timbers and a mine bucket that are actual relics of the area, and an authentic-looking mine tunnel will all challenge your skills.

ELKHORN DRIVE NATIONAL FOREST SCENIC BYWAY (all ages)

Travels in a 106-mile loop from Baker City through the Blue Mountains to the not-so-ghostly ghost towns of Sumpter and Granite and the more ghostly Auburn; (800) 523–1235 or (541) 523–3356; www.byways.org. Always open. **Free***.*

Once a wild frontier town where laws were posted on trees, Auburn grew to become the second largest town in Oregon. Now it's marked only by the gravesites of those left behind. Be sure your gas tank is full. Gas is available only in Baker City, Haines, Sumpter, and Granite.

Top Baker City Event

MEMORIAL DAY, FOURTH OF JULY, LABOR DAY WEEKENDS

Sumpter Valley Country Fair. This outdoor flea market spreads from the fairgrounds to the town area. The tiny town comes to life when literally thousands of visitors come through to look at the wares or enjoy an old-time fiddler's show. When the kids have had enough browsing, they can buy fresh Indian fry bread or barbecued beef sandwiches at one of the food stands set up for the occasion. (541) 894–2314.

SUMPTER

Sumpter, one of the most interesting of area "ghost towns," can be reached by State Highway 7, south of Phillips Lake. You'll pass the **Sumpter Valley Dredge,** a state park where a massive machine was used to dredge up the valley floor to be processed for gold. Point out to your children the long rows of rock piles left by the dredge all along the road. More than $10 million in gold came from dredging the Sumpter Valley alone.

GOLD POST GROCERIES & MUSEUM (all ages)

150 Northeast Mill Street; (541) 894–2362. Open daily, 7:30 A.M.–7:30 P.M.

This mercantile doubles as grocery store, gift shop, sporting goods store, and museum. You'll see old photos and artifacts of the region's gold mining days.

 ### SUMPTER VALLEY RAILROAD (all ages)

Leaves from the McEwen Station, 5½ miles down the valley toward Phillips Lake to the south end of Sumpter and back; (541) 894–2268. Operates the 5 miles between McEwen Station and Sumpter weekends, holidays May to September, call for schedule. $9.00 adults; $6.50 children 6–16; $22 family. Tickets can be purchased at either end.

No trip to Sumpter is complete without taking a train ride on the narrow-gauge steam locomotive as it whistles down 5 scenic miles of track. Vital to the settlement and development of Eastern Oregon, the Sumpter Valley Railroad was one of the most colorful and longest-lived narrow gauge railroads in the nation. Take a trip back in time, to an era when steam locomotives were the main mode of transportation, and logging and mining were the mainstays of the local economy.

John Day

John Day Fossil Beds National Monument is one of the best reasons for traveling to this part of the state. Aside from their vivid beauty, the canyons of the John Day River provide a window on prehistory that will give your children a better understanding of the expanse of time captured in the region's geography. For more information, visit the Web site at www.nps.gov/joda.

 ### KAM WAH CHUNG STATE HERITAGE SITE (ages 5 and up)

Located adjacent to Gleason Park; (541) 575–0028 or (800) 551–6949; www.oregonstateparks.org. Open May through October Monday through Saturday, 9:00 A.M.–noon and 1:00–5:00 P.M.; Sunday, 1:00–5:00 P.M. $3.00 adults; $2.50 ages 6–16; $1.00 under 6.

On personal tours, the museum director explains the purpose of some of the more unusual items housed in the museum. Shrines in each room seek to appease various deities, such as the kitchen god. Do you have any aspiring doctors in the family? They'll be especially fascinated with the collection of more than 500 Chinese medicinal herbs that were dispensed in the building.

An Adventure to Remember The Kam Wah Chung & Co.

building was constructed in the 1860s and served as a trading post on the main east-west highway during that period. The dim lighting that casts an eerie glow in the museum's rooms also beckons the curious to come explore its exotic ambience. You will see that Kam Wah Chung & Co. served as an efficient, multipurpose pharmacy, doctor's office, general store, religious shrine, and opium den. The museum has been left in almost the same state proprietor "Doc" Ing Hay left it when he locked the doors in 1948. Hay and fellow proprietor Lung On purchased the building in the 1880s, and the two men soon became important members of the local community. Lung On was a respected entrepreneur, and Hay was considered the most famous herbal medicine doctor between Seattle and San Francisco. You can spend well over an hour under this tiny roof as your imagination runs wild contemplating the clandestine opium exchanges, and examining sundries that now lay dormant on dusty shelves. More than 500 Chinese medicinal herbs, and gold mining and logging tools, are wedged next to canned goods, tobaccos, and notions. Several Buddhist shrines still coated with incense are housed here too, giving testimony to Hay's position as the region's chief priest for the Chinese. Don't miss this museum, the contents of which are said to provide the best historical account of the integration of Oriental and Occidental cultures in the United States, and the prosperous gold mining era in northeastern Oregon.

 **JOHN DAY RIVER (ages 10 and up)**
John Day Middle Fork intersects Highway 19 about 45 miles west of Baker City; www.nps.gov/rivers/johnday.html. Best times March to June. Always open. Free.
Recreation, from fishing to float trips, is a highlight of this region. Most of the river is smooth-flowing enough for canoes and beginning rafters.

Fun Facts

- The John Day River has more miles of wild and scenic designation than any other river in the United States.

- After **gold** was discovered in 1862, $26 million in the shiny stuff was mined from the John Day–Canyon City region.

SHEEP ROCK UNIT, JOHN DAY FOSSIL BED NATIONAL MONUMENT (all ages)

P.O. Box 126; Located 7 miles northwest of Dayville on State Highway 19, just beyond the junction with U.S. 26; (541) 987–2333; www.nps.gov/joda. Visitor center open daily, 9:00 A.M.–5:00 P.M.; closed weekends from Thanksgiving through February. Monument open daily dawn to dusk. **Free**.

This historic visitor center and museum is a good place to begin accumulating information about the area. The museum has fossil displays of prehistoric creatures that once roamed this region—from saber-toothed cats to elephants and rhinos—between six and fifty million years ago. A fifteen-minute film presents a synopsis of the area's geological history in terms your children will understand. The grounds of the center make a perfect picnic spot. At a small laboratory in an old log shed, park rangers demonstrate some of the tools and techniques used to remove fossil specimens from the stone encasing them. Your children will be fascinated by the tiny jackhammers and will enjoy the idea of dental tools being used to scrape fossil teeth rather than their teeth. Park rangers guide walks on some of the trails throughout the summer. Pick up trail maps and program schedules at the center, then head up the road to explore. The monument covers 14,000 acres in three separate units, the largest of which is the **Sheep Rock Unit.** Trails in this section include two in the **Blue Basin,** with its stunning blue-green canyons, just 2½ miles north of the visitor center. About 3 miles farther north on State Highway 19, you'll see the striations of **Cathedral Rock,** one of the hallmark images of this area.

PAINTED HILLS (all ages)

Located Northwest of Mitchell; (541) 987–2333. Open daily dawn to dusk. **Free**.

The Monument's Painted Hills offer a close-up look at the eroded hills of multi-million-year-old colorful volcanic ash. The best views are at dawn and dusk after a rain, when the moisture brings out the spectacular hues in the mineral-rich clays. A ¾-mile hike leads to an outstanding rim view and a short self-guided walk to **Painted Cove** offers a close view of the colorful claystones.

STRAWBERRY MOUNTAIN WILDERNESS (ages 8 and up)

Located 11 miles southeast of John Day; (541) 820–3311; www.fs.fed/r6/ malheur. Closed winter season. **Free**.

Located in the **Malheur National Forest,** the Strawberry Mountain Wilderness has more than 100 miles of hiking trails as well as several campgrounds. **Strawberry Lake** is one of the more accessible lakes in the wilderness, although the trail climbs steadily for about 1³⁄₁₀ miles and can be tiring for little ones. From Prairie City, head south on Forest Road 60 to the **Strawberry Lake Campground,** about 12 miles south of U.S. 26. You can set up camp here and take a day trip into the lake, or backpack into one of several wilderness sites near the lake, where you must leave behind no trace of your visit.

Top John Day Events

JUNE

John Day Valley Mule Classic. Horses and mules, venerated in this part of the state for centuries, are honored and celebrated in this summer fest. (800) 769–5664 or (541) 575–0547.

AUGUST

Grant County Fair and NPRA Rodeo. This county fair has all the fixings for a family weekend of fun. (541) 575–1900.

Burns

When you get into the southeastern corner of Oregon, you're entering one of the least populated areas of the country. Harney and Malheur counties together account for 20,154 square miles of land—more than Massachusetts and New Jersey combined—and only 34,900 people—fewer than the student population of some universities. That's part of the reason you feel as if you've entered deep Australian outback when you're driving through this country of broad sagebrush deserts and lonely mountain crags. As the major population center in the southeast, Burns is a natural place from which to begin exploring the vast range of outdoor opportunities that awaits visitors. The city received its name because of the fondness early postmaster George McGowen, one of the town's founders, had for Scottish poet Robert Burns.

HARNEY COUNTY HISTORICAL MUSEUM (ages 5 and up)

18 West D Street; (541) 573–5618; www.burnsmuseum.com. Open Tuesday through Saturday, 9:00 A.M.–5:00 P.M.; April to September. Call for admission information.

Look for the armored wagon at the edge of the parking lot. Once a brewery, it's now a hands-on museum where your kids can turn the apple peeler and lift the hand irons to get a feel for the work that had to be done to keep a family together a century ago.

  OCHOCO NATIONAL FOREST, DELINTMENT LAKE (all ages)

3160 Northeast Third Street; lies 42 miles northwest of Burns via Forest Road 41; (541) 416–6500; www.fs.fed.us/r6/centraloregon. Always open. Free forest access, Delintment Lake $2.00 during week, $3.00 during weekend.

This lake was created by damming Delintment Creek. Campsites in the ponderosa pine forest are suitable for tents or RVs. A picnic area and boat ramp are also available.

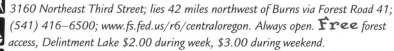

Fun Fact

Close to Delintment Lake in Ochoco National Forest is the largest Douglas fir in the continental United States—standing more than 158 feet tall with a 23½-foot base.

 FISH LAKE (all ages)

 Located about 18 miles east of Frenchglen; (541) 573–4400; www.or.blm.gov/ burns. Open dawn to dusk during season; closed November to May. $8.00 overnight fee.

There's a boat ramp for nonmotorized boats, as well as twenty campsites in both shaded and open areas. A trail joins two sections of the campground, on opposite sides of the lake. The wildflowers here— and all along the loop road—are stunning, especially in July.

Page Springs, another campground, is just 4 miles east of French-glen. Open year-round, it has thirty campsites, toilets, water (seasonally), fireplaces, and limited firewood. There's a $6.00 camping fee when water is available.

FRENCHGLEN

Both the Steens Mountain Loop Road and the Malheur National Wildlife Refuge loop tours take you through this tiny town, perhaps best known for its century-old hotel.

FRENCHGLEN HOTEL (all ages)

State Highway 205, Frenchglen 97736; (800) 551–6949 or (541) 493–2825; www.oregonstateparks.org. Operates March 15 through November 15. Call for rates.

Now a State Historic Wayside Park, the eight-room hotel is an oasis for travelers to this region where many miles separate even the closest towns. The hotel provides lodging and meals for visitors coming to enjoy birdwatching and wildlife. Whether or not you stay at the hotel, you can stop by for sodas or coffee, or just enjoy a picnic in the shaded yard. Breakfast, lunch, and dinner are served daily to residents and drop-in guests. Reservations are a must for dinner meals, which are described as "ranch-house cuisine with a '90s flair."

MCCOY CREEK INN (all ages)

Located 10 miles south of State Highway 205 from Diamond Junction; (541) 493–2131. Reservations required. $60–$75 per night.

The inn is a working ranch that's been in the same family for five generations. Children can explore McCoy Creek Canyon, wade in the stream, or feed the ducks, peacocks, turkeys, chickens, or calves. Watch for the raccoons, beaver, porcupine, and deer that inhabit the canyon and come to the meadows around the ranch to feed.

WARNER WETLANDS (ages 5 and up)

Located southwest of Burns, which borders the western side of Hart Mountain Antelope Refuge; (541) 947–2177; www.or.blm.gov/lakeview. Open dawn to dusk until winter, when area is closed. Free.

The wetlands were established to protect the Warner Valley's unique features and restore critical wildlife habitat. The wetland lakes and ponds go through a natural cycle of drying and filling that increases productivity by recycling nutrients and invigorating plant communities. At Hart Lake, stop and walk the footpaths on dikeways to the viewing blinds. Bring binoculars and a bird identification book to enrich your experience. Boating in this area depends greatly on the water levels, however, and these vary wildly. Even in late summer during high drought conditions, wildlife viewing is terrific—Canada geese, great white egrets, white pelicans, sandhill cranes, great blue heron, cinnamon teal, cormorants, and yellow-headed blackbirds are just a few of the species we spotted from the road alone.

PETER FRENCH ROUND BARN (all ages)

Located southeast of Burns and Malheur Lake near New Princeton, road signs direct you to the site from State Highway 205; (541) 573–2636. Hours change seasonally; call first. Free.

The barn is worth a stop for both historic and architectural reasons. Built before 1884 of native rock and juniper trees, the structure is fascinating. It's shaped like a Chinese umbrella with timbered "spokes" leading to a central truss. Peter French used the barn for breaking saddle horses.

SHELDON NATIONAL WILDLIFE REFUGE AND HART MOUNTAIN NATIONAL ANTELOPE REFUGE (all ages)

Located 37 miles from Frenchglen; the road surface becomes gravel just prior to climbing the escarpment of Hart Mountain; (541) 947–3315; www.wildernet. com or www.pacific.fws.gov. Open dawn to dusk until winter, when area is closed. Free.

This wildlife refuge is also accessible, along mostly paved roads, from the southern Oregon town of Lakeview. All vehicles must keep to the designated roads—for more reasons than the regulation. Established in 1936 to protect the dwindling herds of antelope, the refuge authority now includes the protection of all wildlife in the area. In the higher elevations, you are likely to see mule deer, bighorn sheep, golden eagles, and prairie falcons. Campgrounds and hot springs are available within the refuge.

WILD HORSE CORRALS (all ages)

Just west of Hines, on U.S. 20; (541) 573–4456; www.or.blm.gov/Burns. Open weekdays, year-round, 7:30 A.M.–3:00 P.M. Free.

Wild horses are free-roaming, unbranded descendants of horses turned loose by, or escaped from, the U.S. Cavalry, ranchers, prospectors, or Indian tribes in the late 1800s to 1930s. At certain times of the year, you can see wild horses in the corrals operated by the Bureau of Land Management or at various viewpoints around the Steens Mountain area.

Rockhounding

An activity for all ages, rockhounding is one of the major tourist attractions in this area. Government-managed properties do not charge a fee for removing rocks but call the Harney County Chamber of Commerce first (541-573-2636) about the requirements for each area.

- **Steens Mountain.** *Located 60 miles south of Burns; (541) 573-2636.* Agate, jasper, obsidian, and thunder eggs can be dug near Buchanan Road at the base of the mountain.

- **Burns.** *Located off State Highway 205; (541) 573-2636.* Agates are abundant at the quarry just south near the Narrows, the strip of land between Harney and Malheur lakes.

- **Glass Butte.** *Located 55 miles west of Burns on U.S. 20; (541) 573-2636.* The butte is so named because it is composed almost entirely of volcanic glass, or obsidian. This area was used extensively by Native Americans for gathering obsidian used to make arrowheads. Collecting arrowheads is against federal law, so if you find any, leave them for the next person to appreciate. All kinds of obsidian can be found near here—lace, rainbow, mahogany, gold sheen, black, and banded.

 MALHEUR NATIONAL WILDLIFE REFUGE (all ages)

From Burns, take State Highway 78 south, turn right on State Highway 205 for 28 miles and left at refuge sign; (541) 493–2612; www.pacific.fws.gov/malheur. Visitor center open Monday through Friday, 7:00 A.M.–4:30 P.M.; closed at 3:30 P.M. Friday; museum and refuge open daily, dawn to dusk. **Free**.

Located in the Blue Mountains south of Burns, Malheur is one of the best places to view birds and waterfowl in the state. Before leaving Burns, be sure to fill the gas tank. The refuge encompasses both Malheur and Harney lakes, as well as a narrow stretch of land bordering State Highway 205 south of Burns. Established by President Theodore Roosevelt in 1908, the refuge covers 183,000 acres and is home to more than 350 species of birds and 58 mammal species. Obtain a list of species at the headquarters, located on the south shore of Malheur Lake, 5 miles from State Highway 205 along a paved road. The headquarters consists of both a visitor center and a museum, which contains nearly 200 mounted bird specimens. It's a great opportunity for your children to see up close the birds they might spot through binoculars on the refuge.

STEENS MOUNTAIN (all ages)

Located 60 miles south of Burns on State Highway 205 toward Frenchglen; (541) 573–4400; www.or.blm.gov/steens. Road open July to October. **Free**.

Steens Mountain Loop Road is the best way to explore the mountain; take a full day—or more—and drive the gravel-topped road, which is open only in summer. The road is rough in places, so you'll want to make sure your car is in good condition and has a full tank before you set out. One of the most dramatic geological features of the region, Steens Mountain is a 30-mile-long fault block that rises to an elevation of more than 9,700 feet. A breathtaking view from the rim looks down through the deep gorges of Kiger, Wildhorse, Big Indian, and Little Blitzen canyons, carved by glaciers a million years ago, into the dry Alvord Desert more than one mile below. The highest road in the state, it stops just short of the mountain's 9,733-feet summit. A short climb on foot takes you to the top of the jagged peak. Be prepared for dramatic shifts in the weather and keep a close eye on your children—the walls of the mountain are rocky and steep, and high winds can disrupt balance with surprising swiftness.

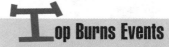

Top Burns Events

JUNE

Old Time Music Jamboree. There's an endless stream of music during this event. Don't miss it. (541) 573-2863.

SEPTEMBER

Harney County Fair, Rodeo & Race Meet. Rides, exhibits, food concessions and broncos will fill your entire weekend. (541) 573-1616.

La Grande

One of the towns settled by pioneers traveling the Oregon Trail, La Grande takes its name from the lush Grande Ronde Valley and the river that flows through its center.

 MEACHAM DIVIDE (ages 8 and up)

Located 19 miles northwest of La Grande near Meacham; (541) 963–7122. Open late, April to mid-December. Call for snow levels and fees.

Wintertime blankets the area with snow, making cross-country skiing a popular activity. You and your children can set out on groomed trails here.

ANTHONY LAKES MOUNTAIN RESORT (ages 5 and up)
Located 50 miles southwest of La Grande on Interstate 84, 19 miles west of the North Powder exit; (541) 856–3277; www.anthonylakes.com. Call for hours. Lift tickets $15–$28.

The resort has rope tows or Pomalifts for beginners, chair lifts for experienced skiers, ski and snowboard rentals, and meals on site. Anthony Lakes also offers 13 kilometers of groomed Nordic trails looping the lake.

LEHMAN HOT SPRINGS (ages 5 and up)
Located in Ukiah, 38 miles west of La Grande on State Highway 244; (541) 427–3015; www.lehmanhotsprings.com. Open year-round; call for hours. $6.00 admission for swimming; 3 and under Free.

The large, hot swimming pool, an unheated pool, and two smaller pools give you many choices for an afternoon soak.

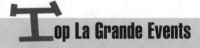

Top La Grande Events

JUNE

Eastern Oregon Livestock Show and PRCA Rodeo. Take the opportunity to enjoy the oldest rodeo in the Northwest. The event also includes horse racing, a carnival, and dancing. (800) 848–9969 or (541) 963–8588.

JULY

Elgin Stampede. Located in Elgin, 20 miles northeast of La Grande. Pro rodeo and a draft horse pulling contest are featured, plus a carnival, parade and races. (541) 437–4007.

AUGUST

Oregon Trail Days, Rendezvous, and Old-Time Fiddler's Contest. Besides good old-fashioned fiddlin', Trail Days features a pioneer encampment, a buffalo barbecue, and a Dutch oven cookoff. (800) 848–9969.

HOT LAKE RV RESORT (ages 5 and up)

65182 Hot Lake Lane, take Interstate 84 to exit 265 and State Highway 203, driving southeast about 4 miles; (800) 994–5233 or (541) 963–5253. Open year-round, call for hours and rates.

A hot spot for summer and winter visitors, the site was once a thriving health spa. The resort now offers RV camping as well as a few tent sites. The natural hot spring produces two million gallons a day at 186 degrees Fahrenheit, which provides heat for the mineral baths, hot tub, steam sauna, and heated pool. Several shallow ponds contain fish that you can try catching. You can also take walks along several trails.

LIONS' BIRNIE PARK (all ages)

Located at the corner of Old Oregon Trail (B Avenue) and Gekeler Street; (800) 848–9969 or (541) 963–8588. Open dawn to dusk. Free.

Once a pioneer encampment, where wagon trains circled to rest and recoup their energy for the steep climb up the Blue Mountains to the west, the park now houses symbolic ceramic columns that mark the route taken by wagon wheels as they climbed out of the valley and a life-size wrought-iron pioneer play wagon. Interpretive displays contain excerpts from pioneer diaries, extolling the beauty of the valley and describing the hardships of the journey.

UNION COUNTY MUSEUM (ages 5 and up)

333 South Main Street, Union, 15 miles southeast of LaGrande; (541) 562–6003. Open Mother's Day through mid-October, daily, 1:00–4:00 P.M. $2.00 adults, $1.00 students. Special tours by request.

Natural history and a "Cowboys Then and Now" exhibit will give you a glimpse into the region's early days and its cultural and geographic evolution.

GRANDE RONDE RIVER (ages 8 and up)

Runs through La Grande parallel to Highway 244; (800) 848–9969 or (541) 963–8588. Always open. Free.

Summer temperatures in this high-country town call for cooling swims in one of several swimming holes along the banks of the river or in nearby lakes and reservoirs. The Grande Ronde River is a natural selection,

Fun Fact The Grande Ronde River, at 180 miles long, is Oregon's second longest free-flowing river.

especially at any of the parks or campgrounds along its shores.

Pendleton

History truly comes alive once a year in this cowboy town when the **Pendleton Round-Up** rears its raucous head. But if you're not in town for the rodeo or didn't plan well enough in advance to get tickets, your children can still get a taste of the Old West with a visit to the **Pendleton Round-Up Hall of Fame.**

 UMATILLA COUNTY HISTORICAL SOCIETY MUSEUM (ages 5 and up)

108 Southwest Frazer; (541) 276–0012; www.umatillahistory.org. Open Tuesday through Saturday, 10:00 A.M.–4:00 P.M. $2.00 adults; $1.00 children; $5.00 family.

Exhibits trace the region's history, beginning with the Native American tribes that settled along the Umatilla River and leading through the arrival of missionaries, sheepherders, ranchers, farmers, soldiers, and loggers. The museum, housed in the restored 1909 railway depot, contains a large collection of photographs and artifacts to accompany the tales from the Old West. Your children might enjoy what's next door most of all. Kids can compare contemporary classrooms with the restored one-room schoolhouse—an elementary, middle, and high school all in one.

 TAMÁSTSLIKT CULTURAL INSTITUTE (ages 3 and up)

72789 Highway 331; (541) 966–9748; www.tamastslikt.com. Open 9:00 A.M.–5:00 P.M. daily. $6.00 adults; $4.00 students and children; under 5 Free.

The word *tamástslikt* means "interpret," and this center interprets the story of three distinct native peoples—Cayuse, Umatilla, and Walla Walla Tribes—whose histories came together over the past 150 years toward an alliance called the Confederated Tribes of the Umatilla Indian Reservation. The museum looks at the region from the perspective of these tribes—often a very different outlook than that traditionally taught in textbooks. Permanent and changing exhibits and regularly scheduled talks and demonstrations provide a rich experience in history. Permanent artifact collections and photography archives look to the past, while contemporary art exhibits display art by local and regional tribal artists. The store offers local tribal crafts, and there's a cafe for light meals.

PENDLETON UNDERGROUND TOURS (ages 5 and up)

37 Southwest Emigrant; (800) 226–6398 or (541) 276–0730; www. pendletonundergroundtours.org. Call for 90-minute tour dates and times. $10.00 adults; $5.00 children.

Descend below street level and get a glimpse of remnants of a time when Pendleton was part of the rootin' tootin' Wild West, once boasting thirty-two saloons and eighteen bordellos. The tours are tastefully presented, but parents of young children might not want to have to explain some of the references. Twice yearly, the underground comes to life. Actors dressed as dance-hall girls, cowboys, Chinese laborers, and gamblers provide entertainment along the tour.

Fun Fact Pendleton's **underground tunnels,** dug by Chinese immigrants between 1870 and 1930, cover more than 70 miles underneath Pendleton's historic district.

PEDALER'S PLACE CYCLE & SKI SHOP (ages 8 and up)

318 South Main Street; (541) 276–3337. Open year-round, call for hours. Adult-size bicycles to rent for $15 per day.

When the weather's fine—as it usually is throughout the summer—rent bicycles and explore the **Pendleton River Parkway.** The illuminated, paved pathway borders the Umatilla River as it flows through town.

BAR M DUDE RANCH (all ages)

58840 Bar M Lane, Adams 97810; located 31 miles east of Pendleton in the Blue Mountains; (888) 824–3381 or (541) 566–3381; www.guestranches.com/ barm. Ranch open to guests April to October. Cost is $900 per week per person.

Home-style accommodations are offered on this working ranch. The main ranch house has eight guest rooms. Other accommodations include three two-room suites and two cabins. Horseback riding, a recreation barn, a natural hot springs, and meals to make any ranch hand's mouth water are all part of the experience.

BLUE MOUNTAIN CROSSING INTERPRETIVE SITE (ages 5 and up)

Located just south of Emigrant Springs; (541) 963–7186. Call for seasonal hours. $5.00 trailhead fee (NW Pass).

During summer weekends here, you can meet some pioneers camped with their wagon at the 4,193-foot summit, awaiting the rest of their wagon train. Dressed as characters drawn from the past, the living-history pioneers tell tales sketched from diaries left by the emigrants. Three short trails take you past signs of their passage. Give your child the interpretive brochure to guide you to the numbered stops along the way.

HAT ROCK STATE PARK (all ages)

Located on the shore of a lake formed by McNary Dam, 29 miles northwest of Pendleton via State Highway 37 and U.S. 73; (800) 551–6949 for information; (800) 452–5687 for reservations; www.oregonstateparks.org. Closed in winter except for boat ramp. ℱᵣₑₑ for day use. Call for camping and picnic area reservations and fees.

This is the first Oregon landmark recorded by Lewis and Clark on their journey. The park has camping and picnicking facilities as well as boat access to the Columbia River. A private campground across from the park has a swimming pool. The large pond is a great place to picnic and spot waterfowl that inhabit the area—great blue herons, kingfishers, and friendly ducks and geese are among those you will be able to spot.

SPOUT SPRINGS (ages 5 and up)

Located in the Blue Mountains on Umatilla National Forest, just off State Highway 204; (541) 566–0320; www.skispoutsprings.com. Call for hours, prices.

Outdoor recreation can be enjoyed all year here. Primarily a ski resort, the area is also popular with mountain bikers during the summer. A map of several routes is available from the restaurant, where you rent both skis and bicycles. In winter the slopes are open for skiing day and night, with 13 miles of groomed and marked Nordic trails.

Clockworks If you walk to the corner of Southeast Fourth and Court, you can view the 100-year-old clockworks through glass panels in the clock tower. The Seth Thomas clock is located in front of the Umatilla County Courthouse.

PENDLETON ROUND-UP HALL OF FAME (ages 5 and up)
*1205 Southwest Court Street; (541) 278–0815. Open Monday through Satur-
day, 10:00 A.M.–5:00 P.M.* **Free** *but donations appreciated. Tours available.*
Displays of photographs of famous bronco riders and rodeo stars
line the walls that commemorate the Wild West. There's even an old
rodeo bucking horse, Warpaint, in full-body mount—a real kid pleaser.

 PENDLETON WOOLEN MILLS (ages 5 and up)
*1307 Southeast Court Place; (800) 760–4844 or (541) 276–6911;
www.pendleton-usa.com. Open Monday through Saturday, 8:00 A.M.–5:00 P.M.;
Sunday, 11:00 A.M.–3:00 P.M.* **Free** *20-minute tours available Monday
through Friday at 9:00 A.M., 11:00 A.M., 1:30 P.M., and 3:30 P.M.*
When some people hear the word Pendleton, they have visions of
soft woolen shirts and blankets instead of rodeos. Although your kids
may not be thrilled to look inside a woolen mill, they might at least
appreciate the benefit of warm winter clothing that can be purchased at
the outlet here.

Top Pendleton Events

SEPTEMBER

Pendleton Round-Up. One of the largest rodeos in the country, the
Round-up includes unusual events such as wild-cow milking and Indian
and baton races. You'll want to don your ten-gallon hat and your cowboy boots (or your baseball cap and sneakers—there's no dress code) and
join in the festivities. The nightly **Happy Canyon show,** in which members of the local Umatilla, Cayuse, Walla Walla, and Nez Percé tribes present pageantry and tradition, is a spectacle to capture even the most
jaded teenage interests. (800) 45–RODEO or (541) 276–2553; www.
pendletonroundup.com; www.happycanyon.com.

Hells Canyon

What is the deepest river gorge in North America? Nope, not Arizona's Grand
Canyon. It's right here in eastern Oregon: **Hells Canyon** on the Snake River.
Forming the border between Oregon and Idaho, the Snake River carved a gorge
more than a mile deep over the last 20 million years. The canyon's oldest rocks
were formed as long as 280 million years ago at the bottom of a vast inland sea.

Designated in 1975 as a National Recreation Area, Hells Canyon offers many opportunities for family fun. The highest point on the Oregon rim of the canyon is **Hat Point,** rising 6,982 feet above sea level. A new road into the scenic overlook has made this vista available to motorists from mid-June through October. From Imnaha, drive east on Hat Point Road. Gas up before leaving Enterprise or Joseph and carry drinking water; you'll drive 23 miles from Imnaha one-way to the Hat Point Overlook.

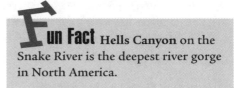

un Fact Hells Canyon on the Snake River is the deepest river gorge in North America.

HELLS CANYON NATIONAL RECREATION AREA (ages 5 and up)

(541) 426–4978; www.fs.fed.us/r6/w-w/hcnra.html. Check first for road access during winter months. **Free.**

To explore the Hells Canyon National Recreation Area more deeply, look into guided trips by boat or on the back of a horse, or with a pack mule or llama. You can take your own float trip or power boat trip along the Snake River if you are an experienced whitewater boater.

HELLS CANYON ADVENTURES (note age restrictions)

Located 80 miles east of Baker City, P.O. Box 159, Oxbow 97840; (541) 785–3352 or (800) 422–3568; www.hellscanyonadventures.com. Open May to September. Call for schedules, prices.

They are one of the few outfitters offering day trips rather than extended overnight floats. With one exception, the trips—either by raft or jet boat—navigate all of the major whitewater on the river, including some Class IV rapids (not for the faint of heart). Children must be at least twelve to take a day-long raft trip. For those with hearts and stomachs made of weaker substances than steel, they offer "soft adventures"—two- and three-hour jet boat trips that take you up to but not through the worst of the whitewater. Younger children are welcome on jet boat trips. All trips involve stops to explore an old homestead, ancient Indian pictographs, an abandoned Indian village, a deserted cave, or the Kirkwood Living Historical Ranch, a museum that was once the home of former Idaho governor and U.S. Senator Len Jordan.

STEEN'S WILDERNESS ADVENTURES (ages 6 and up)

64591 Steen Road, Joseph; (541) 432–6545; www.steens-packtrips.com. Trips run late May to early September. $150 per day per adult, $130 per child for guided trips; $300 first person, $150 each additional, for drop-off and pickup service.

Three- to seven-day rafting and horse and mule pack trips take you into the canyon or into the Eagle Cap Wilderness. With five generations of history in the region, Steen's Wilderness Adventures knows the canyon and its wilderness well.

 HELLS CANYON BICYCLE TOURS (ages 8 and up)

P.O. Box 483, Joseph 97846; (541) 432–2453. Call for prices, tour schedules.

If your family enjoys pedal-powered experiences, mountain bikes are another option for touring the Hells Canyon area. Paul Grow leads one- to four-day bicycle tours through rugged and scenic country. A lifelong cycling enthusiast, Paul can tailor the tour to your experience level, but it's good for riders to be fairly experienced and in reasonably good physical shape. Tours can run year-round, but highlight times are early summer for the wildflowers and early fall for the autumn colors.

 HURRICANE CREEK LLAMA TREKS (ages 6 and up)

63366 Pine Tree Road, Enterprise; (800) 528–9609 or (541) 432–4455; www.hcltrek.com. Call for schedules. Trips range from $590–$875.

Another option for exploring Hells Canyon is one your children (six and older) will love. Stanlynn Daugherty and her gentle, brown-eyed, fluffy llamas make hiking a real adventure on tours into Hells Canyon, on wildflower treks along Bear Creek, or on trips up to the enchanting Lakes Basin in the high Wallowas.

 BACK COUNTRY OUTFITTERS (all ages)

P.O. Box 137, Joseph; (800) 966–8080 or (541) 426–5908; www.eoni.com/~ bcountry. Wallowas July to early October, Snake River May to June. Prices range from $185–$255 per day, five-day photography trip $495 for six-person minimum (they make adjustments for children).

One of the most time-honored means of descending into the canyon is on the back of a mule, those stout and stable but much-maligned creatures with a reputation for stubborn streaks as deep as the canyon. This company takes you down into the canyon on three- to twenty-one-day trips. You'll ride horses, and the mules will pack all the camping gear and supplies, although there are a few riding mules for those who'd like the experience. Custom trips can include children as young as toddlers.

NEE-ME-POO NATIONAL RECREATION TRAIL (ages 5 and up)

Access to the trail by car (high-clearance vehicles strongly recommended) is from Imnaha, about 20 miles over rough single-lane gravel-topped Forest Road 4260; (541) 426–4978; www.tcfn.org/tctour/parks/NeeMePoo.html. Open year-round.

The trail gives kids a strong sense of history as it leads into the Snake River Canyon, downriver from Hells Canyon. "Nee-Me-Poo" means "the real people." The evocative story of Chief Joseph and his flight from the Wallowa Valley seems to resonate through the valley as you walk in their footsteps. The 3⁷⁄₁₀-mile trail ends at Dug Bar on the Snake, where an interpretive sign tells the story of the Nez Percé. When walking here, carry drinking water and be prepared for weather changes. This is a steep trail, with a 1000-foot elevation change at each end of the trail. Be watchful for rattlesnakes.

SADDLE CREEK VIEWPOINT AND CAMPGROUND (ages 5 and up)

Located 18⁸⁄₁₀ miles out of Imnaha; (541) 426–5546 or (541) 425–4978. Open year-round, but check first for snow levels. **Free**.

This area has both camping facilities and terrific viewing spots into Hells Canyon, where you also get a good view of the Seven Devils Mountains in Idaho. An interpretive sign helps you identify for your children the various geologic features they're seeing, and they'll enjoy scrambling over the various rocky surfaces that surround the area. From here the road climbs in twists and turns another 4⁷⁄₁₀ miles to Hat Point. If you're not one for heights, you can enjoy the view from here while your kids climb the 92-foot lookout tower for an all-around view that spans northeastern Oregon and extends to northwestern Idaho. If you're camping, bring your own water, as there's no supply at the campground.

The Wallowas

The lush flatlands of the Wallowa Valley form a contrast to the abrupt rise of the mountains. The variety of choices for family adventure in this beautiful corner of the state is surprising for an area with such sparse population. Magnificent natural beauty, much of it preserved in the **Wallowa-Whitman National**

Forest and **Eagle Cap Wilderness Area,** captivates visitors and residents alike throughout the year. Winter snows cover the Wallowa Mountains—often called the Swiss Alps of Oregon—which offer downhill and Nordic skiing. Spring brings a time for alpine wildflower walks and fishing in the area's many lakes and streams. Summer

un Facts

■ When the **Wallowa Lake Tramway** was constructed, it boasted the steepest vertical lift for a four-passenger gondola in all of North America.

■ **Eagle Cap Wilderness** is Oregon's largest designated wilderness area.

invites hikers, mountain bikers, horseback riders, waterskiers, and swimmers. Autumn colors are spectacular, and so is the fishing during fall spawning. **Wallowa Lake,** formed about a million years ago by glacial drift, is bounded on the east and west by lateral moraines (accumulations of earth and stones collected and deposited by a glacier) and at the north by a terminal moraine. The teardrop-shaped lake is 283 feet deep and 6 miles long. Its name comes from the Nez Percé term for a tripod-mounted fishtrap that was used in the lake. The south end of Wallowa Lake was first commercially developed in 1906. A dance pavilion and bowling lanes have given way to numerous resorts and lodges. Floating platforms dot the lake near the shore for swimmers and waterskiers to rest or picnic. Fishing is excellent both in the lake and in nearby streams for rainbow trout, kokanee (landlocked blueback salmon), Dolly Varden (char), sturgeon, and Mackinaw (lake trout). Hiking trails take off into the **Eagle Cap Wilderness Area,** or you can take horseback trips with a guide. Mule deer roam the area freely and are quite accustomed to people. Please don't feed the deer, as human food is bad for them. Also, these are wild animals, and their antlers and hooves are sharp and powerful.

 WALLOWA LAKE MARINA (ages 5 and up)
P.O. Box 47, Joseph; (541) 432–9115.
Reservations can be made for a 1½-hour lake tour aboard a pontoon boat, which is also available for rent. The marina rents canoes, rowboats, paddleboats, and motorboats by the day, half-day, or hour. The kids will be delighted to find kiddie rides here.

WALLOWA LAKE TRAMWAY (ages 8 and up)
59919 Wallowa Lake Highway; (877) 994–TRAM or (541) 432–5331; www. wallowalaketram.com. Open daily, June through September, 10:00 A.M.–4:00 P.M.; extended to 5:00 P.M. July through Labor Day. Enclosed gondola for back-

country skiing December through March; call for details. $17.00 adults; $10.00 children ages 3–12.

The tram takes you on an alpine ride on an amazingly steep incline. The elevation at the base is 4,450 feet, climbing to a breathtaking 8,200 feet at the crest of Mount Howard. Along the surprisingly brief (about ten-minute) ride, the gondola travels between 3 and 120 feet off the ground—be prepared for children's squeals of mixed delight and terror. From the top, the spectacular vista encompasses **Wallowa Lake,** the **Eagle Cap Wilderness,** the **Seven Devils Mountains** in Idaho, the **Hells Canyon** area, and on really clear days, the **Bitter Root Mountains** of Montana. Let kids work off pent-up energy walking the 2-mile trail that circles the summit, then stop for a bite to eat at the **Summit Deli and Alpine Patio.** June is the peak month for alpine wildflowers on the mountain.

JOE'S PLACE (all ages)
72662 Marina Lane; (541) 432–4940. Open daily, Memorial Day to Labor Day, 11:00 A.M.–10:00 P.M. Call for prices and hours, which change seasonally.

The whole family can load into bumper boats or play mini-croquet at Joe's. And the kids will quickly gravitate to the arcade area. Order one of Joe's "gourmet pizzas" in between sessions.

JACK'S GO CARTS AND SPRING MEADOW RV PARK (ages 5 and up)
59781 Wallowa Lake Highway; (541) 432–9285. Open summers only, call for hours and prices.

The kids will be thrilled to see the go-carts, miniature golf, and arcade tucked into this RV park.

EAGLE CAP WILDERNESS PACK STATION (ages 7 and up)
59761 Wallowa Lake Highway; (800) 681–6222 or (541) 432–4145; www.neooregon.net/wildernesspackstation. Open June to mid-November. Call for pricing on various trips and activities.

This is the oldest horse packing operation in northeastern Oregon. Your family can take a one-hour, two-hour, half-day, or all-day ride as well as a week-long excursion. All rides are accompanied by experienced guides. Deluxe summer pack trips come complete with camp setup, horses, guide, and wranglers (who take care of the horses, cooking, and food). The outfitters have recently added parasailing to their offerings.

Top Wallowa Event

JULY

Tamkaliks Celebration. Held annually, the Tamkaliks Celebration symbolizes the return of Wallowa Band Nez Percé descendants to their homeland. *Tamkaliks* means "from where you can see the mountains." Your children will be wowed by the traditional dancing in ceremonial dress, the rhythm of the drumming and singing, and the experience of a distinctive cultural tradition. The Nez Percé prepare venison, salmon, and traditional fry bread, and other area residents bring potluck dishes to share for the Friendship Feast on Sunday. Visitors are asked to contribute, too, either with a dish or a donation. Tepee, tent, and RV camping available. (800) 585–4121, (541) 426–4622, or (541) 886–3101; www.wallowa.com/visitor/powwow.htm.

SEPTEMBER

Alpenfest. For more than twenty-five years, the Wallowa Lake community has been transformed for one September weekend into a Swiss village. Traditional food, dancing, costumes, and music—yodeling, Swiss cow bells, and 12-foot-long alphorns—bring Bavaria alive in Eastern Oregon. (800) 585–4121; www.wallowalake.net.

Enterprise

This Old West town, named by a committee of early settlers who hoped the name would bring good fortune to the area, forms a gateway for vacationers heading into the Eagle Cap Wilderness.

 EAGLE CAP WILDERNESS (all ages)

Begins at the Hurricane Creek Campground, 6 miles south of Enterprise on Forest Road 8205, a rough road suitable for slow travel with a passenger car but not recommended for RVs or trailers; (541) 426–4978 or (541) 426–5546 for road conditions. Call for hours, which vary seasonally (there's often snow in the area until July). $5.00 vehicle fee (NW Forest Pass).

Besides an easy hike, you'll have great views of Sacajawea Peak and the Matterhorn, Oregon's sixth and seventh tallest mountains, as you pass through meadows and forested areas along Hurricane Creek.

STANGEL BUFFALO RANCH (all ages)
Located about a mile north of Enterprise on State Highway 3; (541) 426–4919. Always open. **Free.**

A wide spot on the road's shoulder invites you to stop and view the herd of 150 or more buffalo that are usually found grazing here. It's a far cry from the days of herds of thousands, but it's an opportunity for your kids to see creatures once native and wild in Oregon. Mules are another frequent sight around here.

Top Enterprise Event

SEPTEMBER

Hells Canyon Mule Days. These long-eared animals are celebrated at this annual event. Mule owners from all over the state come together and your family can join in a halter and trail class or just watch the parade down Main Street. Races, rodeo competitions, and mule rides are also part of the fun. (541) 426–4420; www.wallowa.com/visitor/mules.htm.

Joseph

Named for the famous Nez Percé chief who led his people on a harrowing winter journey to avoid war, the town of Joseph remembers its history. Any resident could tell you the story of young Chief Joseph—the statesman and orator whose Nez Percé name was Hinmut-too-yah-lat-kekeht, which is said to mean "Thunder Rolling in the Mountains"—and his father, Old Joseph, who is buried at the north end of Wallowa Lake, where a roadside historical marker provides a brief history. Young Chief Joseph's peaceful band was ordered in 1877 to leave the Wallowa country, which had been granted to his people by treaty in 1855. After a few angry men seeking revenge for the deaths of two young braves killed some white settlers, Joseph led his people first to seek refuge with the Crow in Montana, and then toward Canada and Chief Sitting Bull. They were pursued and captured after a two-day battle within 50 miles of the Canadian border. In surrender, Chief Joseph spoke words that have rung through time: "Hear me, my chiefs! I am tired. My heart is sick and sad. From where the sun now stands, I will fight no more forever."

Visual Arts

One of the more surprising elements of this small western town is its sizable arts community. While the idea of a trip through an art museum might not excite your children, they'll be enthralled by the bronze sculpture showrooms in Joseph. A number of art foundries specialize in extremely detailed, realistic renderings of western themes, such as wolves, horses, mountain lions, eagles, cowboys, and Native Americans, including:

- **Valley Bronze of Oregon.** *307 West Adler Street (foundry); (541) 432–7551; www.valleybronze.com; E-mail: info@valleybronze.com. Open daily for tours. $5.00 per person.* Stop by the foundry or by the showroom at 18 South Main Street (541-432-7445).

- **Joseph Bronze Foundry.** *83366 Joseph Highway; (541) 432–2278; www.josephbronze.net; E-mail: cast@eoni.com. Call for hours.* Also see the reference for **Manuels Museum Nez Percé Crossing,** which offers foundry tours and workshops.

MANUEL MUSEUM NEZ PERCÉ CROSSING (ages 5 and up)

404 North Main Street; (541) 432–7235; www.davidmanuel.com; E-mail: office@davidmanuel.com. Open Monday through Saturday, 9:00 A.M.–4:00 P.M.; call for winter schedule. $6.00 adults, $3.00 children.

David Manuel's museum combines a large collection of Native American and historical artifacts—including the first wagon to cross into this area on the great Oregon Trail migration. It also includes Manuel's own bronze sculpture, as well as a children's museum, a miniature tepee encampment, and a wagon train.

FERGUSON RIDGE SKI AREA (ages 8 and up)

Located 8 miles southeast of Joseph; (541) 426–3494; E-mail: outdoors@eoni. com. Open weekends only 10:00 A.M.–4:00 P.M. in winter.

Young downhill skiers can spend all day on the rope tow for a couple of dollars; adults ski from the T-bar for less than $10 a day. Equipment rentals and food are available at the lodge. The hill is owned by the Ferguson Ridge Ski Club and operated by members, so opening times are a bit sporadic.

WALLOWA LAKE STATE PARK (all ages)

On Wallowa Lake at the edge of the Wallowa River 6 miles south of Joseph; (541) 431–4185 or (800) 551–6949; for campground reservations call (800) 452– 5687; www.oregonstateparks.org. Open year-round. $3.00 day-use fee; camping $13 tent site; $16 full hook-up; $27 yurt; $55 cabin.

From Memorial Day through Labor Day, this place is packed, so you'll definitely need to reserve your campsite. But if you're staying else-where, come out for the day to enjoy swimming, boating, fishing, or hik-ing the nature trail. There's also a playground, and the area is frequently on the visiting path of the local deer. Never let your children feed or pet the deer. They may seem tame, but they have very sharp horns and antlers.

WALLOWA COUNTY MUSEUM (ages 5 and up)

110 South Main Street; (541) 432–6095; www.co.wallowa.us/museum. Open daily, 10:00 A.M.–5:00 P.M., Memorial Day weekend to third weekend in Septem-ber. Admission **Free** *but donations appreciated.*

The Nez Percé history room contains a large tepee that your children will enjoy sitting in even if museums in general offer little appeal. Look for "buckskin bucks," money produced for trading locally during the Great Depression, when real money was scarce.

Top Joseph Events

EACH SATURDAY IN SUMMER

Great Joseph Bank Robbery. At 1:00 P.M. nearly every Saturday from Memorial Day to Labor Day, enthusiastic performers reenact the 1896 Robbery (always referred to in capital letters around here). Masked ban-dits gallop up to the bank, then come out a few minutes later with guns blazing (blanks, of course). (541) 432–1015.

JULY

Chief Joseph Days Rodeo and Encampment. The events include a three-day rodeo, a ranch-style breakfast, a Nez Percé encampment, a car-nival, ceremonial dancing, and parades. (541) 432–1015; www.chief josephdays.com.

Family Favorites in Eastern Oregon

1. National Historic Oregon Trail Interpretive Center, near Baker City

2. Malheur National Wildlife Refuge, near Burns

3. Steens Mountain, near Burns

4. Nee-Me-Poo National Recreation Trail

5. Warner Wetlands, near Burns

6. John Day Fossil Beds National Monument

7. Kam Wah Chung Museum, John Day

8. Pendleton Underground Tour

9. Umatilla County Historical Society Museum, Pendleton

10. Wallowa Lake Tramway

Where to Eat

IN BAKER CITY

Sumpter Junction. *2 Sunridge Lane; (541) 523-9437.* A miniature replica of the Sumpter Valley Railroad runs on tiny tracks around the restaurant, alongside booths, and over dining tables. Family dining with Mexican specialties. $-$$

Front Street Cafe. *1840 Main Street; (541) 523-7536.* Signature menu items are "flaming pasta salads"—we won't spoil the surprise—as well as more traditional fare. $-$$

Inland Cafe. *2715 Tenth Street; (541) 523-9041.* Downhome cooking specialties are chicken-fried steak and pork chops. $-$$

Oregon Trail Restaurant. *221 Bridge Street; (541) 523-5844.* Family dining with old-fashioned American fare. $$-$$$

IN JOHN DAY

Grubsteak Mining Company. *149 East Main; (541) 575-1970.* Pizza, steak, fish, and chicken specialties; open for lunch and dinner. $-$$

IN LA GRANDE

Foley Station. *1011 Adams Avenue; (541) 963-7473.* Open for breakfast and lunch, this eatery offers gourmet dishes at reasonable prices. $-$$

Wrangler Family Steakhouse. *1914 Adams Avenue; (541) 963-3131.* This place is a bit upscale but happily accommodates families. $$-$$$

North Powder Cafe. *Located at exit 285 off Interstate 84; (541) 898-2332.* The cafe offers smoked chicken, build-your-own omelettes, and—always a country favorite—chicken-fried steak. $

IN PENDLETON

The Great Pacific Wine and Coffee Company. *403 South Main Street; (541) 276–1350.* Get a good deal for your picnic lunch here and buy tasty sandwiches made on bagels or croissants. Then stuff your picnic basket with baked goodies. $

IN THE WALLOWAS

Bob's Cafe. *216 East First Street; (541) 886–6874.* Full breakfast, lunch, and dinner menus, with daily specials. Closed Sunday. $$

Russell's at the Lake. *Located on Wallowa Lake; (541) 432–0591.* Open May to November. Grab a hamburger and terrific fries (from potato to plate in ten minutes) at this old-fashioned burger bar which has both outdoor and indoor seating. Russell's is popular for its almost-too-thick-for-a-straw milkshakes as well as its ranch-style breakfasts. $

TnT Kitchen. *101 West First; (541) 886–7705.* For something different,

have a buffalo burger. This small restaurant also serves dynamite homemade cinnamon rolls. $

IN ENTERPRISE

House Cafe. *307 West North; (541) 426–9055.* Family-style meals served in a casual setting. $–$$

Toma's. *309 South River Street; (541) 426–4873.* Family cooking. $–$$

IN JOSEPH

Old Town Cafe. *8 South Main Street; (541) 432–9898.* This tiny lunch and breakfast place offers hearty food at reasonable prices. It's the place to stop and fill up before heading out for a round of outdoor activities in northeastern Oregon. $

Cheyenne Cafe. *209 North Main; (541) 432–6300.* Country cooking seven days a week. $–$$

Magonis. *500 North Main; (541) 432–3663.* Italian specialties served family style for all you can eat. $$

Where to Stay

IN BAKER CITY

Best Western Sunridge Inn. *1 Sunridge Lane; (800) 233–2368 or (541) 523–6444.* One hundred fifty-five units. An outdoor pool waits for you in the summer, and an indoor spa will warm your bones during the cold winter months. $$–$$$

Eldorado Inn. *695 Campbell Street; (800) 537–5756 or (541) 523–6494.* Fifty-six units. A restaurant and indoor pool are among the amenities here. Pets are welcome. $$–$$$

Quality Inn. *810 Campbell Street; (800) 221–2222 or (541) 523–2242; www.qualityinn.com.* Fifty-four units. The inn serves continental breakfast and welcomes pets. $$–$$$

Super 8. *250 Campbell Street; (888) 726–2466 or (541) 523–8282.* Seventy-two units. Laundry facilities, an indoor pool, and a spa pool help make family stays here more comfortable. $$–$$$

Union Creek Campground. *Located on Highway 7 on the shores of Phillips Reservoir about 20 miles southwest of Baker City;*

(541) 523–4476. Fifty-eight campsites for tent and trailer camping. The swimming beach is a great place for your kids to enjoy a summer dip while mom and dad soak up some of this area's seemingly endless sunshine (in the summertime, that is). *$*

IN JOHN DAY

Budget 8 Motel. *711 West Main Street; (541) 575–2155.* Fourteen units. Your family will settle in nicely here, with a restaurant and laundry services, plus an outdoor pool for those hot summer days. *$$–$$$*

John Day Sunset Inn. *390 West Main Street; (800) 452–4899 or (541) 575–1462.* Forty-three units. You'll find a restaurant here, plus laundry facilities, an indoor pool and a sauna pool. *$$–$$$*

Lands Inn Bed and Breakfast. *Star Route 1; Kimberly 97848; (541) 934–2333.* Located 10 miles northeast of Fossil Beds National Monument headquarters off State Highway 19, this bed-and-breakfast has two quaint cottages for rent. *$$–$$$$*

Riverside School House Bed and Breakfast. *Route 2, Box 700; Prairie City 97869; located 6 miles east of Prairie City, 19 miles east of John Day; (541) 820–4731.* Here's a bed-and-breakfast that will give your children a new experience in going to school. Originally a one-room schoolhouse, it is now part of a working cattle ranch. *$$$–$$$$*

IN BURNS

Hotel Diamond. *10 Main Street (take Highway 205 south toward Frenchglen); (541) 493–1898.* This century-old hotel has both charm and tradition. Adja-

cent to the Malheur Wildlife Refuge, it receives regular visits from deer and great-horned owls. The restaurant serves breakfast, lunch and dinner. *$$–$$$*

Silver Spur Motel. *789 North Broadway; (800) 400–2077 or (541) 573–2077.* Twenty-six units. A health club, microwaves, and refrigerators make this a convenient place for families to settle in for a day, or more. Best of all, they offer a full breakfast buffet. *$$*

IN FRENCHGLEN

Frenchglen Hotel State Heritage Site. *Located on State Highway 205, 62 miles south of Burns; Frenchglen 97736; (541) 493–2825 or (800) 551–6949; www.oregonstateparks.org.* The hotel provides lodging and meals for visitors coming to Malheur to enjoy birdwatching and wildlife. Breakfast, lunch, and dinner are served daily to residents and drop-in guests. Be sure to make reservations for dinner. *$–$$$*

IN LA GRANDE

Anthony Lakes Recreation Area. *Baker Ranger District, on Forest Road 73; (541) 523–4476.* You can camp at Anthony, Mud, and Grande Ronde Lakes. Campgrounds are available for tents and trailers, and there are boat ramps for nonmotorized boats. *$*

Stang Manor Inn. *1612 Walnut Street; (541) 963–2400.* Four units. A stay here will add to your list of memorable travel experiences. The stately Georgian manor was the home of a local lumber baron in the 1920s and is furnished with antiques. The spacious grounds are ideal for children to let off pent-up energy. *$$–$$$$*

Hilgard Junction State Park. *Located on the Grande Ronde, at the edge of the Blue Mountains, take Interstate 84 northwest about 9 miles to the Highway 244 turnoff and head west about ¼ mile; (800) 551–6949; www.oregonstateparks.org.* The park lies along the path taken by pioneers of the Oregon Trail, and you can use the interpretive panels to share some of its history with your children. $

Lehman Hot Springs. *P.O. Box 187, Ukiah 97880; (541) 427–3015.* If you plan ahead, you can camp or rent a cabin or tepee here. A large swimming pool heated from a natural hot springs and a mineral bath adjacent to the pool will keep the whole family content for hours. $$$–$$$$

Super 8. *2407 East "R" Avenue at the Interstate 84/Highway 82 interchange; (800) 800–8000 or (541) 963–8080.* Sixty-four units. The simple rooms are comfortable, and the indoor pool and spa pool offer a nice respite after a day of outdoor activities. $$–$$$

IN PENDLETON

7 Inn. *Interstate 84, exit 202 and Barnhardt Road; (800) 734–7466 or (541) 276–4711.* Fifty units. Continental breakfast is served. Kitchenette and laundry services are available. Pets are welcome too. $–$$$

Holiday Inn Express. *600 Southeast Nye Street; (541) 966–6520 or (800) HOLIDAY.* Sixty-four units. Indoor and outdoor spa and indoor swimming pool are offered. Continental breakfast is served too. $$–$$$$

Emigrant Springs State Heritage Area. *Located near the summit of the Blue Mountains of Interstate 84, 26 miles southeast of Pendleton; (541) 983–2227 or (800) 551–6949; (800) 452–5687 for reservations.* Your family can stay in the Totem Bunkhouse, with two bunk beds (four single beds) in each of two units. It's available year-round for winter cross-country ski holidays and summer camping. The campground offers a self-guided nature trail, a kitchen shelter in the day-use area, a horse camp with two corrals, and a horse trail that doubles as a cross-country ski trail in winter. $$

IN THE WALLOWAS

Wallowa Lake Lodge. *60060 Wallowa Lake Highway; (541) 432–9821; www.wallowalakelodge.com; E-mail: info@wallowalake.com.* Thirty units. Lodge rooms and rustic cabins are for rent. Open year-round (weekends only mid-October through Memorial Day) for all-weather recreation, the lodge has a dining room for breakfast and dinner, and you can order picnics to go. $$–$$$$

Eagle Cap Chalets and Park at the River RV Park. *59879 Wallowa Lake Highway; (541) 432–4704; www.eaglecapchalets.com.* Twenty chalet rooms, twelve cabins, five condos, plus full RV hook-ups (no tent camping). All rooms and cabins have TV, coffeepot, microwave, and fridge. Indoor pool and spa at chalet. $–$$$$

IN ENTERPRISE

Best Western Rama Inn & Suites. *1200 Highland Avenue; (800) RAMA–INN or (541) 426–2000.* Fifty-three units. Continental breakfast is offered, plus an indoor pool, spa, and an exercise room. Pets are welcome too. $$–$$$

Lick Creek Campground. *29 miles southeast of Enterprise on Forest Road 39, Wallowa Mountain Loop Road; (800) 585–4121, (541) 426–4622, or (541) 426–3151.* At the 5,400-foot elevation, nights are chilly, but the views from the ridge above the campgound are terrific. You can fish or hike from this campground, which also has trailer sites and drinking water. **Free**.

Wilderness Inn. *301 West North Street; (541) 426–4535.* Twenty-nine units. This newly remodeled inn has private saunas, kitchenettes, and an adjoining restaurant. $$

IN JOSEPH

Collett's Cabins. *84681 Ponderosa Lane, Joseph; (541) 432–2391 or (866) 432–7300; www.eoni.com/~smcollett; E-mail: smcollett@eoni.com.* Cabins with linen, utensils, microwave, fridge, coffeepot, and barbecue. Sleep from two to eight. Artist owners provide art work in rooms and sell art supplies in gift shop. $$–$$$$

Flying Arrow Resort. *59782 Wallowa Lake Highway; (541) 432–2951; www. flyingarrowresort.com; E-mail: flyinga@ oregontrail.net.* Twenty units. This family-oriented resort with all the amenities—heated swimming pool, hot tub, sun decks, and barbecues—is open all year. Cabins range from rustic to modern, with one to four bedrooms. Most are located on the Wallowa River, and all are fully equipped. $$$–$$$$

For More Information

Baker County Visitor & Convention Bureau. *490 Campbell Street, Baker City, OR 97814; (800) 523–1235 or (541) 523–3356; www.visitbaker.com.*

Eastern Oregon Visitors Association/Oregon Trail Marketing Coalition. *P.O. Box 1087, Baker City, OR 97814; (800) 332–1843; (541) 523–9200; www.eova.org; E-mail: eova@comports.com.*

Grant County Chamber of Commerce. *281 West Main Street, John Day, OR 97845; (800) 769–5664 or (541) 575–0547; www.grantcounty.cc; E-mail: questions@grantcounty.cc.*

Harney County Chamber of Commerce. *76 East Washington, Burns, OR 97720; (541) 573–2636; www. harneycounty.com.*

Joseph Chamber of Commerce. *Box 13, Joseph, OR 77846; (541) 432– 1015; www.josephoregon.com.*

La Grande–Union County Visitors and Convention Bureau. *1912 Fourth Street, #200, La Grande, OR 97850; (800) 848–9969 or (541) 963– 8588; www.visitlagrande.com; E-mail: visitlg@eoni.com.*

Pendleton Chamber of Commerce/ Visitors & Information Center. *501 South Main Street, Pendleton, OR 97801; (800) 547–8911 or (541) 276–7411; www.pendleton-oregon.org; E-mail: pendle ton@pendleton-oregon.org.*

Wallowa County Chamber of Commerce. *P.O. Box 427, 936 West North Street, Enterprise, OR 97828; (800) 585– 4121 or (541) 426–4622; www.wallowa countychamber.com; E-mail: wallowa@eoni. com.*

Activities Index

HORSEBACK RIDING

MUSEUMS

OUTDOOR RECREATION, OUTFITTERS, AND GUIDES

RODEOS

SCENIC DRIVES AND VIEWPOINTS

SHOPPING

WINTER SPORTS AND PLAY AREAS

About the Author

CHERYL MCLEAN is an Oregon native who spent a great deal of her childhood exploring the state on family vacations. She received a bachelor's degree in English from Oregon State University and a master's degree in journalism from the University of Oregon. Cheryl worked for several years as a stringer writing travel articles for *Sunset Magazine*'s northwest office. She also taught writing at Western Oregon State College before starting her own design and publishing company. She is the author of *Oregon's Quiet Waters: A Guide to Lakes for Canoeists and Other Paddlers* (Jackson Creek Press). Since 1979 she has served on the book and journal editorial boards of CALYX Books, a women's literary press. Cheryl currently lives in Corvallis, Oregon, with her husband and daughter.